FROM THE GROUND UP

First published in 2006 by

WOODFIELD PUBLISHING
Bognor Regis, West Sussex, England
www.woodfieldpublishing.com

ISBN 1-84683-015-X

From the Ground Up

ALF COMMONS

Woodfield

*This book is dedicated to my wife Pat,
who single-handedly moved our home 29 times during
the 20 years of marriage covered in this book, and to our
son and daughter, who together went to some 25 different
schools and thus destroyed the myth that changing schools
is detrimental to a child's education.*

Contents

Foreword

It is easy to think that the history of any century is best described by the momentous events for which it is famous. The twentieth is no exception and is prone to be described solely by wars and great social events such as revolutions. While we cannot completely decry that approach, it is one that has severe limitations and it is good to see that the stories of the ordinary individuals who were the lifeblood of, and shaped the great events, are now a very popular form of historical narrative.

Alf Commons has added greatly to this theme of a people's history with his remarkable autobiography. He takes us on a journey from childhood to maturity and, amazingly, his style allows us to see his world at each stage as though we actually were the child or the anxious but optimistic teenager – a term that was not used in those days – and then to share his life as he becomes a typical "other rank" in the RAF; the people in all three services who really run the show!

Running through the book is the theme of Alf getting on with his life no matter what is thrown his way and we are invited into several scenes that give us a real feel for the times in which he lived. As one whose earliest memories of Brighton are of the beaches mined and relatives in uniform, I was fascinated by Alf's wartime stories. Here he was, trying to overcome the problems of a working-class kid projected into what was, in effect, a private school environment, with all the traditions to absorb and follow, while simultaneously being part of the greatest war ever fought. The vicissitudes included the loss of uncles killed – I shall never forget my own father's last leave in 1944 – and evacuation of the school from Brighton to Yorkshire. Alf and his mates forgot that tiresome fellow Hitler and demonstrated the bulldog spirit in many ways. With the world completely mad around him, it is not surprising that this obviously highly intelligent boy did not progress along the usual narrow academic route and his successful life was carved out independently, without the cushion of matriculation. He started work at fourteen years and from then on went for the best he could achieve.

Alf invites us to follow him through his development from a boy into a man and brilliantly evokes the old-fashioned romantic image in his description of his wife Pat and their splendid love affair that has lasted to this day. But Alf developed a sterner side as he gradually matured, until he was prepared to tell a senior officer to stuff peacetime aircrew training – my words – when the service "bull" became too much to swallow. With this courageous action Alf demonstrated that he was, of course, just the sort of guy who, a few years earlier, would have been certain to complete wartime training and doubtless would have been one of those who took their heavy bombers night after night into the hell of northern Europe.

I could write another book just describing Alf's literary work and am immensely privileged to have been asked to prepare this foreword – a first for me – but I must round up my poor efforts with one thought about Alf's modesty in the way he decries himself when comparing his lifetime efforts with so-called "successful Old Varndeanians". The work gives enough insight into the author to say "Forget it Alf, your life has been immensely successful and you have travelled paths and immersed yourself in experiences that might have been impossible if greater academic success had come your way". This book is the record of that success and it comes straight from the heart.

I am sure that the "old school" was important, but basic character is the reason Alf could produce a treasure of truth describing all these years. Anyway, there is still a possibility that he could achieve fame in Academe. Alf should, in retirement, study the process of physiological telepathy that gave him morning sickness with each of his wife's pregnancies while Pat remained symptom free! There must be a Nobel Prize somewhere in that. But I must not disclose any more of the wonderful anecdotes that are the backbone of a book that will make readers laugh and cry, but leave them feeling warm and happy about the best in our often-blighted human race.

Jack Beavis
Consultant Orthopaedic and Trauma Surgeon
Past Hunterian Professor Royal College of Surgeons of England
But most of all, and proudly, An Old Varndeanian
June 2006

Acknowledgements

Where does one start with acknowledgements? It seems that during the process of writing a work of nearly 89,000 words over about eight years that I have done it all by myself. Then, thinking back over that time, I realise that others were involved. Of course firstly there was the inventor of the computer. Couldn't have written it all by hand and, not being a terribly bright fellow, I doubt that I could have done it without my Apple Mac. So thanks firstly to Steve Jobs, for Apple, which made it so much easier.

Closer to home though I must thank my kids and their kids for firstly making me think seriously of putting it all down on paper and later for encouraging me to continue. As well, for the occasional clarification of facts, dates and places that had become blurred memories I must thank Pat, Andrew and Susan. Pat has also had to put up with years of my laziness in the house. Friends who suffered the indignity of being asked to read the seemingly dozens of re-drafts must also be acknowledged. Rob Polglase (Carshine) for his suggestion that I should put more of my own thoughts into it; until then it was just a chronological list of events. Pam, who said "Alf, it is just like talking with you" deserves a special thanks. That was exactly the style I was aiming for. Bob Edgar who unloaded all his 'aids to authors' onto me and told me to turn it into a novel. No go Bob, but thanks for the enthusiasm. I must get them back to you soon. My 'little' sister Rene also spurred me on when she published her Ronnie Rabbit childrens' picture stories at around the age of 65. I didn't even know that she could draw!

Old Varndeanians have also assisted. Initially Jim Franks who, when we were discussing the 9/11 disaster suggested that we swap our bio drafts. He then said "This should be saved for posterior" or something like that. Photos supplied by Ted Brooke from his recent visit to our wartime retreat in Yorkshire, and Clive Henly who kindly provided a few days accommodation for my grandson Brendan, in Brighton, and took him on a tour of the school and my old homes; hence the 2003 photos, have also served to 'bulk it out'. A desire for achievement came about when Professor Jack Beavis became the President of the Old Varndeanian's Association. His work around the world's disaster spots was truly inspirational and I felt that the Charity IDEALS, which he co-founded, must be supported. I hope to dedicate this book to IDEALS and, should it ever receive any royalties, I know they will be well used. I must thank Jack for his very generous personal offer of publication costs and for agreeing to write the Foreword. He probably thought that it was just another disaster. As well I must thank OV's Ron Denman and Mike Chick for agreeing to take care of the Pommie end of the logistics.

Lastly I wish to thank friends in the Springwood Bowling and Golf Clubs who have shown an interest in the project. I hope that they will take the opportunity to assist a wonderful charity when publication is a fact.

Alf Commons

Blue Mountains, Australia 2006

Introduction

For a number of years now, when we have had family get-togethers, a few drinks, a couple of questions and I have told stories about various events that have happened in my lifetime. My wife, Pat, has added to these and the kids have said to us, "You ought to write it all down." I did start writing it down in 1969 but it fell away during the trip to Oz.

For my 70th birthday Siobhan, our oldest grandchild, bought me a thick hardbound notebook with instructions to "Get it started, now!" At the same time our other two younger granddaughters bought me some 'stickies' to make quick notes on. Well, I never could refuse a pretty face, and when there were three of them, I surrendered.

This autobiography covers only the first 40 years of my life. Of course I should also point out that it was written as an autobiography and so, only brings in my family where they had a bearing on that life. In the first 40 years we were likely to be living different lives for much of the time. Pat has also written some details of her life over this period. I wonder if they will agree?

This is mainly the story of an airman. There are two kinds of airmen. The one that everybody has written about and hero-worshipped, with some justification I hasten to say. He has won his wings and has been featured in every war story and movie for the past 60 years. He has won his battles the hard way. There are also the 'other airmen'. These are the men that provide all the support required to ensure that the fliers are equipped with fully functional aircraft and that the ground radio and radar navigational aids and communications facilities, so necessary for the successful execution of their tasks, are always to be manned and relied upon. This is the story of an 'other airman'.

I shall be writing this slowly because I know that you can't read fast. Which is an appropriate way to start because that terrible joke was around when my story began...

1. The Early Days 1929-40

May 19th 1929. Born, screaming and kicking, number five of a family that eventually reached seven kids; an eighth was stillborn. I was the third of four boys and we had three sisters. Memories of this occasion are rather dim and enquiries to the County Archivist at the East Sussex Records Office have failed to revive them. I know I was born at the Buckingham Road Hospital in Brighton, Sussex, England. My mother told me that I was born with a broken collarbone, and in my infancy suffered a very severe bout of gastro-enteritis. I was on the verge of carking it. Good job I didn't or you'd be looking for something else to read tonight!

The family at the time of my birth consisted of Mum and Dad of course, with Frances the eldest child, she was 7 years older than me, and then in just seven years there were Eric, Rita, Ronald and myself. At this point Dad must have been running short of lead in his pencil because it took another seven years to produce Peter and Irene.

My earliest memory is at the age of about two, being held up, probably by my mother, to see an airship fly over our house, 27 Firle Road, Brighton. This was a council house. In Australia it would be called a Commission home. A lot of work was being done on airships at that time and it seems that they were massive machines. Its presence over the houses would certainly have attracted much attention.

Mum reckons that, at this time, her greatest fear was when neighbours would knock on the door and start their conversation with "Your boys..." I think at this time, as well, one of the neighbours knocked on the door to tell Mum that my next older brother, Ronnie was hanging by his feet, upside down, from a workman's ladder. Of course I was too young at this time to be involved in any of this.

Sometime around 1931/32 we moved to 74 Carlyle Street, Brighton. Recent family history records uncovered reveal that this had been my paternal grandfather's home. It was not a council house. My first memory of this time was on my fourth birthday when I had a whole packet of Dolly Mixtures given to me. Hey man don't laugh. That would have been a whole two cents worth. Surely you know what Dolly Mixtures are. A rare treat.

In September 1933 I started at Finsbury Road Infants School. I was probably escorted by Ronnie or my older sister Rita in the first term or so but do not remember this. They'd have been in the Junior Mixed School during my first few years. I do remember walking to school later. Finsbury Road was probably a half hour walk from home. We went up Carlyle Street, along Queens Park Road, down Bentham Road, along Wichelow Place, down Islingward Road and either along Finsbury Road or Southampton Street. Of course there was far less traffic in those days. School times then were 9.00am to 12.00 mid-day, home for dinner then 2.00pm to 4.00pm for infants and 4.30pm for juniors. In winter it could be dark by 4.30pm! The main meal of the day was Dinner but it was eaten at mid-day. Breakfast: porridge, Dinner: cooked meat, potatoes, cabbage followed by rice pudding, macaroni or tapioca (afters). On good days we would have a slice of apple pie for 'afters' instead of rice. Tea: bread and jam. Then off to bed for the littlies. Littlies were the under 14's. Non wage earners.

I think that it was in the Education Act of 1948 that 'School milk' became free for all children. Prior to that the one third of a pint bottles of milk cost a halfpenny. Twopence halfpenny (Tuppence ha'penny) per week. We never had school milk. The family just couldn't afford it. This cost could have been a County Council impost.

In about 1936 I moved up to the Junior Mixed School where it seems I was an exceptional student with, as one school report said, 'a sweet disposition'. It was probably right. I did have this disposition towards sweets (lollies) but no one could afford to buy me any; hence my clear memory of the Dolly Mixtures. As a student I remember getting three first places and three third places and of course, my crowning achievement, being awarded a 'Special Place' Scholarship to Varndean Secondary School for Boys. Varndean was seen then to be the second best school in Brighton (Population then 145,000) but its record of scholarship has since shown it to be probably the best. Except for me.

I should mention here that in those days I was a real weedy type who suffered constantly from chest complaints. These were usually diagnosed as Bronchitis. I was as skinny as a rake, ate like a horse and never put on an ounce. Mum had me down the School Clinic time and again suspecting that I had Tuberculosis (TB), which was fairly prevalent in those days. My Uncle Wally suffered from it and I suppose Mum thought that it could have been hereditary. Thankfully it was not so.

In other matters of that time I recall being in the School swimming team in the inter-school sports. The race was over two widths of the North Road Swimming Baths. I knew that good swimmers swam smoothly, and almost leisurely, so that is the way I went about it. I came fifth. People had to ask the question directly before I would tell them that it was out of six! There was also a Swimming Bath at St. Lukes School, much nearer to Finsbury Road, and we went there, once a week for the School swimming training program.

By now I was the only one of our family to still be attending Finsbury Road School, so it was considered safe, as we walked home from the Queens Park past Mr. Brown, the Headmaster's home, for the older ones to sing:

"Old Daddy Brown is a nice old man,
He goes to church on Sunday.
He prays to God to give him strength
To bash the kids on Monday".

I would immediately run ahead so that he wouldn't see me.

For some reason or other Peter, three years younger than me, was enrolled at Elm Grove School so the Finsbury Road tradition in our family was broken.

Most of our spare time in the summer was spent on Brighton Beach, swimming and playing by the fishing and pleasure boats. Most of these were manually powered! They were very heavy and we used to help bring them up the beach by putting bits of timber at the front for the boat to slide on, and as a piece was left behind, picking it up, rushing it to the front again. A game of leapfrog with timber planks. Everybody would hurl their shoulders into the heave ho! I also remember that at a very early age, I was down the beach by myself and there was a religious group doing the old "Come and join us" business. I stood up on a chair and sung "I'm not too young to go to Jesus for he loves a little child", et al. for which I received a medallion. Jesus must have known that I was 'on the make' 'cause I lost it down the lavatory soon afterwards and no-one would put their hands down for it. Nobody had rubber gloves in the kitchen in those days. Years later that could have been the medal that, added to my RAF Long Service Medal (on which umpteen pages some time later), would have gone 'chink, chink!' when I came to a halt, and I'd have happily marched in Sydney every ANZAC Day.

Brighton also boasted a fine Race Course, which held several race meetings each year. It wasn't a loop course. To get to the start the horses had to be cantered up to the starting post past all the spectators, then race back again. There were no starting stalls in those days so the lining up behind a rubberised tape for the start was a very exciting part of the race. The great jockeys of the day, Gordon Richards, Scobie Breasley and others, trying to get their mounts in the best possible position to give them an advantage, calling out to the starter "Hang on sir!" "Not yet!" "Yes now!" The last race was timed to start at 4.30 pm, so we were sent home from school at about 3.45 pm on Race Days to avoid the traffic. We all immediately ran up to the Race Hill, as it was known, to watch the last race. We were completely oblivious to the fact that the Race Course was notorious for it's razor gangs. Graham Green's 'Brighton Rock' referred to these if I remember rightly. There was a very well known tipster, a Zulu, whose name was Prince Monalulu (or something like that). He would stand there shouting "I gottanarse, I gottanarse" and we used to call back "So what? So have I."

Queens Park would have been on our way home from school.... if the school had been built on the other side of Queens Park Road. That didn't seem to deter us. We often came home via the Park, especially if we were with the girls. We used to have kissing competitions to see who could kiss the girls the most times. I think scores of 75 with a girl either side of me on the park bench were not uncommon. Well, we thought they were kisses. That came to an abrupt end when, having sated our appetites one day, though the girls were screaming for more, we were walking along Queens Park Road by the 'Pepper Box", a very ornamental set of Public Toilets, when my mother saw me. I was in double trouble. Firstly for going with girls and secondly, because she had been going to catch the tram along to Carlyle Street, but couldn't afford to pay for me as well. So she had to walk. Mum suffered badly from bunions and rheumatism and had great difficulty with walking.

Something that I should have got the blame for, but was too scared to say anything about, was when, one day, I'd arrived home from school and there was nobody home.

I thought it would be a magnificent gesture if I had a pot of tea ready for when Mum got home. I was obviously too small to manage the job and made a big mess all over the scullery. I immediately ran out of the house and didn't come home again for a while. By this time Ronnie had been given a walloping for the mess. There was no point in me saying anything by then, so I kept quiet. Poor Ron. I hope he forgives me. Thinking of that I realise what a tremendous change has come over the world. None of us kids had house door keys. The doors were just never locked! I could walk in. Anybody could walk in. The world was a much safer place, except for the fact that people like Adolf Hitler were beginning to make their presence felt in Germany.

I should explain the type of house that we were living in. Carlyle Street consisted of terraced houses with no side entrances. There was an outside lav at the rear, kept stocked with paper cut into squares from the News of the World and Daily Express. The dustbin was also kept out in the backyard. We never put the dustbin out the front. On dust collection day the dustmen would just knock knock on the front door, walk straight in through to the back, take out the dustbin, empty it and bring it back. It is hard to imagine such a thing now. As well, the milkman used to deliver milk from a churn carried on his man-powered milk barrow. Mum would leave a glass jug just inside the front door; the milkman would just look inside the door, if the jug was there he would fill it from his churn. One day, I raced into the house, accidentally kicked the empty jug and smashed it. Mum was at the top of the stairs facing the front door. She nearly collapsed. That jug had been a wedding present. There was no running hot water. The only taps were in the scullery, one over an stone sink and the other over the copper. I believe there may have been a gas stove also but wouldn't swear to this.

We didn't have any mains electrical appliances at that time. The laundry and bath water was boiled in the stone copper in the corner of the scullery. One of my jobs on Mondays was to go up to Mrs Westons, the corner grocers shop at the top of Carlyle Street, and bring back a sack of packaging. Cardboard boxes, egg separators, often smeared with broken eggs, all the rubbish that she could spare and then I'd light the copper and keep it going till the water boiled for Mum to do her washing.

Mealtimes at our house were silent occasions. Mum said that every time you talk you lose a mouthful. She kept a big wooden spoon on the table alongside her plate and any misbehaving copped a wallop from it. You also had to say "Yes" immediately if she asked if you wanted something. I remember Ronnie dithering about whether he wanted some more rice for 'afters' one day. He decided too late and went without. Poor Ron again.

Things my Mother told me. Could be a song title. Well, close to it anyway. I always meticulously wash behind my ears. You're bound to if; every day for about twelve years your Mum says, "Have you washed behind your ears? You could grow potatoes there!" Another philosophy of mine is that when a thing is 'lost' don't bother looking where it 'should' be. Rather look where it 'should not' be. I wonder if this comes from another of Mum's expressions. "Mum, where are my socks?" "Under my arm." would be the response. In other words, "Look for them yourself." Years later my son would have immediately lifted her arm to look. He was very cheeky with his Grandmother. Once threatened to stand her upside down in the corner if she didn't behave.

Just before the war started, Dad's brother, our Uncle Harry finished his time in the Navy and became a bread roundsman for Groom's bakeries. He drove a horse and cart around our area and I started going round with him on Saturdays. It was different. At this time the modern mechanised bread roundsmen were driving chain-driven vans with solid rubber tyres. Other tradesmen who had street rounds were the Sunday Winkles and Whelks man who sold these straight from the rocks at Blackrock beach. They were sold by the pint and scooped up in an enamel pot. Shrimps would also be available. As well there was the Muffin man. He was also a Sunday special. The muffins were not like those sold in Australia but more like crumpets. These would be toasted in front of the fire and buttered or, more probably, marged whilst hot, and spread with jam for Sunday tea. This was all done in the kitchen which was equipped with a wide coal fire range. This range was kept looking posh by 'blackleading'. The 'blacklead' was a black paste that was scrubbed on with a brush then brushed hard until it was shiny black. Like polishing shoes. The dining table, well, really a kitchen table, was also there. The tablecloth was either a sheet of oilcloth or newspaper. Knives, forks and spoons were polished with 'Brasso' or 'Silvo' every Sunday then washed and dried. Kids' work.

Our spare time when not at the beach or the race hill (where we often went for a game of football played with an old tennis ball with our coats as goal posts), would be spent playing in the street. Marbles or alleys, the former were of a stone/clay composition whilst the latter were made of glass, which we would roll along the gutter trying to hit the other player's alley, was also popular and fairly cheap. They could also be set up on a flat pavement with the same aim in mind. One very foggy day, we were up the Race Hill playing football when we heard an aeroplane fly low overhead followed by a crash. We ran home and learned that a young man had pinched a plane from Shoreham (I think) and crashed it on a home in Freshfield Road. Just down from where we were playing.

'Conkers', horse chestnuts, with a hole through them, through which was threaded a piece of string or a bootlace, and secured by a knot at the end, were also a favourite sport. The aim was to smash the opponents 'conker'. Each in turn would hold his conker by the top end of the string whilst the other would aim his conker at it. There were various methods of ensuring a hard hit and a good aim. The winners at this were usually kids that had the know how and facilities to harden their conkers. They would soak them in soda water for a while then let them dry hard. A conker was known by the number of others it had smashed. So a kid might have a 'sevener' or a 'tenner' or even a 'twenty-fiver'. If you didn't particularly like the kid you were playing conkers with you would 'accidentally' hit the hand he was holding the string with. Ouch!

Hoops cost money so we had to make do with wheels. These would be pram wheels, which we found at the Corporation Tip at Woodingdean. We would push a piece of wood through the spindle hole and use another piece of wood to drive the wheel along the road. Four-wheelers were also made of wooden boxes nailed to planks. These in turn were affixed to a fixed spindle and pram wheels at the rear and a movable plank, spindle and wheels on the front. The vehicle was steered by a piece of rope similar to the reins of a horse. There is no question that we were far better able to entertain ourselves at nil cost than any following generations have managed, or perhaps, had the need to.

Skipping was also a favourite and sometimes quite dangerous pastime. It was safe enough with a small piece of skipping rope but when someone had half-inched a length of builders scaffolding rope from a building site, it was a different matter. One person stood at each end of the rope, either side of the road, and started twirling it. It gained some pretty hefty momentum and many a sprained wrist or ankle resulted. There could be half a dozen or more of us skipping on the same rope. The skipping would be to the cry of "Salt, Mustard, Vinegar, Pepper, 1, 2, 3, 4, 5 *et seq*" and the rope would get faster and faster as the numbers got higher. It's a wonder that necks weren't broken.

On the subject of half-inching I suppose we were really all minor thieves because one of our favourite occupations, at the right time of the year, was 'apple scrumping'. This was not your safe pinching apples from an orchard out in the country somewhere. No way. With our scrumping you had to go through someone's front gate which probably squeaked, creep up the side passage of their house (posher street than ours) into the back garden, by now the dog would be barking, (all rich people had dogs), scrump the apples before anybody in the house caught you, and get out the same way where, as like as not, they would be waiting for you. That's the way all thieving should be. A clip round the ear and on your way.

Other dangerous games were getting hanging rides on the back of lorries (later replaced by getting free tows by lorries whilst on our bikes) or jumping onto the rear platform of trams as they started off and jumping off again as they reached dangerous speeds. I had an accident when I went to hang on the back of a lorry. It reversed instead of going forward. My recollection is that it went over my leg but, on hindsight, that seems impossible without leaving me crippled. I think it must have hit my head knocking me to the ground and pressed against the leg when the driver heard my screams. I was still very lucky though.

Radios, and electrification of homes, were still in their infancy. I think we had a D.C. supply to our house and I'm pretty certain that it was as a supplement to gas. There was a gas meter just inside the front door, which took shilling pieces. The shilling would be held in a certain position until its allocated amount of gas was used when it would drop into the 'money box'. You could hear it drop. Unfortunately, if you crash banged your way into the house, shoving the front door into the wall by the meter, that would also cause the shilling to drop. Mum didn't have very many shillings. I remember seeing her almost in despair when this had happened. Most houses had either 'Radio Relay' an audio version of today's 'Cable T.V.' or a D.C. Radio. The latter ran on accumulators. These were small batteries, similar to car batteries but the outer casing was glass and it had a sliding handle. When the electrolyte was below the marked level it had to be taken up the corner shop (grocery) and put on charge. The shop would provide us with a recharged one. I think that the cost was tuppence. When we arrived home from school in the afternoons Mum would be listening to Radio Luxembourg, the name 'Della Street' as a program comes to mind, but I could be way out in this.

Two events outside the family occurred during these years. The first that I can recall was a Council Election. Two of the contestants were Mr Lux who I imagine was the Conservative and Mr Frank Ingman (or something like that) who would have to have been the Labour man. We kids, of course, had not the faintest idea of what a Council election was all about but I recall that we went through the streets to school singing at the tops of our voices:

Vote, vote, vote for Frankie Ingman,
Chuck old Luxy out of town,
If it wasn't for the law we'd sock him on the jaw
And you wouldn't see old Luxy anymore.

An alternate third line was

If it wasn't for the King, we'd punch him on the chin

I think the tune was one that is still used in American political conventions by one of their parties.

The other event was that, with a new unmarried King, Edward VIII, on the throne, an American divorcee, Mrs Wallace Simpson, appeared on the scene to throw Britain into turmoil. Again we kids had a song to sing about it. This one went:

Who's that walking down the street?
Mrs Simpson's dirty feet.
She's been married twice before
Now she's knocking at Windsor's door.

Of course it is history now that Edward VIII abdicated in favour of his brother, George VI and became the Duke of Windsor. Mrs Simpson married him and became the Duchess.

At this time my father was a bit of a roustabout. Alternating between beach photographer, illegal street vending and spending the night in gaol. I remember that at the time of the Silver Jubilee of King George V he had had a photo of the King on the wall and took a photo of it. He then printed out hundreds of copies to sell. Another venture I remember was seeing our tin (galvanised) bath in the front room, the same that we had our weekly bath in, and him and a mate sloshing around some red liquid in it and filling bottles. He had gone into the soft drinks industry.

I think the gaol incident arose from some illegal (unlicensed) street vending activity. It would not have been anything terrible, even vegetables on a barrow, without a licence was illegal. He didn't get the goods out of sight quick enough when the coppers appeared. He was hauled off to Lewes Prison for the night, presumably to face the magistrate next day. However the cops and prison staff had not reckoned on my mum. She went to Lewes and refused to leave the prison until they gave her back 'her childrens' father'!

Another incident which indicates just how poor we really were, was when Mum sent Frances and Rita down to the School Canteen, in Southover Street or Albion Hill I think, with a big china wash-basin jug to get free soup for our dinner. The School Canteen was the children's equivalent to the Matthew Talbot kitchens for homeless people in Sydney. They arrived back home with a full jug of cold greasy liquid which none of us could eat. I don't know how Mum fed us that day but it is probable she sent up to Kit Weston's corner shop and got something 'on the book' for us. I think everything we ate was 'on the book' for varying periods.

I'm sure that by today's standards we would have been classified as living in poverty.

Another memorable incident, for all the wrong reasons, was a case of child abuse by a man living in Picton Street. I believe he had made his son pick up bits of burning coal with bare hands. The police went to arrest him and he wouldn't come out. They, and a few hundred lynch hungry Brightonians, including myself, lay siege to the man's house. I do recall that I was there until well after dark. I would almost certainly have been in trouble when I got home but have no memory of that aspect. I believe he was arrested later.

It would have been about this time that World War ll started. September 3rd, 1939 at, I think, 11 am. I recall that we were playing in the street outside the house when the announcement was made. Within minutes the air raid warning sirens started to wail and I think we all thought that this was probably 'it'. It is well known now that it was a private plane coming across the English Channel from France that triggered off the panic. I believe that it served to prove that the then, secret, Chain Home radar system was working effectively.

Everybody was now issued with an Identity Card, Ration Book and Respirator (gas mask). My ID card number was EGNS18/6. I don't know what the system was for determining the first six characters of this but, if you take my brother Eric out of our family, he was now in the Royal Navy and would have had a Royal Navy service number, then I would have been the sixth oldest in the family so it is reasonable to assume that the '18' was our family designation and the '6' was my personal number. It wasn't long before we kids realised that you could make some disgusting noises whilst wearing the gas masks. The sort of noises that would make the wearing of a gas mask seem advisable.

Air Raid Precautions (ARP) became the watchword. Everybody learned how to put out an incendiary bomb before the fire could spread. Every building including homes had a bucket filled with sand close to hand, plus a bucket of water and a stirrup pump. With a few people filling up spare buckets and topping up the one being pumped from, a pretty good continuous stream of water could be directed on a fire whilst waiting for the Auxiliary Fire Service to come. Comic posters were displayed to assist in this training. I recall one that said "If an incendiary bomb falls near you, don't lose your head.... put it in a bucket of sand." We learned how to rewind a rubber hose so that it could be run out without kinking. I still try to do this but with the modern thin plastic hoses it doesn't work so well. We also had a house evacuation exercise from the top floor of the Patchings' house down the street. We kids volunteered to be casualties and lay down in the top bedroom. The ARP men would mark us with our 'injury', then tie us to a stretcher and lower us out of the window. After the first few scary days it all seemed good fun. For a while!

Other Wartime Posters I recall were those for the 'Spitfire Fund'. They were appealing for money to enable more Spitfires to be made. Then there was the fear of 5th Columnists. Posters all over the place showed a wall with a man hiding behind it. The punch lines were, "Walls have Ears" and "Be like Dad, Keep Mum". I suppose that the war would be lost nowadays whilst the feminists argued that the last one was sexist. Then there were the ones entreating people not to travel unless they had to. "Is your journey really necessary?" As well there were organised "Holidays at Home". These could be great fun. All sorts of events would be organised and the valley at Wild Park would be crowded during holidays.

In one of the earlier air raids on Brighton an 'Oil bomb' hit the front of a house in Wichelow Place. I think the idea was that it should burst, catch fire, and then spread the fire all around. I don't believe the fire and spread occurred but I remember that there was a stain on the front wall of the house for some time which I could see as I walked to school. I was the Bell Monitor at Finsbury Road for the first year of the war. I had to be in the school ten minutes before everybody else to ring the bell for five minutes. My bell rang 'Di-ding-Di-Dong Di-ding-Di-Dong' which I thought was quite a skill. At 8.55 am I would stop and the St Lukes School bell would ring with a much more strident and urgent 'Dong dong, Dong dong, Dong dong' for five minutes. After the fall of France and the evacuation from Dunkirk we were under the threat of a German invasion. On the radio news one night (no TV in those days) it was announced that no bells were to be rung in future. The ringing of bells would be the signal of an airborne invasion by German paratroops. I went in the next morning as usual, had the cupboard door open and the bell rope hanging down, watching the clock, when the Headmaster, Old Daddy Brown, a portly man, came running up the stairs. "Don't ring the bell! Don't ring the bell!" I have been unable to ascertain whether or not the school bell was ever rung again.

Shortly after this time Finsbury Road School, along with others, was taken over to be converted to a Military Hospital. Our schooling for the rest of my time there was spent in half days at Elm Grove School with the other half at the Elm Grove Labour Club. We alternated weekly between mornings and afternoons at the school.

During this time, as well, the Battle of Britain was building up. It reached its climax on September 15th, 1940. It was a beautiful summer. We had spent most of the school holidays down on the beach and up on the Downs. That's not as stupid as it sounds! The South Downs and the North Downs are two ranges of rolling, grass covered, chalk hills separated by the Weald of Kent. The South Downs are behind Brighton (the Race Course is situated on them) and are probably about 500 feet above sea level. There had been brilliant blue skies, which, as each day progressed, became clouded with vapour trails as the RAF fought off the bombers of the Luftwaffe. By this time Emergency Water Supplies (like the modern above ground pools) had been erected all around the town to be used to fight fires. The Auxiliary Fire Service (AFS) had been formed and a true 'Dad's Army' of commercial vehicles had been converted into fire engines. Each area had it's own AFS station. Our nearest one was in Luther Street. Its stand-by position was up past the top of Carlyle Street so, every time the sirens sounded, the fire engine would chug up our street. On that final big day we had in excess of twenty air raid warnings and all-clears. The latter frequently coming within minutes of the former. So we were standing out the front of our house cheering the firemen on and yelling at them to turn back if the all clear had gone before they reached our house. It seemed great fun at the time. Of course it could have been the end of civilisation as we then knew it. On the BBC News bulletin that night it was announced that over 180 enemy aircraft were destroyed. The figures have since been vastly modified. The fact is that it was the sort of news that we needed at that time. It is glorious history now that the RAF, assisted by many airmen from all over the Commonwealth and some over-ridden European countries, won the Battle of Britain.

2. Varndean 1940-43

My time now came to start at Varndean. As a winner of a Scholarship and being from a very poor family, I was issued with a free set of clothing to start with. It did not include a school blazer but did include vests, pants, shirts, School socks, tie and cap, a pair of 'house shoes', gym shorts and plimsolls. It also included a set of geometry instruments. I'd never been the owner of so many fine clothes. The 'house shoes' were changed into on arrival at the school each day. I was also to receive free bus tickets as the school was right over the North West side of the town and I lived at the South East part. The only trouble with the bus tickets was that we received two tickets per day but had to catch four buses, two in each direction. No one had thought of transfer type tickets then. We had to decide whether to bus half way and walk half way or to bus all the way there and walk all the way home. As it was more important to get to school on time, that is what we usually did.

Varndean had been a pioneer school in its original premises at York Place in Brighton in about 1886. It was one of the first to introduce science, higher mathematics and engineering subjects into a school curriculum and was the first (I believe in the country) to abolish the compulsory leaving age of 14 years. I believe that a contract was signed that I would stay at the school until at least the age of 16.

It seems that the headmaster in 1940 was a product of the English Public School system and wanted Varndean to be a replica of a Public School. Public Schools in England are the schools of the very well heeled. Eton, Harrow, Winchester etc. At Varndean you didn't start at the 1st form. It was probably assumed that you were a product of a prep. school (I have no source for that statement) and your first year at Varndean was in the 3rd Form. This went on to the 4th, Lower 5th, Middle or Transitas 5th, Upper 5th, Lower 6th, Middle 6th and Upper 6th. Upper 6th scholars would have expected to go on to Uni. Unlike today, very few children expected to go on to University. The 'red brick' Uni hadn't been invented.

So it was at this time, as a 3rd Former, that my Achilles Heel came to light. I didn't even know I had one. It must have been those new 'house shoes'. The Headmaster, 'Butch' or 'Bunny' Hutchins obviously saw it.

A message came round the classrooms 'All boys who catch the Trolley Bus on route numbers 41 and 42 (both went along Queens Park Road) to report to the Headmaster's study. Note that we had replaced the trams with Trolley Buses by this time. About forty or fifty of us turned up and what followed was the most superb piece of detective work I have ever seen. Butch looked at each of us in turn. To some he said "You can go" and to others including me, he said nothing. There were eventually about twelve of us left there. We were the ones who would play around on buses. There had been complaints. The dozen of us left were fairly evenly spread among 3rd, 4th, Lower 5th and Middle 5th forms. We were duly given two and a half hours detention. This meant going to school on Saturday morning. No extra bus tickets! It also meant writing out the School Code, Varndean's equivalent of Chairman Maou's little Red Book. It was a little Red Book and contained little black print. I never got past writing the first page so I still don't know what it was all about. The truth is that, at that age, I was far too meek and mild to open my mouth loudly let alone play up. I was certainly unjustly punished. However the incident was, without doubt, prophetic.

I worked fairly well during that first year. I remember topping the class in Maths and not having too much trouble with other subjects. One of my problems was that my exercise books were usually unreadable. This was not due to my poor handwriting, though that could have been improved, but because I could not afford to buy shin pads to play football. I had to stuff my exercise books down my socks to protect my legs. With football usually being played under wet or icy conditions the books received quite a battering.

In March 1941, we had nearly lost the war. The German Army was massed on the other side of the English Channel after the miracles of the evacuation of the British Army from Dunkerque and the Battle of Britain, and the Channel was just twenty two miles wide at it narrowest point. It was decided to do a voluntary evacuation of Brighton School-children. I went, with about 100 others from Varndean, to Yorkshire. Few of us had ever been away from our homes before. I suppose we must have looked like refugees. We were refugees! Cardboard suitcases with all our worldly belongings. Gas masks, at that time in cardboard boxes slung over our shoulder with a string shoulder strap. I had a tooth brush for the first time in my life. We boarded a steam train at Brighton Station in the morning and puffed slowly up through London and on and on until we reached somewhere around Leeds. It was now dark night. We were put on buses and taken to a hospital on Ilkley Moor where we slept the first night. Whenever people talk about the romance of travelling on the old steam trains I think of that journey. If you opened the windows and allowed the steam into the carriage it had a special unforgettable taste. I suspect that we were hungry and thirsty as well.

Back on to buses the next morning to four different villages. I went to Gargrave and was fostered, with a boy named Albert Beadon, by a dear old lady named Mrs Churchman. She lived in Church Street and of course, it was right opposite the church. She had a beautiful granddaughter who was also about 12 years old and who was my first love. How easily I forgot those stolen kisses in Queens Park. Unfortunately whatshername lived in Keighley with her parents so I only saw her occasionally. I have recently resumed my friendship with Albert Beadon via the Varndean Internet list. He is now in Whiterock, Vancouver, Canada and President of the Victoria Bowling Club. No further contact with whatshername. But I digress. Whilst living with Mrs Churchman I became a very good churchgoer and choir boy. Always keen on hitting piano keys (we had a piano that nobody could play in the front room at home) I used to creep into the church, when I believed there was nobody else around, and thump out marches on the organ. No one ever told me off so either they understood that it was not doing any harm or I really did have the place to myself.

All of the evacuee students from Varndean went to Skipton Grammar School. We were four and a half miles (about 7Km) from Skipton so we went by bus. Note that word carefully. Just writing about it has got me sneezing. There was a war on. All the able bodied men were either in the armed forces or on essential war work. The buses were being neglected and we were all from house-proud families. We decided that the bus seats needed dusting … en route! We sat on one seat and, singing and shouting, pounded our feet onto the opposite seat. The dust rose in clouds. We done good. Obviously our efforts were not appreciated by the driver.

The next day, and again, I don't know why I was selected, but at least this time I was guilty, we were caught up with in the Gym and made to bend over and received two very nasty strokes of the cane on our nether regions. That's not funny. The skilful schoolmaster could swing a cane with the minimum of effort. Almost no back swing with the arm but an almighty flexing of the cane. It came in from about five feet. I play golf with people who hit the ball in the same way. Goes miles farther than mine. I often wonder if they are retired school teachers.

I said earlier that I now owned my very first tooth brush. With it, of course, I had to have tooth paste. Now remember that this was a kid who never had money to buy sweets. Toothpaste, on the other hand, was essential ... and nice tasting. Full marks for innovation anyway. I used to buy Skuse's toothpaste because it was only fourpence ha'penny a tube… and really cleaned my teeth often! A habit my son was to adopt many years later.

The war wasn't left behind entirely by our evacuation to Yorkshire. I recall that we were playing a game of football on the village green near to the Johnson & Johnson Band-aid factory when a German bomber, probably a Heinkel 111, flew so low over the pitch that we could see the gunner sitting in the ventral gun position. Thankfully he never fired on us. Perhaps he had kids of his own at home and didn't really want to be there anyway. Dropping bombs from 15,000 feet is one thing; machine gunning children on the ground is another.

I think that two young boys were too much for Mrs Churchman and after a short while we were passed on to a Mrs Lowther. She was a younger lady with a little baby, who lived next door to her in-laws, who owned a farm. I think that Mr Lowther was in the Army. Here we learned why, or rather, how, farmers did things to the back ends of sheep and lambs. We learned that sitting on top of a big farm horse was like sitting on a skyscraper as it swayed in the wind. We learned that sheep do not like being herded into pens and will find the smallest gap to escape from. I learned that that gap was usually the side on which I was herding them. The sheep knew a coward when they smelled one.

The Varndean boys were known by the local kids as the Redcaps. Our School cap was red with a black edging and black peak with the School crest on the front. There was a fair amount of rivalry, probably because, coming from the South of England, we spoke English. They spoke this foreign gibberish like "Put wood int'oil", which roughly translated means "Shut the door." Anyway, in March or April of that year we heard that they were planning to beat us into 'breaking the ice'. Further enquiries resulted in us understanding that the first person to swim in the River Aire each year had 'broken the ice'. We couldn't resist. We went up in a group with Mrs Lowther one Sunday, early. She had her camera with her. On the count of three we all plunged in. I thought I would die. It was like having a steamroller run over my chest and squeeze every last puff of breath out of my lungs. How we got to the surface and back to the bank I'll never know but there is a photo of me, still in my cossie, freezing. It is in the family album. Of course, we 'broke the ice' that year.

I remember visiting a place called Malham with the class and seeing the source of the River Aire. The river flows out from the foot of a high cliff and the water was perfectly clear. I had a nasty stomach ache and drank some. The ache cleared! At the top of the cliff there is a plain consisting of flat limestone rock with crevices between. I seem to recall that at the foot of the cliffs there was also the carcass of a dead sheep. Probably got too inquisitive. The place is worth a visit. But don't go too near to the edge.

After a few months I was returned to Brighton. I don't recall too much about the events at school for a while. At the age of 13 I got a paper round at Beale's in East Street. They were a posh paper shop. Not one of your corner shop places. I had to ride a bike all around the western boundaries of Brighton before going to school. It was all new territory to me. The pay was three shillings a week. I wasn't very good at it and, after wearing out a pair of shoes in just three weeks Mum decided it was cheaper to keep me out of work than in work. I never went back for the fourth week. I can't recall giving anybody any notice. Just didn't go back.

Of course, by now we were getting air raid warnings at fairly frequent intervals. The Blitz had started, and, although we weren't a big target, the Luftwaffe went over Brighton going to or coming back from major targets.

Sometimes they were frightened off their major target by Ack Ack or fighters and had a go at Brighton just to get rid of their bomb load. Whatever, the Air Raid Warning would sound night after night and we'd hear the unsynchronised engines of the Jerry planes. That was how we could tell the difference. I am not ashamed to admit that whenever I heard the Scream or Whistle of a bomb dropping, I was terrified. The Germans had a nasty device fitted to the fins of their bombs, which caused them to scream instead of whistle as they fell. Horrible! In the book, 'The Brighton Blitz', (written by a Finsbury Road boy) it reckons that 381 high explosive bombs were dropped on Brighton, and many hundreds of incendiaries. I was a very poor sleeper and I heard every rotten one. I distinctly remember that I went to Wolf Cubs or Boy Scouts once, can't remember which because I never owned a uniform, and just at the end, as the boss man was saying prayers, there was a whistle of a bomb dropping. All my instincts said "Get down flat and cover your head" and my body started to follow my instincts. My left foot went forward with a loud slap on the wooden floor and the only other noise was the boss continuing with his prayer. It's is a funny fact that the fear of being seen to be scared can overcome the original fear. I stayed upright.

In one of the daylight raids a bomb landed near to our grandfather's house in Bedford Buildings, Kemp Town. His home was badly damaged and he had to come and live with us. He said that he saw the bomb whiz past the back door as he was shaving. I never believed this until I read (again in The Brighton Blitz) that a lot of bombs actually bounced on hitting the ground and went through buildings and out the other side before hitting something else and exploding. We were already over-crowded with about eight of us living in what I think must have been a three bedroom house. Eric, my oldest brother, being in the Royal Navy. Anyway, in the kitchen, which as I explained earlier, was also the dining room and everyday sitting room (all the washing, cooking preparation, washing up etc was done in the scullery) we had a very wide coal fired range which served as the normal sit-around fire, with integral cooking oven and cook tops. The front grill was used for roasting chestnuts or toasting bread on a toasting fork. Grandfather would sit there and spit into the fire. Actually he used to gob into the fire but that doesn't sound very nice, does it? Hell! It wasn't nice so Mum said he had to go. He went. I don't think Mum ever wore a pair of trousers in her life (see Pat around 1947) but she wore the trousers in her own house.

I do remember that we boys, there were three of us left at home by then, used to sleep two up and one down in a double bed. If you were the one down you had two lots of stinky feet to rest your head beside. We only had a bath once a week and feet were only washed on bath night! Except of course when we went swimming. This was only available now in the Municipal Swimming Baths. Beach swimming was out of the reckoning because the beaches were mined and barbed wired against the threat of invasion. Our two famous piers, the Palace Pier and the West Pier, had had large lumps blown out of their respective middles so that they could not be used as invasion piers. Another change that was taking place around all British towns was the removal of iron railings around parks and schools and wherever else they existed. These were to be melted down to make tanks and guns. We were getting quite serious about this war.

This would have been the first war in which every home owned a radio so propaganda also played a part. Whilst it was a serious medium, the voice of 'Lord Haw Haw' an Irish-American traiter, William Joyce, who broadcast English language propaganda for the Nazis, became a laughing matter. His "Jarmany calling, Jarmany calling, Jarmany calling" was imitated by us all. I recall that he mentioned the bombing of Brighton Harbour once. Actually Brighton didn't have a harbour. The nearest were at Shoreham or Newhaven. He was hanged as a traitor in January 1946.

Probably around 41/42 we moved to a council house at 32 Moulsecoomb Way, East Moulsecoomb. This was pure luxury. We had a bathroom, a full front to back Lounge/Dining room, a separate kitchen, electric Burco boiler for washing, electric hot and cold running water for baths. A toilet upstairs. No more creeping through the house and out to the back garden in the middle of the night. Probably still used newspaper though. I think it had four bedrooms.

Moulsecoomb was built as a garden suburb by the Council. It consisted of hundreds of semi-detached houses, each with a sizeable front and back garden. All the homes were rented but I believe that there was an arrangement whereby tenants could eventually buy their home from the council. Not that that interested us at the time.

A big house meant extra duties. We could not afford carpet so we had linoleum throughout the house. On Saturdays Peter, my younger brother, and I had to wash (scrub) the big front to back room and polish it. None of this pour on/rub off stuff. Floor polish was in a flat tin. Ronuk or Mansion Polish. You rubbed it on with a cloth and you polished it off with another cloth. It was hard work on your hands and knees after the scrubbing, which was also on hands and knees.

By this time all homes were encouraged to have their own air raid shelter. These were free. There were two types. The Anderson Shelter was dug into the back garden, lined with corrugated iron and with deep soil over the top. The Morrison Shelter was an indoor contraption which formed a table. About six feet long, five feet wide and three feet high. The frame was lengths of around five inch steel angle. The top was a sheet of steel to form a table top. The bottom was a spring bed. I think that there could also be a steel mesh 'curtain' around each side. The thing served as a shelter, a dining table and a bed. Being a born coward, I spent the rest of the war sleeping in the Morrison.

I still had to catch two buses each way. The trip from Moulsecoomb on a Southdown Route 13E to St. Peters Church, where we caught the Route 35 bus to school, was longer than from Carlyle Street. It's funny but I've just remembered a bit of fun we had on that bus. We had to pass the Cox's Pill Factory (as it was known) and there was a clock on the top of the wall of the factory. We boys would sit at the back of the top deck. To see the clock you had to dip your head to below the top of the bus window. As we went under the railway viaduct just before the factory we would say loudly "What's the time?" and watch all the heads ahead of us dip down to check the time. An auto-suggestion game I repeated many years later. Walking home from Varndean to Moulsecoomb was more pleasant. Varndean was about the same distance North West of the town as Moulsecoomb was North East. Between was the Varndean Girls School, Hollingbury Golf Course, Wild Park, and most of Moulscoomb. So walking home was mostly a walk through the countryside without roads. There was an anti-aircraft gun site on the hill which we might visit on the way.

One night some bombs (I think it was three) were dropped behind the library at Lower Bevendean. We got up next morning and from our front window could see white chalk holes (bomb craters) in the ground. We decided to walk to school that day. We visited the bomb sites as we went and picked up some big bits of shrapnel for souvenirs. We couldn't take them to school with us as it was against the rules. Instead we hid them in some bramble bushes and walked home again that afternoon. One bramble bush is very much like another and the hillside was littered with them. Either we didn't find the right bush or somebody had got there before us. Whatever, our souvenirs had vanished. We, in this case was Frankie Homewood who lived just down the road, and myself.

It wasn't long before my heel started to cause trouble again. This time it was on the Route 35 bus. All the buses were getting very old and were probably not getting as good maintenance as they should have. There was a hill which climbed from Preston Road to Surrenden Road, probably Varndean Gardens, and our bus was having a great deal of trouble negotiating it. They were always overloaded and I was one of the passengers standing on the back platform. I decided to jump off the bus, put my shoulder to it and help it up the hill. Doing my bit for the war effort, you'll understand. Everywhere there were posters entreating us to help the war effort in a multitude of ways. Later, when we were in class, a message came that Robson, a prefect, wanted to see one of the boys. We all laughed and wished him the best of luck. Robson had a bit of a reputation as a strict disciplinarian. A few minutes later he was back to say that it was a mistake: Robson wanted to see me. It seems that he had been on a second bus, immediately behind my bus, and had seen the whole incident. It took him the best part of a week to get me into Butch's office. I would stand outside morning and afternoon and be dismissed to my class until the next morning. Eventually I went in and received yet another two and a half hours detention. The fleet number of that bus was 6235. I remember because I said it would only last a minute and on Route 35 it was aptly called the sixty second 35. 'Robson' is now the late Brian Robson C.B. Noted military historian. Former Deputy Under-Secretary of State, Member of the Army Board and Commissioner of the Royal Hospital. If you are going to be caught, then get caught by somebody who is going to be somebody. That's what I say.

There were a number of funny things that happened in the classroom. You must remember that I had led a very sheltered life and though I was 12 or 13 years old now I was amazingly innocent of the ways of the world. Mothers of seven children are, of necessity, very strict mothers. I was a 'street kid' but not a 'street-wise kid'. I still thought that the birds and the bees were things that flew and I would avoid a gooseberry bush like the plague in case a baby popped out.

Varndean had four classes of 30 pupils starting each year. Foreign language studies for the first two years consisted of two of these classes studying French and the other two, including mine, studied German. Ich bin, Sie sind, Der, Die or Das ist. Easy. Years later I wondered why they didn't teach it in German schools. But I digress. There were a pair of twins in my class. Tom and George. They were entirely different in every way except for their sense of humour. They had a very modern, with-it, mother who has, at the time of writing, recently turned 100! I think that they knew all about the birds and the bees. It was in a German class one day, we had a very young lady teacher, when one of the twins asked that, "as the French class had had some French letters for homework, could we do some German prose?" I didn't comprehend but joined in the laughing just the same. Honest!

We also had a Physics master who told us that he had been to a seance to discuss with a dead Indian Chief about Acetyl Salicylic acid. It was as if he was about to invent something. Years later I was reading the label on an Aspirin bottle and found that it was the main ingredient of Aspirin. Hm! Everything was at a premium and wastage was a crime. Hence when I was arguing with another boy, in a physics lab, over who was going to do an experiment with a 'U' tube containing some mercury, he pulled on one side and I on the other with the result that the glass tube broke and mercury spilt all over the floor. We spent the rest of the lesson trying to capture the tiny balls of mercury on sheets of paper, to tip back into a container.

Miss Arkell, the German language teacher was also our form Mistress for the first year. We led her a merry dance, and I remember once, when we were out of control, she went out declaring that she would get a master in. Just at that moment the air raid warning sounded and we all cheered and rushed out to various parts of the shelters to get together again, just in time for the all-clear. Because many of the air-raid warnings were 'general area' warnings it was decided that too much factory production time was being lost by people going to the shelters at every event, so they introduced a new 'Local Alert'. This became known as 'The pips' because that is what it sounded like. The Pips were sounded when an air raid was developing in the local area. Varndean sat at the top of a hill, well out of town and was never threatened by hit and run raiders. These were typically F.W. 190 Fighter Bombers which would streak across the channel at just above wave height, swoop over the town and fire machine guns or cannons wherever. A lot of the boys would watch out of the windows, the fighting that was going on over the town. Not me. I used to be under my desk. Not a mark on me! Cowardice? Nah! Intelligence!

By now my father was a bus conductor with the Brighton Corporation trolley buses so Mum had a regular weekly wage coming in. Food rationing was at its meanest. Two ounces of butter, two ounces of sugar, one shillings worth of meat. Eggs were on 'allocation'. If a ship managed to get through from Canada with a consignment of eggs, a new allocation was announced. I believe it would have been one egg per person but cannot remember the details. Tropical fruits were impossible to get. We didn't see a banana for five years. Clothing was on a points system and quality controlled by regulation CC41. Each person had an allocation of clothing points which you spent as you wished until your allocation was used up, then no more clothes. The same system applied with most tinned foods. Each item was worth a certain number of points and when your points were used for the month that was that. Sweets (lollies) were also on points and we used to have our ration on the first Sunday of each month. Funny really. Before they were rationed we couldn't afford sweets. Once they were limited we had our full ration every month. One great thing about the war was that it brought some goods that couldn't be afforded before the war into our rations and therefore, we just had to have them. We almost certainly ate horse-meat and whale meat and were glad of it. As well as food and clothing rationing, there was also a restriction of the amount of bath water you could have, the restriction was not more than five inches of water. Not sure who was supposed to police it. Just imagine a woman copper going into someone's bathroom "Oohps! Sorry sir. May I measure that?"

One day in 1942/43 I was walking down to my Aunt Elsie's place. At the southern end of Queens Park Road you could see quite clearly over the coast to the English Channel. On this day there were hundreds of aircraft going to the East. It was the 'Dieppe Raid' taking place. It is worth reading about.

Whether it was a terrible failure or a useful exploratory raid will not be known for a number of years. And then it will depend on the opinion of the historian. Many Canadians were lost.

My best friends at Varndean were Arthur (Fooey) Ford and Frank Homewood. Both lived in Moulsecoomb. Fooey and I spent many years as best mates and he was later my Best Man. Our greatest joy was riding our bicycles of which more later.

Soon after the war started my Uncle Harry, was recalled to the Navy and was killed whilst serving on HMS Valencia and another of Dad's brothers, Uncle Les, went down on HMS Wren. It wasn't all fun. Dad had had a medical discharge from the Army during or just after WWl so was not called up. Mum's brother, Uncle Will, was in the army and I believe he took part in the D-Day landings in Normandy.

Oldest brother Eric, as I stated earlier, had joined the Royal Navy as a boy sailor at the age of 15 and served around the world ending up in submarines.

Oldest sister Frances had married a soldier in the Royal Artillery from Sheffield. Sam Stoneham was a very nice man and served with the Eighth Army in North Africa and Italy.

Youngest sister Irene was also at home now but what young man of fourteen years admits to having a little sister? She is the older of the children in the front row of our wedding group photo.

Around this time the war was slowly beginning to change. We had Bomber Command which was equipped with four engined heavy bombers. The Lancasters and Halifaxes. Bomber Command was beginning to hit back. Wicked though it may seem today, we were delighted to see these bomber forces building up in the skies over Brighton as they were setting off on their long and dangerous flights towards Berlin, Cologne and the railway yards at Hamm. We were at last hurting Germany. We'd been hurt for some years. Small wonder that we were so pleased. Never for a moment did I think that these cities would mean much to me in later years. I have recently spoken to a former Royal Australian Air Force pilot who was flying Halifaxes in these raids. I mentioned that we watched the build up over Brighton. He told me that sometimes during the briefings, the crews were told to deliberately fly over London as a morale booster to the population. He also remembers well the Metropole Hotel in Brighton in which, with the Grand Hotel, many Commonwealth Airmen were housed.

I remember an air raid that occurred one evening. We kids all prided ourselves on our aircraft recognition skills. Suddenly two aircraft shot very low over our house towards the Hollingbury Golf Course and the air raid warning sounded. I assured Mum that it was OK. There had been some Air Raid exercises recently up north and this was probably the same thing. The planes were Hurricanes. We watched them swing to the south towards the town. A couple of big bangs and the Hurricane myth was smashed. So much for my aircraft recognition skills.

By now my Dad was working for a food manufacturing company, Times Food Products, in Hove and, one day, during an air raid, a stack of sacks of flour collapsed and pinned him down causing a multiple fracture of the pelvis. Rita was now married to Jacky Almy and Jack worked with Dad. He evidently threw himself into pulling the sacks off Dad but the damage was already done. So again, the family income would have dropped. The Welfare State was yet to come. Add that situation to the fact that by 1943 my school results were very poor and I was considered a lost cause, I didn't pass a single exam in the end of year tests, received an 'F' (Fail) for every one. It was rightly decided that I should be out earning my living. So at the end of July 1943 at the age of 14 years and 2 months I left school. I don't know who made the decision. I don't recall any fond farewells at the end of term so I must assume that, as with the paper round, I just didn't go back.

Why did I fail so miserably? Without attempting to apportion any blame, I believe that to learn one needs to live in a learning environment. Nobody in our family, as far as I know, had ever reached the level that I'd reached. Latin, German, Physics, Chemistry, Biology, Trigonometry. Where would I have turned for help? Nobody's fault. Just circumstance. School was something that we had to do until we were fourteen years old. It had always been that way. Old enough to go out to work. I don't believe that I was ever asked if I'd done my homework and I certainly was never asked by any of the teachers if I had any learning problems. The word 'career' was never mentioned either at home or at Varndean. I think my ambition at that time was to be a long distance lorry driver. The War? Could have had something to do with it. It was a bit of a worry, at the time. I have re-read the Varndean History, see the reference below, and I see frequent mentions of School Societies, trips to places around the town, around the local rural areas and even overseas to Paris. I read of contributions, to various projects and after school activities in the school. Teachers taking a personal interest in a student's progress. Many things that brought the pupils and teachers together, out of the classroom. They all required the expense of a few coppers or sixpence or shillings. I'm pretty certain that I can say with all honesty (perhaps with the exception of the three week newspaper job), I never went to school with a penny in my pocket. There was no such thing as pocket money in our family. It just didn't exist. Apart from Detention spells, I was never at the school at any time other than normal school hours. I reckon that we were just too poor for me to go to Varndean and gain from all its activities. Of course, there is always the possibility that perhaps I could have worked a little harder. Who knows?

I didn't realise it then but, as the years have passed, it is obvious that the standard of education at Varndean was so good that, even as a failure, and with just three years at the school, I could usually hold my own, at the level on which I chose, or was destined to travel, in the big bad world outside. Of course, that could have been because of my 'sweet disposition'. From the School History "Onward and Upward - York Place to Varndean 1884-1975" it is apparent that it was an amazingly successful school. It can claim one Life Peerage, at least 5 Companions of the Order of the Bath (CB), including an Undersecretary of State, The Master of the Queens Rolls (Head of the Old Bailey), an Oscar winner, (Paul Scofield for his role in "A man for all seasons"), Dep. Ch. Scientific Adviser to the M.O.D, a number of professors, an Olympic champion in Steve Ovett, a Commonwealth Games Silver Medallist, Mike Winch, the successor to the Australian, Des Renford, to the crown of 'King of the Channel' and Olympic swimmer, Mike Read and numerous others. Jack Beavis, past Hunterian Professor Royal College of Surgeons of England, renowned for his work on trauma in disaster areas around the world is, at the time of writing, on the ground in Pakistan setting up 'repairs' for broken limbs and crushed bodies and minds from the October 2005 earthquake. Just another OV. Then, of course, there were the successful ones. Oh Yes! Then there was me.

3. Work experience 1943-46

I looked in the Evening Argus and saw a job at Payne & Cox in North Road for one pound a week, about $A2.50 (Nineteen shillings and eight pence after National Health and Pensions contributions were deducted). Those contributions, gradually inflating over a period of twenty six years, paid for my current English DSS aged pension. Of the remainder I gave fourteen shillings to Mum, spent two shillings on bus fares, two shillings in the Post Office Savings Bank (POSB) and one and eightpence pocket money. I suspect that the POSB didn't last too long 'cos I can't remember there ever being any money in the account.

Payne & Cox made small timber household products such as towel rails, garden baskets, table mats etc. My job was to operate a sanding machine alongside an old fellow who ran the big circular saw. He would cut the legs and dowels to size and I sanded them smooth for the assembly workers to put together. They were supposed to be straight utilitarian items cut and sanded square. It wasn't long however before I decided that they looked better if I sanded the tops rounded. There were no complaints so I suppose they added another shilling to the rounded ones when they sold them. The sanding machine was a big belt sander, like an upside down floor sander. If I was careless and split the belt the 'Slap, slap, slap' as it tore itself to pieces was quite frightening.

I remember that I was working with a fellow who lived down the road from me in Moulsecoomb. A very keen Army Cadet. He was the scruffiest individual in the world until he put on his uniform when he was the perfect soldier. Anyway, one day he decided to join the real Army. He would have been about fifteen and a half years old (I wasn't even that much round the tops of my legs) and suggested I go up to the Recruiting Office with him. The Office was just up the top of North Road on Queens Road. I went with him and hung around whilst the recruiting sergeant dealt with him. The Sergeant then looked at me and asked "You too?" I was horrified! Well, it was bloody dangerous. I told him "No, I'm not yet old enough" which was, thank goodness, true.

As well, at that job, there was an upstairs office on the other side of North Road in which my cousin Peggy Goddard, Uncle Will's daughter, worked. She was a very attractive girl and this would-be soldier and I used to ring her up at lunch times and chat her up. Years later I heard that she had 'got religion'. Probably never got over the fact that she had lost me.

By now I had a bicycle, and Fooey and I were the terror of Brighton. We could literally do anything on our bikes and were apt to do so. Imagine the incredulous looks when, on London Road, one of the two main shopping Roads in Brighton, two young lads would dismount, remount, but now sitting on the handlebars and riding backwards, and go merrily down the road oblivious of the horror that they were causing. These days with the modern bikes, dismounting by lifting the front wheel high into the air and sliding off the back of the bike is not unusual and fairly easy. With the old 'sit up and begs' it was not so easy. We perfected it. We would also, in a main shopping street, pull over, get off the right side of our bikes, walk around the bikes and get on again on the left and ride off again. Of course this was done in perfect unison. I suppose we were proving something or other. The only damage to property that I can ever remember was when we were doing another of our favourites. Suddenly one of us would force the other towards the pavement, up onto the pavement and going almost at a standstill pace, remain standing upright on the pedals trying to force the other off or to give way. We once went into a paling fence and broke one of the palings. Of course we were off like a shot, but I can honestly say that vandalism was the farthest thing from our minds as we did it.

Of course with all these close encounters we damaged our bikes a bit, but in those days any ten year old kid could repair most of the problems with a bike. Probably as easy to us as breaking into a car is nowadays to modern ten year old kids. I remember once we had a race out to Falmer, up over the Downs to Rottingdean (Kipling's hometown), back along the sea front road and along Lewes Road to the football pitches near the barracks, where we stopped to rest. Probably ten miles or sixteen kilometres. Whilst resting we counted the spokes left in my front wheel. I seem to remember a figure of around seventeen. I think the correct number was around thirty two. Time for repairs.

Black-out restrictions were strictly enforced, so after dark we were supposed to show just a very heavily shaded front and rear lamp. It was nothing unusual for Fooey to suddenly turn off his lamps, go shooting off ahead of me, (he had a faster bike), and to start doing lefts, rights around the houses until he lost me. I think it was at such a time that a copper shouted to him, "Hey, where's your lights?" to which Fooey replied "Next to me liver!" Of course coppers were usually on foot and did not have two way radio. Having said that I believe the Brighton coppers were the first in Britain to have some sort of radio in their helmets.

Sussex, in those days, had many square miles of woods and forests, I'm not sure what the difference is, and the wild flowers in Springtime were beautiful. We would go out on our bikes and collect bunches of Bluebells, Primroses,

Cowslips and Daffodils to take home to our Mums. These would hang in bunches from our handlebars as we rode home.

The only newspapers that came into our house were the 'Daily Express' on weekdays and the 'News of the World' on Sundays, this is more accurately dubbed today as 'Screws of the World'. Divorce then was a very dishonourable thing. There had to be a guilty party and this had to be proven in court. As a consequence the Divorce Courts provided a never-ending stream of salacious reading for the 'News of the World', which published it fearlessly. The Daily Express, on the other hand, was a respectable paper. Not up to the Times or Telegraph (English type) yet not down to the Daily Mirror. As well, the Daily Express had 'Giles' every day. Giles was one of the greatest cartoonists ever. We have, even now, thirteen Giles Annuals, a collection of his best cartoons in any year. Of course many of the cartoons were topical and would not seem so humorous today, his 'family' characters however lived on for years.

Now that I was earning my keep I could afford to buy a weekly boys magazine. My favourites were the 'Champion' and 'Hotspur'. I never failed to read 'Rockfist Rogan, RAF' first. Rockfist was a fighter pilot who, in between shooting down German Me. 109's thought nothing of landing in enemy territory to go 15 rounds with the Luftwaffe heavyweight champion, then quickly escaping again after putting him 'on the canvas'. Meanwhile, from the Brighton Library I was an avid 'William' (Richmal Crompton) fan (with Violet Elizabeth Bart being sick everywhere) and a firm believer in 'Biggles' (W.E. Johns) together with Ginger and Archie.

After about six months at P & C I saw a job advertised for a Transport Clerk at the Danish Bacon Company. They were a national company and their Brighton branch was down the bottom of Moulsecoomb Way. Just right for me. All I had to do was walk past a few houses, then past the Allen West Moulsecoomb factory to be at work. As soon as I said that I was educated at Varndean I got the job. I think the pay was about twenty two and six. My first job each day was to record everything that was loaded on to the four delivery vans, three four tonners and one three tonner. I still remember part of the registration numbers: FLN 196, DMD 626 and two others. FLN was driven by Fred Lacey and DMD, a new vehicle, was driven by Vince Marcantonio.

Every order was already printed on a delivery form on a comptometer, the forerunner of today's computers, and I had firstly to check that each item was ticked off as being loaded. If it was an item of variable weight, such as a side of bacon then I had to record its weight. There would be all the drivers and mates loading the first van, then two less for the second and so on till the last van pulled out leaving just the warehouse staff. I had to write every item down on foolscap sheets and put a weight down for each item. This meant that I had to train myself, when we were not loading, to go round, take a case of every item to the scales, weigh it and memorise the weight. Thus a fifty six pound case of butter weighed sixty three pounds. A case of thirty packets of Corn Flakes weighed thirty three pounds. When all the vans had gone I had to use a Burroughs Adding Machine, a bit like the old one arm bandits, to calculate the weight in each vehicle to show that they were not being overloaded. Of course if they were it would have been too late. I then had to take the next days delivery dockets and put them in order so that the last shop on the run was the first to be loaded on to the van. This again was a memory job because I had never been on any of the runs and most of them were spread throughout the Sussex countryside. I soon became adept and recently heard a name which I said straight away to myself, Partridge Green. I think the name was Mercers. I did the refuelling of the vans when they came in after the day's runs and kept the fuel records (very strictly rationed).

On one occasion Jimmy Nickless, remember that name, one of the van-boys came to me (aged about 15 ½) and said that there had been an extra ham loaded on his van that day and the driver had decided to keep it. He asked if he should report it. He was about a year older than me. I think I told him that it was up to him. A ham would not show on the stock lists as missing because there was always a weight wastage factor.

I also did a daily check of the measurable rationed goods such as butter, margarine and cheese. I had the previous days stock, subtracted today's orders then counted today's stock. This led to a very sad result. I was still only about sixteen years old and one day the stock was a half pound packet of butter short. After rechecking my records and calculations it had to be true. Of course there was no weight wastage factor with packeted or boxed goods. I reported it to my boss the Transport Manager. He asked me who had been in the Cold Store that morning cleaning and it turned out to be an ex-policeman who with his twin brother, also a copper, had been well known and loved around Brighton. As he left that evening my boss asked him to open his bag. He was fired on the spot. It was so silly. There was no secret to the fact that I counted the cold-store stock daily.

At about this time I had a very severe attack of my chest problem. It was on the day of a full warehouse stocktake. I had counted in the morning and was feeling very bad at lunchtime. Mum tried to stop me going back to work in the afternoon but I said that it was too important to do the stocktake. After work I started walking up Moulsecoomb Way. Allen West's had a low brick wall with a high wire fence behind it all the way along their property. I sat down on the wall and took some breath. Then I went a little further and sat down again. As I got farther up the hill I sat down more frequently. Once past the end of the factory I walked all the way home. Outside the house I only had three small flights of steps to go up. I went up them and into the house. Mum was at the table and I stood in front of the sofa. I must have passed out because I don't remember anything else about it except that, years later, Mum told me that the doctor had said that if I 'pulled through the night' I would be OK! This was why when, just before the end of the war, DBC asked me if I would like to be their permanent on-call Fire-Watcher for ten shillings a week extra, Mum wouldn't let me take the job. It would mean getting out of bed whenever there was an Air-raid warning and going down to work to deal with any incendiaries that may be dropped on the place. As it happened we never had another Air-raid. Another medal chance gone. I'd have been entitled to the Defence Medal if I'd done it.

But that is not in chronological order.

I learned two other valuable lessons at DBC. Both connected with hazardous situations. In those days, electric power plugs weren't all earthed. Two pin plugs were common. In my office I had an electric fire with a round two pin plug which I decided to plug in one day. As I plugged it in my fingers were touching the pins and I received the whole 250 volts. Lesson one. The second was when I was burning off a load of packing materials outside the warehouse and drew off some petrol (naughty lad) to get it started. With my eyebrows singed I had learned lesson two.

One day in 1944, Fred Lacey had been on the Eastbourne run. When he came back he said that people in Eastbourne had been crouching against walls looking up at the sky and there were terrible sounding aircraft going over: Dozens of them. That night it was announced that Hitler had unleashed his secret Victory weapon, the V1. These came to be known as Doodle bugs. They were pilotless aircraft, driven by a blow-lamp. They were just flying bombs. Their engine (ram jet) noise was distinctive. They were fired from ramps all round the European coastline and aimed generally at London. They had a pre-set engine run time. When the engine cut-out they glided to the ground and exploded. If you could hear the engine you were OK. If you heard it stop you ran for cover. I can only remember hearing one stop and that was because it was shot down by a fighter. It exploded in mid-air. If we youngsters were out on the Downs when they flew across and we saw some Typhoons or Spitfires racing after them, we would wave our hands and point to the direction in which they'd gone. I doubt that the pilots had time to notice us but it would be nice to think that we may have guided them once or twice. I believe that the practice of Deception flourished with advent of the Doodle bugs. If a batch landed on London the BBC would announce that they had landed 20 miles north or south of the city. Then if the Germans rectified the engine run, the probability was that they would indeed land 20 miles off target. Hopefully in country areas.

The V1's were followed by the V2's and though they were far more destructive, the fact that they were a rocket, soundless and invisible in flight, meant that we never really worried about them in Brighton. Again they were aimed at London.

A couple of weeks before my sixteenth birthday the war in Europe came to an end. Most companies took the day off but we had to get our scheduled food deliveries out so it was work almost as usual. The difference was that the boss asked me if I'd like to go out with the country run that day. I accepted, and saw for the first time, some of the places that I knew by heart from my office desk. I don't remember taking part in any other Victory celebrations.

Behind our house there was a small wood and beyond that a steep valley. We often tried to sit on our bikes and let them go down the hill. It was typical downland. Lots of grass, gorse and bumps. Most times we finished up being belted in the crotch by the cross-bar. It is a wonder that any of the family came into being when you think about it. It hurts me just to think of it.

Dad was now back at work at Times Food and decided to go back into the Wet and Dry fish trade. Much of his early life had been spent as a fishmonger working, I think, for an uncle. He opened a shop in Brunswick Street East, Hove and talked me into leaving the DBC to help Mum to run it. I had a trades carrier bike. Small front wheel with a tray above it and a normal size rear wheel with another tray above that. You could carry two boxes of fish on the front and one on the back. A box of fish would have been about a metre long, half a metre wide and thirty centimeters deep. Each box would be filled with fish and topped up with ice. They were bloody heavy. I would have to be down the Fish Market at the sea front by just after five each morning and, with Dad, attended the fish auctions. He would help me to load up then go off to work, leaving me to go to the shop in Hove, unload and, with Mum, run the shop. In the evenings I would do the books for the shop. One set for us, one for the Ministry of Food. After I had done that, I would help him to do work that he'd brought home from Times Food. I was working, probably, a sixteen hour day.

After a while he gave up the Times Food job and came into the shop. The main trouble was that there were two pubs up the top of the street. Both were customers. Huh. That cheeky face of mine came up again when, one day when I was delivering fish to the nearest pub, I was leaning on the counter of the Bottle and Jug Dept. Dad was in one of the bars talking to an important looking man. The man looked up and saw me and said "D'you know Chris, that kid over there has the cheekiest looking face I have ever seen." to which the old man answered "That's my son."

I became quite adept at cleaning, scaling and filleting fish, but never succeeded in getting rid of the fishy smell that must have clung to everything I wore. I still didn't own many clothes.

Fooey Ford's aunt and uncle, who lived in East Barnet, invited Fooey and myself up to their place for a holiday. We were about sixteen I suppose. He was (to us) an old man but very likable. He took us round the Abbey at St Albans and many other interesting (I suppose) places and then one day asked us if we'd like to go to a theatre 'Up West'. That is the London term for the West End. This was living with a capital Wow. Of course we accepted; he was paying. Imagine our surprise when we went to the Duke of Yorks, right in the heart of London's theatre land. Even more surprising was that the show we were to see was one of Brian Rix's famous bedroom farces. Sort of 'what the butler saw'. This was extremely risque for the time and our age. We probably blushed all the way through but it was certainly enjoyable. I almost said memorable, but I can't remember a thing about it!

Another disgraceful incident was when Ron and I told Mum that we were going to the Imperial to see 'I walk beside you' or something like that. Actually we went to the Hippodrome to see the best known English Strip-tease artist of the time, I think she called herself Venus. I wonder why? When we got home I wandered around the house, trying to cool my blood down, humming and whistling the tune 'I walk beside you' whilst Ron kept nudging me and saying that that was not what the film was about!

When I was around sixteen I started going to the local dance hall. Moulsecoomb Hall was a shilling 'hop' every Saturday night. There was a three or four piece dance band and they served tea and cakes during the interval. My reason for starting was to chaperone Frances who's husband Sam was still in Europe with the army. It became a habit and I started to learn how to dance the waltz, fox-trot and quickstep. I never did get round to mastering the exotic dances. After a while Fooey and I made it a weekly do. We had lots of fun and used to have competitions as to who could dance with the most girls in one night. We especially liked Xmas when there was lots of mistletoe around to be kissed under and people carried a twig of it in their hands while they were dancing. We would dance with a girl, hold our hand above their head and get a kiss. They would then notice that we didn't have any mistletoe and we'd ask "Who needs mistletoe when you've got technique?".

Around February 1946 I decided that I was going to get out from under. I was talking to the fellow that owned the greengrocery shop next to the fish shop. He said that I wouldn't dare give Dad a weeks notice and anyway where would I get another job. I said I'd go back to DBC. He asked why would they take me back and I told him that I knew they would. That day I gave my notice to the old man and went to DBC. My old boss was standing on the loading dock and asked me what I wanted. I told him that I wanted a reference for a job with Stewarts, (bloody liar!) another food distributor in Hove. He asked me if I would like to go back to DBC. I said, tongue in cheek, that they wouldn't be able to pay me enough. He asked how much and I took a plunge and said twenty five shillings. He was gone for a few minutes and when he returned I was re-employed as a Warehouse and Transport Clerk at twenty five shillings a week.

By now I was beginning to notice girls. Probably dancing had awakened instincts that I hadn't known existed. In those days we danced with a girl, not just on the same dance floor! I was already dancing with Pat at the Hall though nothing steady as yet. Now at DBC there was another bird, two in fact, who I found that I could fancy. Joan and Sheila, both acquaintances (members of the Womens' Junior Air Corps) if not close friends of Pat. In fact, I think that at this time Fooey was more interested in Pat than I was. However he couldn't dance as well as me. His waltz was like a military manoeuvre. Done with precision and quick fire action. Left! Right! Together!, Right! Left! Together! Hardly the stuff that romance would be born of. We were also now branching out a bit and going to the Regent or Princes Hall. The Regent was famous for its sprung dance floor and had a very good orchestra.

At work I was going along well, I had even done a few evening classes in shorthand and typing. Frances was now expecting her first child. Obviously Sam had been demobbed! Eric's wife Ruby had come over from Ireland to live with us. She was a wild thing and I believe that she sometimes scared me but we got on very well. I recall that some evenings, after work, I would get home and ask for some tea. Mum would sit at one end of the table cutting bread, Ruby would sit in the middle buttering and jamming and I would sit at the other end eating it as fast as they could go!

A weird experience occurred late one night. Mum and I were the only ones home downstairs. Peter and Rene were probably in bed. We were listening to a play of 'The Invisible Man' on the wireless. Very creepy. Then from the kitchen there came this strange noise. Mum looked at me, I looked at Mum. I was now too big to hide behind her skirt so I had to creep out to see who was there. It was the Burco electric wash boiler boiling over. Mum had put some washing on and forgotten it!

Probably the most important event, one that could have changed my life entirely, now occurred at work. I was seventeen years old. The only employees in the company younger than me were a couple of van boys a couple of office girls and one of the warehouse boys. The warehouse staff were mainly well into their fifties and sixties except for the supervisor who would have been forty. They knew the bacon smoking and food distribution industries inside out. One of the Salesmen resigned and the Warehouse Supervisor was offered the job. He accepted. To my surprise, my old boss, the Transport Supervisor asked me if I would be interested in the Warehouse Supervisor's job. I was only seventeen! Many of my friends were still at school! Branch (in reality County) Warehouse Supervisor at that age, in a nationwide company, could have seen me as National Warehouse Manager at some time. I had to say "Yes". Never even thought that there would have been a million complications for me. He went into the Branch Manager and there were very lengthy discussions. Eventually he came out, very disappointed, and told me that the top men had decided that I was too young for the job. On hindsight, it is obvious that they were right, but at the time it seemed that the end of the world had come.

A few weeks later, three of us warehouse boys decided to ask for a rise. I don't know if you know the Franz Schubert song that has a chorus which goes " Arise, arise, my lady sweet arise", well we went round the warehouse all day singing that, then went into the boss and asked for one. We got half a crown, which took me up to twenty seven and sixpence a week.

War stories were still all the go in the cinema, masses of propaganda. One of these was a story about the RAF's Air Sea Rescue service starring Tyrone Power. Pulling 'downed' fighter pilots out of the channel seemed a very rewarding career. Anyway, the war was now over, so it was fairly safe. The cold war had not yet begun in earnest, as far as the general public was concerned. A few days later I went to the RAF recruiting office and asked for signing on papers. Mum and Dad tried to dissuade me, I think Dad offered to give me a job back in the fish shop with a van instead of the bike but my mind was made up. I was soon going to be roaring around the English Channel in a high speed launch, wearing big white roll neck jerseys and white woollen socks hanging over the tops of sea-boots.

4. Sons of the Lords of the Air 1946-47

My papers came through in due course and on November 27, 1946 I travelled up to Croydon where I joined a crowd of other young boys and girls with similar high ideals. I got friendly with a girl named Johnnie (honestly) from Kent and carried her bags for her when we were sent to Euston (I think it was) and put on a LMS train to Bedford. The girls were sent to RAF Wilmslow in Cheshire. At Bedford we were picked up by RAF transport and taken to RAF Cardington. Cardington was the home of the old ill fated British airship R101 and the airship hangar was, and probably is still, there. Cardington was the intake centre for new volunteer recruits, as opposed to National Service types. It was the end of November, it was in England and worse still, it was in the region written of by John Bunyan (I'm told) as 'The Sloth of Despond'. I don't know what that means but I certainly knew what it felt like. It was wet and foggy and cold. We never walked or marched, we sloshed around doing all the preliminary bits required to put handcuffs on ex-human beings.

We were issued with uniforms. As a lad of average height, average weight, average shoe size etc. it was difficult to get anything to fit. We were taught how to form up into three ranks and the beginnings of how to march. We also took the oath of allegiance to the King, his heirs and successors. And then came the bit we'd all joined for. To be checked for suitable trade training. This started with a series of Intelligence Tests from which I emerged unscathed and with a somewhat enhanced set of papers. These were followed by interviews by Senior N.C.O's for trade suitability.

"You wanted Motor Boat Crew."

"Yes, Sergeant."

"You'd be wasting your time."

"I'd what, Sergeant?"

"Waste of time. Why don't you try a Radar and Wireless Fitter test?"

"Yes, Sergeant."

I did a 20 or 50 (a lot anyway) question test on physics, mechanics and other sciences that are part of radio engineering. I did know that Tungsten had a higher melting point than Lead. I may have known one or two others but 2 or 3 out of 50 wasn't the result they were looking for.

"You didn't do too well at that did you." It wasn't a question it was a statement.

"No, Sergeant."

"All right, we'll send you along for a Morse Aptitude test."

"A what, Sergeant?"

"Never mind, go along the corridor there."

This was a different matter altogether. I had to put a pair of headphones on and had a sheet of paper with 50 sets of boxes headed SAME or DIFFERENT. From the headphones pairs of combinations of dashes and dots issued. After each pair I had to determine whether they were the same or not and mark the sheet accordingly. This I could do. As the test went on the combinations got more and more complex but I found that I could make a sort of rhythm out of them. No problems. I think I probably got them all correct.

"That's better lad. Now you've got two choices. Coxswain, Motor Boat Crew, or into Signals as a Wireless Operator."

"What would be best Sergeant?"

"Dead end as MBC, big future in Signals." ....They needed Wireless Ops.!

So that was it. After a week we moved up to No. 4 Recruit Centre, Royal Air Force Station, Wilmslow, in Cheshire. I was now 4014453 AC2 Common. A.W. (note there is no 's' on the end!). Wilmslow was the square-bashing and basic service training unit. Every new recruit had to do 8 weeks of square-bashing. This consisted of marching, halting, wheeling, turning, saluting on the march with and without rifles, rifle drill, rifle shooting, hand grenade throwing ("Get back up lad, you've got seven seconds with these, NOW GET DOWN!"). One of the weapons we were trained on was the Sten Gun. A very light, very cheap and very unstable weapon. It used to pull diagonally upwards as you fired off a burst. To hit anything on the 25 yard range was, for me, almost an impossibility. One of the Drill sergeants could place a small piece of wood on the range and shoot it continuously up the bank. Wilmslow was farther North than Bedford by a hundred or so miles and colder by about 5 degrees. We are talking about the seriously cold degrees now. Those around the -3 to +2 region. As well we were at the start of one of the worst English winters in many years.

It was at Wilmslow that I first came across what Air Force discipline meant. At 9.30 every night you were expected to be standing by your bed whilst the corporal Drill Instructor inspected the billet and ensured that every airman was in. At that time I found that it was better if I shaved at night instead of in the morning. Lights Out were at 10.00 so it was usually a rush after the corporal finished his inspection to get out to the 'ablutions' and do the necessary. About the end of the first week we were standing waiting for him to turn up. It was getting later and later until eventually I told the chap in the next bed that I was going out for my shave and to let me know when the corporal turned up.

I had got my faced well and truly lathered and started to shave when a fellow rushed in and said the corporal wanted me in the billet. I told him to tell the corporal to hang on a minute as I was shaving. You know. I said it nicely. He was gone about ten seconds when he was back to tell me that the corporal said "NOW!" I couldn't understand what the rush was all about suddenly. After all, it was him that was late not me. I went into the billet and into a massive storm. Next morning I was in front of the Flight Commander where I was told a little about Air Force discipline. When he'd finished the Flight Commander asked me if I had any questions. I said "Yes Sir, is there any chance of being transferred to a Commonwealth Air Force?" I didn't have the temerity nor probably the wit to respond to his answer, as I would now, "I can take that as a definite 'No' then, can I?"

To ensure that you got rifle movements perfectly correct there was a training method called Rifle Drill by Numbers. The rifle is 'at the slope' when it is against the left shoulder and supported by the left hand. Bringing it down to the ground again is known as "Order Arms". The command was "Ordering arms by numbers, By numbers, ONE!!!" at which command you brought the rifle straight down the left side of your body with the left hand and holding it upright by bringing your right hand up and across the chest. You then held this position whilst the sergeant walked round the flight and checked/corrected every airman. Thirty airmen usually to one flight. If and when he was satisfied he would give the next movement, ("Ordering by numbers, By numbers TWO!!!"). As I said earlier this was a very bad winter and around December 15th or so we were standing at the "ONE" position for one hell of a long time, whilst the little Welsh SOB of a sergeant did his fancy thing. Gradually I could feel my feet freezing, then my legs, then my.... well to cut a long story short, the next thing I knew I was lying face down on the ground, my rifle butt between my legs and blood pouring from my chin. I had blacked out. Luckily we were still training with 18 inch (450 mm) bayonets affixed to our rifles. The foresight of my rifle had gone into my chin. If we'd had the later 6 inch bayonets (pig stickers) I'd probably have come off much worse. Of course I still have that scar. The little Welsh sergeant used to stand in front of the flight, look at us with disgust registering on his face and in his voice as he would say "Sons of the lords of the air, Huh!"

Girls. Well there was no shortage of kaifer. I had a 'sort of understanding' with Pat at this time. I would arrange to see her INSIDE the Moulsecoomb Hall on a Saturday night (this was before joining up). There were no Saturday nights for the first two or three months in the Air Force. Inside because it was cheaper than outside. I didn't have to buy her ticket. I had a similar understanding with Joan C, also at the Moulsecoomb Hall. At Wilmslow I had bumped into Johnnie again. We used to see each other in the Church

Army hall. Here you could eat cakes and drink tea till about 9.00 pm when it closed. This was to allow time for the bed-check and lights out. It was in the Church Army hall that they had the 'Two foot Rule'. No airman was allowed to sit with a WAAF with their knees closer than two feet. It ruined many a promising romance. So I had three 'girlfriends'. This was to increase come the New Year!

After four weeks at Wilmslow we were given a 48 hour pass. The nearest place was Manchester where there was a big new NAAFI (Navy, Army and Air Force's Institute) Club. These were a new thing at that time and were more palatial than anything I had ever experienced. We all rushed off to the Club and spent the week-end gorging ourselves silly with posh nosh, having photo's taken in our uniforms at Jeromes, trying to 'get-off' with Waafs and Wracs, unsuccessfully I might add, we were too obviously 'sprogs' and as such, very poor. I had my first private RAF photo taken there. I can't believe how young I looked in it. I was still under eighteen. That photo features again later!

Back to camp for another week or so when we were granted Xmas and New Year leave. I spent Xmas in Moulsecoomb and had been to the Hall for the dance. I'd arranged to see Pat on New Years Eve INSIDE. Then I received an invitation from friends of Dad's who lived in Kent to spend New Year's Eve with them. They were well off and had a big enough house to allow me to stay the night. They had a piano which one of the sons could play properly. Y'know, from music sheets with all the digits of both hands. I remember that because he played a piece of music and asked if I knew it. I proudly said "Yes, it's 'I'm always chasing rainbows'." He promptly showed me how ignorant I was by saying that actually it was Chopin's Fantasy Impromptu, or something like that.

We went to the New Years Eve Ball there where I was introduced to their friends and finished up spending most of the evening dancing with a very tall girl. My nose came up to her 'wotsits'. Fascinating! Anyway she wanted to write to me afterwards so I took her name and address back to camp with me.

There was another bird somewhere in the offing because I know that there were now five on my books. Can't remember who the other one was. Probably another Waaf. Trouble with having 5 birds is that you have to write to 5 birds and that's too much. When conversations got round to women in the billets, as it invariably would, I was looked upon as a bit of a god. Anyway I started farming out names and addresses to mates who had not got girl friends. I suppose it's lucky that I didn't farm out Pat's.

Of course while all this was going on Pat went to the Moulsecoomb Hall on New Year's Eve and I wasn't there. I don't suppose she'd have been miserable for too long!

By now I had written on the emulsion side of a copy of my photo "To Johnnie, with all my love, Alf." Somehow or other I never gave it to her. I can't remember why.

Towards the end of January we completed our recruit training. This is normally finalised with a 'Passing out parade'. When our turn came the whole of Cheshire and Lancashire and most of England was under ice and snow. The parade was cancelled and early one morning we trod our way carefully out of camp in Indian file to the railway station to get our various trains home for 'end of course' leave.

I was now an AC2 u/t w/op.tpo. That is to say an Aircraftsman 2nd Class, Wireless operator and Teleprinter operator, under training. Unfortunately courses don't start just because there are would-be trainees waiting, so I was sent to RAF Fairford in Gloucestershire to mark time. I said earlier that the winter of 46/47 was to be one of the hardest on record. The train travel for a forty mile section of the journey from London took me eight hours!

At Fairford the accommodation was Nissen Huts, corrugated iron clad, semi-circular, constructions. Snow forms naturally to their contours so the camp looked like one great mass of snow hills. Fuel for room heating was still very much rationed, I think that the ration per billet was two buckets of coke per day. A bucket would not fill up a single stove, there were two stoves in each billet. The billets had rooms at each end which served as the NCO's i/c Billet's room and store rooms. These were separated from the main big 'dormitory' accommodation by doorways. By the end of the winter of 46/47 not one billet had doors or shelves inside the main front and back doors. Everything that could be burned was burned. As well there was a wood, within the airfield, owned by some private landowner. He lost many, many trees that winter. If you'll excuse my French, it was bloody cold.

Fairford's purpose in 1947 was as a glider towing unit. There was a squadron of Halifax four engined bombers, converted for glider towing, and the Army had a lot of Horsa Troop Carrying Gliders. I was attached to the Halifax Squadron, or so I thought. I reported to the Signals Section for work each day. I learned my next big lesson. If you had diesel oil and water and a pot bellied stove, you didn't need to be cold. It was probably the most dangerous and hottest fire I have ever seen. A drum of diesel oil and a drum of water were placed on a shelf about five feet off the floor. Both were fitted with taps. The taps were positioned immediately over the opening in the top of the stove. The lid of the stove was removed. In the stove, where you would usually light the paper, wood and coal there was a tin lid sitting on a small amount of paper and wood. The lid was facing upward so that it acted as a shallow bowl. The paper and wood were lit and the tin lid got very hot. The diesel oil was then turned on so that a tiny drip, drip, drip would fall onto the hot tin lid. It immediately vaporised and burned. Then the water was turned on to drip, drip, drip. The combination created a roaring inferno which had the skin of the stove red hot in minutes.

The snow had cut off villages in the north midlands and it was decided that the Halifaxes would attempt to drop food to them. Every officer and airman on the camp was sent onto the runway with shovels and brooms and we had to clear the runway to allow the kites to take off. When eventually one took off it returned to camp saying that it had been unable to get down low enough to identify the village of Buxton. The Derbyshire moors are pretty high. The Wing Commander was disgusted and said that he would do the job and an Army Major went for the joy-ride in the rear gunners spot. The Wingco ploughed the Halifax into the hillside and all on board were lost. My introduction to the sort of tragedy that can suddenly hit a service establishment. I'm glad to say that they were few and far between.

It was then decided that I should not have been in Squadron Signals but in SHQ Signals. I moved across and watched while everybody did things. SHQ Signals also controlled the telephone exchange and I was in there one day when the operator asked me if I'd like to ring anybody, anywhere in the U.K. I don't think I had ever made a trunk call before so I said that I would like to call my dad in his shop. The operator connected me and I heard my dad answer. I said "This is Alf" to which he replied "Alf Who?" I know that he had a friend named Alf Pierce but it did rather hurt at the time.

I saw the winter out at Fairford. The only other thing I can remember was getting a lift in a jeep one Friday to go home for the week-end. The ice was like glass on the road and as we went into Swindon around a corner the jeep did a 180 degree slide. The driver thought this was great fun and did another to get it back on track. I, sitting in the back seat, hanging on for dear life, (no seat belts in those days) was not amused.

In April of '47 I was posted to No 3 Radio School, Compton Basset in Wiltshire. The nearest town was Calne whose fame was made on Harris's Sausages. Like most small towns near RAF Stations, it's train service was known as The Flier. The Calne Flier. Next to Harris's sausages the most famous thing near Compton Basset was the White Horse at Cherhill. This was one of the ancient carvings on the hillside and can be seen for many miles from the air. We went up to there for walks a few times.

I think that by now the girlfriend stakes had been whittled down to just the two. Both in Brighton. Both known to each other. Talk about living dangerously. I can't put a date on the time that Pat emerged as the only contestant. She was certainly 'my girl' at the end of '47. I rubbed out the "To Johnnie" on the photo and added "To Pat" around this time. The trouble was that I had written it on the emulsion side of the print with a hard pencil. The indentation was still there and, I suspect, is still there to this day.

Training at Compton Basset was scheduled as a 30 week course with mid-course leave after week 15. There would have been many hundreds of airmen trainees there at any one time. The school area was in the middle of the camp. A mass of very large wooden huts. The living accommodation which were the standard RAF wooden huts were the furthest from the entrance whilst the Station Headquarters and Administration area were the nearest. The main road that ran past, near the camp, was the Great West Road, the A4. A walk from the billets to the Guardroom would have taken about 10 to 15 minutes.

To move this many airmen around every morning, every lunch time and every afternoon it was necessary that they be marched. To achieve this Compton Bassett was fitted with a massive 'Tannoy' Public Address system which, apart from being used for making important announcements as on most RAF Stations, and sounding reveille, was used for broadcasting stirring marches at all major movement times. It was the only camp that I ever went to that had this. So we learned all the most famous march tunes over that 30 weeks.

We studied three major subjects. Morse, Typing/teleprinting, and radio and direction finding theories. The radio theory was fairly basic and was more concerned with the ability to tune and operate various types of service receivers and transmitters. Morse was the thing that most ex trainees will never forget. It was literally pounded into us. We started at 4 wpm (words per minute) and had to pass out at 18 wpm. Most of the training was in alpha/numeric coded groups. This meant that you couldn't anticipate what was coming. We also, after a few weeks of both Morse training and typing training, started to do TAM (Typing Aural Morse). Our Morse Instructor, Mr. Tickle, was a civilian ex-Royal Navy operator, usually considered the best there is. He took us all through our course and in the thirty weeks only made one sending mistake. He'd had a tooth out that morning!

As we started each lesson he would say in his broad northern accent "Six (eight, ten) words a minute. Slow, easy and coomfortable". When we were doing sending practice, keying, he would pound the desk with a thick cane, with the rhythm that we were supposed to be matching. There is no doubt that he was a top quality instructor.

Typing, on old Imperial typewriters, also had to be rhythmic. For this we would have the material which we were to type alongside our machines, wear earphones and type to the music of a slow waltz, which in time became a faster waltz! Later, of course, the waltz was replaced by Morse code.

In teleprinting we had to be able to type at 25 wpm. Whilst this seems slow compared with normal typist speeds, the old teleprinters could only operate at a maximum of 66 wpm and rhythm was again very important. A word was considered to be five characters and one space so 25 wpm was 150 key strokes per minute. Not too slow.

The last part of the training, Direction Finding (D/F) was my favourite. It used words like 'goniometer'. Real show-off talk. People talk about Mathematicians seeing beauty in figures, I had the same feeling for the theory of D/F. It was known as the 'Development of the Cardioid' and seemed so natural to me. Years later ... but that is to come.

Most week-ends we were allowed a 36 hour pass. This was from Saturday at mid-day to midnight on Sunday. This was not long enough to go home so we would spend those week-ends on camp or in Calne, swimming in the river or perhaps going to Chippenham a bigger town than Calne. Every fourth week we were given a 48 hour pass. With a 48 hr pass we also got a 48 hour food ration ticket which helped our families to keep us over the week-end. Everything was still very much rationed. Britain may have won the war but was having one helluva time winning the peace.

Of course we were still on minimal wages, I think it was still 28 shillings a week of which I had allowed 7 shillings to Mum so I had just over a pound a week to live on. We therefore could not afford to catch a train home. The Great West Road at 4 pm on a Friday afternoon became a long stream of airmen hitch-hiking towards London. Compton Basset was not the only RAF station in the area. Most people would start from the camp and start thumbing it toward London, 87 miles away. Me? I was crafty. I walked away from London towards Chippenham. This way any lifts had to see me first. We invariably got a lift. We were all in uniform. The fear of hitch-hikers was not as it is now and the wartime idea of giving a serviceman a lift was still strong. We could finish up in or on anything. A lorry with twenty or thirty airmen sitting in the open back was a common sight. Our forage caps could be unclipped to make a balaclava and they usually were in winter when on such a lift. We would reach London or somewhere in the suburbs late at night usually. I would then get on an all-night tram and go to the end of the line at Coulsdon North. From there I would start the thumb going again. Sometimes the trip would go easily and I would be in Brighton by late Friday night. They were the good ones.

The lifts from London to Brighton very early or not so early on a Saturday morning could be very interesting. I once had a lift from a lady who assured me all the way down that she knew she was safe because I was so young. She stopped half way to go into the bushes for a pee. I stayed where I was and got to Brighton unsullied. Another interesting one was with two fellows in a Sunbeam-Talbot sports car. We shot Bolney X-roads at in excess of 100 miles per hour (160 KPH). That was scary in an entirely different way.

The best lift I ever got was in a Rolls Royce going through London. It was filled with very rich men and girls going from a party. It would have been early Saturday morning. The ride was so smooth I could have stayed there all night but they had other ideas and dropped me off somewhere or other.

Going back to camp meant leaving Brighton at about 5 on Sunday afternoon on a train to Victoria. Tube to Paddington and train to Swindon and thence to Calne. There were usually buses to take us back to camp. Into bed by about half past midnight and up again for reveille.

Of course we were still airmen. Some C.O.s would even go as far as to say that we were first of all soldiers, then airmen. Soldiers? Pongoes? Brown Jobs? What an insult. Our billets were inspected daily so, before we went to school, we had to pull our beds to pieces, place the biscuits (3 piece straw mattresses) one on top of the other, then have our blankets and sheets folded blanket, sheet, blanket, sheet, and blanket, all wrapped around with a fourth blanket. And regardless of the fact that they were all made of very pliable materials they had to be absolutely square! These sat on top of the biscuits. Our spare clothing was stored in ammunition boxes under the bed. No such things as wardrobes. A room-job roster was pinned to the notice board and we had to do our allotted room-job every day of the week.

During the fifteenth week, my room job was to clean out the fire grates. I did this assiduously each morning. Imagine my surprise, then, when half way through the mid-course exams our room sergeant, another five foot nothing load of whatever, came bursting into the classroom, yelled out my name and screamed "You're on a charge!" It seemed that some lousy bastard had eaten an orange just before going to work and had thrown the peel into the already cleaned fire. It was no use me pleading that I had cleaned the fireplace out; the evidence that I hadn't was there. I went before the C.O. and was awarded 5 days 'jankers' – the common term for Confined to Camp (CC). But we were due to go on mid-course leave next day. I decided to appeal to the Wing Commander "Pecker" Smith, the most feared man in the school. Funny, he was also five foot nothing. I was marched into his office and put my case. He yelled at me that there was no way I was going to go on leave with my hair as long as that. Get it cut! Then come back! I went to the School Office and asked for an 'out of school chit'. When asked what for, I told them that it was for a haircut. They nearly died laughing until I said that it was on Wing Commander Smith's orders! I had the chit in my hand in seconds, got my hair cut, went back to Pecker's office, got his approval to delay my Jankers until I got back from leave and went off for a 'you beaut' two weeks.

Butting in here, more on jankers in a while. You may recall in Chapter 1, I said that Mum never wore trousers in her life. At this time it was still a little bit avant garde for a girl to wear trousers (slacks) unless she was in the army, the land army, a bus conductress or a factory worker. Pat owned a nice pair of check patterned slacks. We met one day with our bikes and were going up to my Mum's. Pat was wearing her slacks. I told her that she couldn't wear them to go visiting my Mum. She was immediately huffy and wanted to know why not? I said that I just wouldn't take her to my mother's home wearing slacks.

It was our first row and the first time I'd seen her hot temper. We rode back to her place to allow her to change into a skirt and rode back towards my Mum's. There was a bus conductor stopped on the side of the road trying to replace the chain on his bike. Pat crashed into his pedal and just rode on. Didn't even say "Sorry". That was the first time her wild streak nearly got me into trouble. It happened again many years later, around 1965.

Jankers. Best to be avoided if possible. Especially on a very widespread camp. For five days I had to get up at about five, wash and shave, polish my brasses and boots, put on full webbing kit (packs and water bottle filled) and 'best blue' uniform. Go down to the Guard-room which was by the main gate, as far as possible from the billets, parade with the other 'defaulters' to be inspected by the Orderly Officer, return to my billet, change into working clothes, go to breakfast, then to work. At dinner time (mid-day) immediately after eating I again had to go to the guard-room, parade and inspection, return to the billet and march off to afternoon school. After school we went to tea, then again change into best blues with full webbing, go to the guard-room be inspected, allocated fatigue duties, which could be washing up the 'tins' in the mess or peeling tomorrows potatoes or scrubbing somewhere clean. These started at six thirty and lasted a couple of hours (after we'd been back to change our uniforms again). Then it was back to the Guard-room at about 9.30pm for a final inspection. Same again next day, for five days.

As a matter of interest, full webbing kit consisted of belt with brass buckles, two shoulder straps with brass end tabs, bayonet frog, back pack, side pack and water bottle. All buckles and tabs were brass and had to be polished. All webbing parts had to be 'blanco'd' with blue/grey blanco. All packs had to be filled. After five days I was a physical wreck.

It would have been just after this that a kit inspection was rostered. All your service issue kit is laid out on the bed, neatly folded, cleaned and numbered. The inspecting officer comes round and checks each airman's kit whilst they are standing by their beds. Every airman hates kit inspections. (See 1952 later) My mate Sparks Pile and I decided that we were going to skive off this one. We went on Sick Parade instead. There was nothing wrong with us and, until the time that I stood in front of the M.O., I hadn't the slightest idea of what I was going to say. When he asked I blurted out something like being all uptight. Losing my temper very easily. Being generally run down. He did a few checks on me. Asked me if I was going home at the week-end. I said I was. He asked me which way I went and I told him via London, to Brighton. He put me on three lots of medication and advised me to go via Southampton and Portsmouth instead. I was learning.

In November we were passed out as AC2 Wireless/Teleprinter/D.F. Operators. Most of us were sent on two weeks embarkation leave and told to report to RAF Personnel Disposal Unit at Burtonwood at the end of the leave. Burtonwood was again up near Manchester and bloody cold.

I spent the leave living at Frances' home in Upper North Street which was quite a way from Lower Bevendean where Pat lived. The old bike was again very handy though I often walked as well. Can't remember why. Could be getting my chronology a bit wrong.

One night I was cycling home at about 1 am when, by The Level, a park in the centre of the town, I was stopped by a copper because I had no front lamp. Of course I assured him that it had been working when I left. He asked me how long I had been in the 'mob' and I told him about one year. He had been an airman during the war. We had a little chat and he asked me which way I was going. I told him and he said "Well if you go along here, up there and round there you won't bump into any more of our fellows". We wished each other goodnight and I carried on home, sans front lamp.

A favourite trick, if I was walking home in the early mornings, was to go past the army barracks (Preston Barracks) looking suspicious. Furtively glancing over my shoulder at the Army Guardroom until the M.P.s came out in a Landrover and asked for my leave pass. Of course I had one and more than once they gave me a lift most of the way home.

I believe that during this leave The Queen, then Princess Elizabeth, was married to Prince Philip, and not a moment too soon! As a young Naval Officer he is reputed to have held the speed record for driving from Corsham (near Bath) to London. We listened, avidly, to the ceremony on the wireless.

Burtonwood, as I said previously, in November and December was bloody cold. Our daily routine consisted of parading in the morning where a sergeant would read out the drafts for those who's postings had come in. The rest of us would then stand while the sergeant picked half a dozen for fatigue duties. Those left were then free for the rest of the day. Most played cards but I was never a card player and I would just lie on my 'pit'. It was so cold that when I did this my wristwatch would stop! I really think that it thought that I had died.

The ablutions were long huts spaced between the accommodation huts and were warmed with coke braziers. This was not to give airmen comfort whilst attending to the calls of nature but to stop the water pipes from freezing. Burning coke gives off very acrid fumes. To stay in the ablutions for long would have you choking and eyes streaming. When I wanted to poo I would go out to the entrance of the ablutions, undo my braces and fly buttons (no zips), take a deep breath and race in, hoping to find a clean seat immediately, sit down, strain as hard as possible, grab paper, you know what, and try to get out again without taking another breath. Of course it was not possible but that didn't stop me trying. I think I've only been to one worse place than the ablutions at Burtonwood, but that comes in 1969.

5. Near East Air Force 1947-49

Eventually my draft came through and, with a crowd of others, I entrained for Southampton and embarked on the Arundel Castle bound for Malta. We had all our own normal kit in the normal kitbag, plus an extra kitbag full of Khaki Drill clothing (K.D) tropical kit and in addition every airman was issued with a rifle. The ship was a Union Castle Line vessel which had a 'troop deck'. As a troop-ship it would have been top of the pops. We sailed from Southampton on or around 14th. December and had an uneventful trip arriving in Grand Harbour, Valletta on the 19th. Disembarkation was into barges in the middle of the harbour. We had to balance ourselves, our two kitbags and our rifles down a set of steps hung down the side of the ship. Most of us made it O.K. but there was one corporal who also had his fishing rods with him. Half way down something had to go. Later he said that it was either the fishing gear or the rifle and he had paid a lot of money for the fishing gear! The rifle slid neatly down the side of the ship into the harbour and could be there to this day for all I know.

In Malta we were billeted at the RAF Station Luqa where we again awaited further instructions. I was still very un-streetwise and went along with the fellows for company. I was also broke. There are two streets of ill repute in Malta, both known to servicemen as 'The Gut'. There is the Sliema Gut and the Valletta Gut or Strait Street which is its official name. The boys said that we would go down to the Valletta Gut, I strung along. On either side of the street there were 'bars' rather like stables and girls sitting in the top windows calling "Steak, egg and chips RAF, upstairs, half a crown". Out of the question for me. I only had a shilling. The lads chose a bar to go in and I sat down with them. I was teetotal so just sat and talked with them. Some music was playing and a girl asked me if I would like a dance. Innocent me said "Yes" and we danced. When the music finished a Maltese man came up to me and said "Buy the lady a drink". I said that I was sorry but I had no money. The boys quickly got me out of there.

It's a small world. Some British sailors were coming up the Gut as we walked down and there was Ginger Turner, one of the van boys from the DBC and a Moulsecoomb Hall boy. I don't know who of us was most embarrassed.

On the 23rd December we were embarked on HMS Striker, a Landing Ship (Tanks) (LST) and at mid-day sailed for Tripoli in Libya. As it was a Royal Navy vessel all servicemen had to 'line the decks' as we sailed out of harbour and a Royal Marine trumpeter saluted us from a tower overlooking the harbour entrance. Very impressive. We were quite tickled to be involved. An L.S.T. is designed to run straight up on to a beach in an invasion and its tanks and lorries drive straight off into battle. Today's car ferries do a similar thing. To do this it has to have a flat bottom and a flat front. It doesn't cut its way through the seas as would a destroyer or ocean liner. It bumps into the waves, slows almost to a stop, then shudders back as it regains seaway. As well, with no keel, there is very little lateral stability so it heaves from side to side whilst doing the aforementioned shuddering. This seemed to be great fun ... for the first four hours. Unfortunately we were to suffer it for twenty four hours. At four pm I was seasick for the first time and remained in that state for the rest of the trip.

Accommodation in an LST is along the sides of the ship. All the centre space being reserved for the tanks and trucks. Our 'cabin' was a space about 8 feet wide and about 30 feet long. Along both sides were stacked bunks. I think they were three high and about five stacks this meant we had thirty men sleeping or spewing in a space 30 feet by 8 feet. As well as sleeping we had to eat there. A table was scraped in between the two rows of bunks. But who wanted to eat? Well my mate 'Sparks' had been a wireless operator in the Navy on Torpedo Boats. He loved it. He went to the galley each meal time, picked up food for thirty airmen, chose his favourites and chucked the rest away.

I was lying on my bunk, feeling extremely miserable, when he came up to me with a Heinz baked bean on his finger and said "Have something to eat Alf." Off to the 'heads' again! Some mate! It seems that it was an unusually rough crossing and most of the crew were also sick. We were told that we were so late that the RAF had had an aircraft looking for us.

LST's do not have a nice deck rail of the type that you get on passenger liners. The edge of the deck is marked by iron spikes, about knee high, with a ring on the top. Through the rings is threaded a chain. Next morning Sparks came to my bunk and said, "Come up on deck Alf, get some fresh air. It will do you good." I begrudgingly agreed. As we reached the deck the ship heeled over to one side and took me with it. I went flying across the deck and just grabbed the chain before going overboard. Sparks grabbed me and got me straight down below again. That was a close one!

We had to line the decks again as we entered Tripoli harbour. There were still a number of sunken ships in the harbour from the war. We got no salutes from them. In fact we got no salutes from anybody. There were no other Royal Navy ships in harbour. It's a good job Rommel's Afrika Corps weren't still there. We airmen were a sorry sight. We stepped ashore in Cyrenaica and were trucked to the RAF airfield at Castel Benito (now Idris). The main airfield for Libya. I recall, as we stood in the Orderly Room being checked in by the sergeant, I grabbed the desk top and asked him to keep it still. My balance was still way out in the ocean, or rather, sea. It had been the Mediterranean we'd just crossed.

Castel Benito was an RAF staging post. About a couple of thousand miles from England, it was just about at the end of most military aircraft's endurance. There were four of us AC2 W/ops in the draft and we were told we would be taking over the High Frequency Direction Finding (H.F. D/F) watches. They were currently being done by sergeants and corporals. We were each allotted to one of the present operators and 'double-banked' with them for about a week after which we were left alone.

The H.F. D/F hut was about a mile out from the main camp into the desert. About four hundred yards nearer the camp was the V.H.F. (Radio Telephony) D/F hut. Between us and the airfield there was an old wartime tank-trap that we had to cross. We were taken to and from work in a Signals Gharry usually driven by one of the corporals. Our job was to pass bearings in Morse code to any aircraft that called our callsign, CB. Dah di dah dit Dah di di dit. The aircraft were a complete mixture of military and civil aircraft. British Overseas Airways Avro Yorks, Sabena DC4's, RAF Yorks, Lancasters, Lincolns, Scottish Airways Liberators and lots of others. Each had their own national or company callsign which we soon got to recognise. The BOAC Yorks were in a series starting with G-AGOA to G-AGOM or something. Once communication with an aircraft was established we'd shorten it using just the first and last two letters thus G-AGOA became GOA. I remember that on Easter Sunday I was on watch between 11 pm and 8 am on the holy Sunday morning. BOAC York, G-AGOD, on its way from U.K. to Kano in Nigeria called me for a bearing. I went into the mess after work and very seriously told the boys that I'd had a call from GOD that night. They all thought that I was nuts.

Of course, it was a job that required constant attention as all signals aren't loud and clear. Sabena call signs were in the series O-OCBA, O-OCBB et seq. One early morning, I must have dropped into a doze when through my earphones I heard CB. I woke up immediately and sent the message "Aircraft calling CB call again". I did this a few times and got no response. I was by now quaking. If anything had happened to that aircraft I was very seriously in the soft stuff. After a while I got a call from Sabena O-OCBA. The CB I'd heard was the middle of his callsign while he was calling somewhere else. Phew!

For our protection we had a .303 rifle in each of the D/F. huts with plenty of rounds of ammo. We also had a dog, a German Shepherd. I've no idea who it belonged to but it used to hang around and get fed by us. We collected rations from the ration store for snacks and drinks. The NAAFI van, a mobile tea and cake vehicle which visited all sections on camp every morning, never came out of the camp so we had the rations. Every morning a young Arab boy who we called 'Chunky" would turn up at the door and we would give him any left-over rations.

At about 100 yards range from our hut there was an old World War ll machine gun post. It was made of concrete and had slots for windows. We would often fire off rounds to try to get one in the window. If you got one in you would hear it ricochet around the inside. At least that is what I was told. As well, if you were lucky, you would see an Arab and his camel come flying out. They'd have been resting there in the shade. The camels were hobbled and it was quite funny to see a hobbled camel trying to get out of range. Well, we were still only boys.

Wild dogs roam around the desert. They were called Pyards (could be the wrong spelling). They could often be seen standing at the top of the tank trap. This was yet another invitation to get the rifle out, put one just behind him and watch him try to get away from the follow up rounds. Again it was not unusual to see an Arab and camel go flying in the opposite direction to the Pyard.

This 'sport' had its dangers for us. The mast at the rear of our hut was neatly drilled by a .303 about two feet above ground level where the VHF operator had once got a bit careless. The only other dangerous wildlife there were scorpions. They were a yellowy-corn colour and if you touched their backs with a twig their stingers in the rear would shoot over to poison the offender. There were also some neatly drilled holes in the path outside the D/F hut which had me puzzled. They went straight into the ground and one day, to find out how deep they were, I started dropping old .303 bullet cases in the hole. I think I reached over thirty. Never did find out what they were.

Meanwhile there was a life after work. We would work either a three man or four man watch roster. Watches were from 8am-mid-day.(Morning), and 6-11pm (Evening) on the first day then Mid-day to 6pm (Afternoons) and 11pm till 8am (Middles) on the second day. In a three watch cycle we would do Morning, Evening first day, Afternoon and Middles second day then off till Morning of the fourth day. Two days on, one day off. A four watch system was more generous giving you a two day break. This was never-ending. No such thing as week-ends or Public Holidays. In the one or two day break we were more or less free to do as we wished as long as it didn't interfere with the C.O's wishes such as guard duties and parades. I was on guard duty one night and decided to walk out to the DF hut for a cuppa with the on duty W/Operator. I was about a hundred yards from the hut when a big whitish animal came towards me. It was almost touching me by the time I got my rifle in position and shot downwards at it. I must have just missed my own foot. It ran away and eventually turned out to be our own Alsatian.

We had lots of football and other sports and a swimming pool to keep us fit.

I achieved what I believe is probably a world record during this time. I was watching the Station hockey team practising. The sergeant in charge came across and asked if I'd like to have a try. I'd never played hockey in my life but said that I'd have a go. He went through the rudiments of the game with me, put me in the same position as I played in football, right wing, and I got stuck in. At the end of the practice he asked me if I was free on the following Saturday and I said that I was. He invited me to play for the RAF against the Army in Tripoli. On Saturday I went with the team to Tripoli. We changed into our strips, practised for a bit while waiting for the Army team to turn up. They didn't show and eventually we went back home again claiming a win. I never watched them again and was never contacted again. So my world record is that I represented the RAF against the Army in a winning game of hockey, having never before, then, or since played a game of hockey.

Swimming proved to be nearly fatal for me, and indeed was fatal for another airman. My problem started with an ear-ache which gradually got worse. I went sick and was taken into the camp hospital where the M.O. treated me with all sorts of ear syringes. I got worse. Suddenly my temperature was over 105 degrees and they plonked me into an ambulance and shot me down to the British Military Hospital in Tripoli. There I was put on a course of Sulphonamide tablets (M & B). I had to take (I think) 16 tablets a day and had to drink a full large glass of water with each tablet. The treatment worked but the sight of a tablet and a glass of water by the end of the second day was horrifying. The fatality occurred sometime later when I was no longer on D/F shift work. A group of airmen including the camp's top swimmer formed up on the diving boards and did a simultaneous dive. The top swimmer dived from the top board and struck another as he landed and broke his own neck. I had to send the signal to AHQ Malta advising of the death. Very sad.

We had a couple of exciting periods on D/F watch. One of the boys was on when a USAAF B29 Superfortress had engine failure over the Med. and our operator guided him successfully back to Castel Benito to land. My most exciting shift was when I had 12 Lancasters flying out to Egypt for a bombing range practice and 12 Lincolns flying home from the same bombing range. These were all diverted to search for a light aircraft that had been reported missing. This gave me 24 aircraft circling and ranging all over the Med. and the desert, constantly calling me for bearings. Routinely, when an aircraft starts calling for bearings, he will be en route from A to B, the subsequent calls are usually from the same approximate direction as the first contact unless the aircraft has overflown the base. As well they would normally be asking for the same type of bearing viz. Course to steer to base, magnetic bearing from base or true bearing from base. With these aircraft doing search patterns I had to check every bearing from scratch. It was my busiest watch. After a few months we were replaced in the D/F hut by civilian operators and were assigned to SHQ Signals. This involved the sending and receiving of administrative, technical and operational signals between us, AHQ Malta, RAF Benina (near Benghazi) and RAF El Adem (near Tobruk). We also received 'broadcasts' from H.Q. Middle East Air Force. It was not the same sort of shift work so we found ourselves doing more parades and guard duties.

It was on one of these guard duties that I was out on Runway Guard. Supposedly to prevent the 'wogs' from pinching the electric cables or paraffin gooseneck lamps that lined the runway. We would walk up the runway and back again, making sure that we were well clear if an aircraft came in to land or to take off. I was walking, at the time, about fifty yards the camp side of the runway, when I heard a noise that I cannot spell, followed by an almighty crack. The noise was that of a .303 bullet whizzing past, not far from my head. The crack, of course, was the explosion of the bullet being fired. I immediately went to ground and screamed at the camp that I was one of them. No more bullets were fired. I must have reported it but nothing happened until, some months later, two fellows in front of me in the NAAFI queue were talking about shooting at this 'wog'. I very politely told them that the 'wog' was me. I'm sure they apologised. The best guard duty to get was Hangar Guard. If you were careful and be sure not to fall asleep, you could get up into the seat of a fire engine and do the job from in there. Much warmer than walking around outside. Of course if you fell asleep and went past the two hours on duty the Guard Commander would come looking for you and you were in the cacky.

I must have been a very scruffy airman. I was twice told so by consecutive Senior Admin. Officers. I recall the first time. I had just come off guard duty and was waiting for the Armoury to open to hand back my rifle and unused rounds of ammo, before going to work. I was very tired and had my hands in my pockets leaning against the armoury door when I noticed him, too late to be ready. I pushed myself more or less upright and slung him one up (saluted). He told me that I was the scruffiest airman on camp. I was in no mood to argue so left it at that. I can't recall the details of the second incident but do remember that it was a new S.Ad.O who said almost identical words, so I took it that I must have been.

National Service was still very much on the go and every month a 'Demobform' would come in on the broadcast from H.Q. MEAF detailing the demobilisation group numbers for the various trades that were to be released that month. That was a very useful document. The cooks were all Nashos and were keen to get the first news of dates. A copy taken into the

Airmen's Mess, following a phone call to the Mess that we would be coming in late for tea with the Demobform, usually resulted in a very special meal.

Xmas I hated at CB. I was still a non-drinker and non-smoker. The general aim at Xmas was to get smashed on Xmas Eve and stay that way till Boxing Night. Drunk British servicemen are not a pretty sight and often not nice to know. Their behaviour, whilst sometimes funny was more often disgusting. We were hated all over the world and with good reason. Luckily, being in Signals, we never closed down for any holidays (see also Christmas 1963) so it was a simple matter to volunteer for duty allowing one of your mates to enjoy a drink with his mates.

Two things I remember that were funny at the time. The Officers serve the airmen at Xmas dinner. The Station Commander puts in an appearance etc. I recall this airman, p ... d out of his brain, holding a piece of wire with a loop on the end, going up to the Group Captain and telling him to watch out for his dog 'cos it could get vicious. The other was a Radar Tech corporal going on a 3 day bender with his airman mechanic staying with him and keeping a record of the hours that he had been p ... d and the amount of drinks he'd had. He called the airman his 'statistical queer bloke', and, no matter how long it went on for, he never once faltered over the pronunciation of 'statistical queer bloke'.

About the middle of the year Ray Baker and myself went down to the British Army's Leave Camp 'The Lido' in Tripoli for two weeks leave. Ray was a Radio Telephony Operator from VHF D/F. There sitting on the beach was Jimmy Nickless, the van boy from Danish Bacon, now a soldier. I said it was a small world.

The NAAFI in Libya was staffed by Expeditionary Forces Institute girls (NAAFI/EFI).They would come down to the beach some days and we had lots of fun swimming and generally messing around, all strictly platonic. They were a good bunch of very dedicated women doing an excellent job. There's some photos around somewhere of us and of Jimmy Nickless on the beach at the Lido.

In Tripoli, horse drawn 'gharries' were the normal taxi type mode of transport. It was quite common for airmen to hire two of these and make their Arab drivers race along the Tunis Road. Like many Middle Eastern cities, Tripoli was a mass of small hole-in-the-wall shops. They all sold the same things. Silks, leather goods, and masses of bottles of scent. I remember my introduction to being a nasty British serviceman by my corporal Jock K. We would go into the first shop and he would point up to the scent bottles and say, "Lets smell that one". He'd open it, smell it, and say 'Shit" pointing to the next bottle and going through the same procedure. With ten or twenty bottles on the counter he would walk out of the shop and go into the next. On a good 'shopping trip' he would leave at least two hundred bottles of scent on ten counters in ten shops without buying a thing. My own nasty British Serviceman act was when little kids chased you to sell leather wallets for 100 Lira, knock them down to 25 Lira then say "No!" Not terrible, but nothing to be proud of either.

Aircraft crashes were, thankfully, rare whilst I was in the Air Force, so it was very perplexing when we had two civil airliners crash on landing within a few days. The first was a BOAC York, 'Mansfield' and the second a Continental Airlines troop carrying DC4 Skymaster. I did crash guard on both of them and it was a weird experience. It would have been in January 1949 and the desert was very cold. I had been on crash guard at the York crash site with a RAF fireman and we were about to be relieved when it started to snow. It was the first time in living memory. When our relief arrived we set off on our bikes back to the guardroom. The fireman decided to go the short way across the airfield whilst I chose to go around the perimeter track. I beat him in by quite a long while and was amazed to see that when he got in he was in tears with the cold. I have a funny effect on weather! As a matter of interest, during the preparation of photographs for this autobiography, I have realised that 'Mansfield' was the same G-AGOD (GOD) that had called me at Easter.

One of the RTO's, Ginger Forbes, went over to Malta for a couple of weeks leave. At that time Lord Mountbatten was based there. He was probably C in C or something. Anyway Ginger went to a dance in the Castle Club. During the evening he says he danced with Lady Mountbatten, then later danced with a young lady and said that her face was familiar. She laughed and said she was Lady Pamela Mountbatten (Daughter of Lord Louis). He said "My God, I only have to dance with the old man now and I'll have danced with the whole family." She responded "That could be arranged!"

During my time at CB I sat and passed my AC1 exam, having been given a bit of pre-exam help by my sergeant. I later went to Malta for my LAC (Leading Aircraftsman) promotion exam. This I also passed. As well during this time a pay rise was announced for all the services. I think that at my level at the time it was six pence a day. The trip to Malta and back this time was by a DC3 Dakota. It was a lot more pleasant than the LST. I believe that it was on this trip that I bought my first camera, a Kodak Brownie Box.

As well, in 1948, the Palestine conflict was reaching one of it's earlier crises. At that time 'Palestine' (there was no State of Israel) was a British protectorate as was Egypt and much more of the Middle East. The Jews were waging a constant war against the British and the Arabs. The Arab part of this spilled over into Libya and the British Army in Tripoli came under a bit of pressure. They had to stand with fixed bayonets around the big fountain in the middle of the city and have stones thrown at them by the Arabs without responding. It didn't last for long but was nasty. We weren't affected other than not being able to go into Tripoli for a while.

Towards the end of my time there we had an exercise whereby the Royal Marine Commando were to attack the base. I and most of the Signals types were put on guarding the Air Traffic Control Tower. It was a very disorganised affair. No one was actually in charge, to our knowledge, and we did more or less as we wanted. I remember that Sparks decided that he would go out on a recco, foraging on his own, and came upon a group of commandos in a small gully. There was an 'Umpire' there and he declared that Sparks had captured the soldiers. The night wore on and by about five in the morning we were all thoroughly bored with the whole idea. I and another mate, can't remember who it was now, were on the roof of the Air Traffic Control Tower. He had a searchlight which he switched on every so often and swept around the area about two hundred yards out. I had an Aldis signalling lamp. He did a sweep and just caught something moving out on the airfield. I told him to carry on as if he hadn't seen anything then switch off. He did this and after about five seconds I switched on my Aldis aimed at the spot where the movement had been. We caught the Commandos fair and square and started shooting off rounds wildly. At this point, of course, we showed that we were airmen and not soldiers. We hadn't a clue what we should have done. I never did find out whether it was considered that we'd won or not.

I still did not drink alcohol so had a rather strange experience one day when four of us decided to walk out into the desert. We came across an Italian farm. The Italians welcomed us, sat us down, gave us food and red wine. I was undoubtedly a little intoxicated when we left them. On our way back to camp we decided to climb the water tower. It was pretty high and I have never had a head for heights. We all got to the top OK and enjoyed the view, then it was time to come down. Forget about coffee as a sobering device. Nothing can beat shock and fear. I was terrified. How the hell had I got up here? I grabbed the ladder very tightly, put my head up into a level position and commenced a very careful descent. I made it and swear that I was dead sober by the time I reached the ground. After I had changed my underpants ...

There was a room somewhere not too far from camp with a painting of a beautiful woman, nude, in a classical reclining pose. She was known as 'The Lady of Garian'. The landscaping of the deserts of North Africa includes many rocky water courses, usually dry, which are called 'Wadis'. One that comes to mind now is Wadi Halfar. The painting of the lady was covered in drawings of soldiers and tanks coming over, out, in every bump and crevice on the girl's body. All the crevices were named Wadi Y'know, Wadi Y'care etc. I should have bought one of the postcards that were available but it all seemed too rude to me then. I still hadn't heard the word 'sex' spoken out loud! I have since learned that the painting was done by a British Army artist and is quite well known now.

The RAF tried to eat as much fresh food, local produce, as was possible, subject to hygiene considerations. As a result it was considered that eggs and grapes, well washed, were suitable. As a result of this policy, at one stage, the ration of eggs per airman was something like six per day. RAF cooks, being slightly below cordon bleu standard, only knew one way to cook eggs; watery poached! Every meal seemed to include watery poached eggs. After a while we started to buy more meals in the NAAFI in the evenings. This would usually be Spaghetti with tomato sauce and ... fried eggs!

Thinking of the Airman's Mess at CB always brings back the smell of diesel oil. Every airman, when a recruit, received a knife, fork and spoon, known collectively as his 'irons', and an enamel mug. The irons were stamped with the airman's service number and went with him for ever. Outside the Mess Halls were big tanks of hot water, rather like horse troughs but bigger. These were kept close to boiling by heaters which in the case of CB were diesel burning. When an airman finished his meal he would put his plates in the appropriate area then walk out and wash his irons and mug in the hot water. There was no such thing as washing up liquid or detergents in those days. I used to wash my stuff in the water then go out into the 'garden' which of course was sand, dig my irons into that to finish them off then rub sand around the inside of my mug.

Diesel also figured in the appearance of our rooms, and myself. We were billeted in two or three man rooms which had 'quarry tile' floors. The easiest way to make these shine for inspections was to rub them with a rag soaked in diesel oil, so we ate and slept with the stuff. It also contributed to the loss of my front tooth! I was demonstrating to my mates how the Ice Speed Skaters came to a halt by turning their skates sideways on and sending up a massive spray of shredded ice. I went running across the floor, flung my feet sideways and went down flat on my face coming up with only half a tooth. My mates couldn't stop laughing.

As well by this time the 'Cold War' had well and truly been declared. We had been told of it in a lecture as soon as we'd arrived in Libya. It was only the public that didn't know. The Berlin Airlift was started. The regular flow of RAF transports was reduced to a trickle as they were all diverted to Berlin.

I saw my first jet aircraft at about this time when two Vampires flew into Castel B. We were amazed at their speed and were thrilled when they took off from our place, went down to Tripoli to 'shoot up' the USAF Air Base at Mellaha and returned within minutes. I was a bit concerned by the fact that they had to be tilted at one stage in their start up to spill out all the loose kerosene onto the ground which promptly caught fire when the engines started.

Pat and I were now unofficially engaged. The fact is that we never did become officially engaged because that would have meant buying a ring and neither of us could afford to do that. I wanted to get back to England so that we could get married. There was only one way to get back before my two and a half year tour was up, so I applied to re-muster to a Wireless Fitter. This is what I'd failed the tests on at Cardington in 1946! Surprise, surprise, my application was approved and I received my papers to return to U.K. in about February 1949

My trip back was different. Someone approached the A.O.C., who was visiting the station at the time, to ask if he could find room for me on his return to Malta. He agreed, so I went to Malta in style. VIP! Even had a WAAF Flt. Sergeant serve me with tea and biscuits en route! After a few days again in Malta (my third four day stay) I was put on a Lancastrian (a Lancaster fitted out with inward facing, canvas seats down each side) with a load of reporters and photographers and took off for England. There was no pressurisation in those days so the height limit was around 12,000 feet. There was cloud from about 3,000 to 15,000 feet all the way except for a small clearing over the Rhone Valley in France. It was the LST all over again. I was sick for most of the trip. We flew into Lyneham in Wiltshire and I went on a couple of weeks disembarkation leave.

6. England 1949-53

Pat and I spent most of that leave together I think. There was now only one girlfriend.

My next posting was to H.Q. Central Signals Area at Bletchley, Buckinghamshire. This was the famous Bletchley at which the code breakers worked during the war and broke the German Enigma codes. My work area was at the Main Signals Centre at Stanbridge, a few miles away. We lived at Bletchley and were taken by bus each day to Stanbridge. Stanbridge was a massive Signals establishment with dozens of circuits going all around the world. Most of the operators there were Teleprinter Operators so as a LAC Wireless Operator I was given the chance to work in the W/T (wireless telegraphy) room. They only had about 5 Morse circuits. Of course as a Main Signals Centre it was 24/7 as they say these days. Back to the old shift work.

I was on watch one night and, at about 3 in the morning, the Army in Austria came through with a very long coded signal. These were usually in five figure groups. This message was to be hundreds of these groups long. I started taking the message at a very slow pace with the operator at the other end obviously not very good. After many mistakes I sent the Q signal for "Put on a competent operator". Well, that's what the Q signal was designed for! I think it was QOO2. He sent back the signal for "Unable to comply". I carried on for a while and then after another twenty or thirty mistakes I sent the Q signal for "Put on your supervisor". I think it was QOO1. Yes, I know. How could I be so nasty? This was at 3 am remember. He again sent the signal "Unable to comply". So in desperation I sent in plain language "Oh. Go home" to which he responded "Unable to comply". I saw the funny side of this and settled down to a long night.

Sometimes I worked up in the Tape relay room. This is where the tapes that had been punched by the Teleprinter operators were fed into tape sending machines and transmitted to all parts of the world. On night shifts, I noticed, that as the shift wore on I was attending to more and more machines. Sometimes there'd only be three or four of us in the room. I found out later that there was another big room, not used for any technical purposes with lots of long tables. The Airmen and Waafs would quietly retire to there leaving muggins to do the work.

I was only at Stanbridge for a couple of months awaiting my Wireless Fitter course but, whilst I was there, the Berlin Airlift came to an end and I had the honour of sending the tape, from the Chief of Air Staff, advising of the finish and congratulating all concerned etc. It was one helluva big signal.

Being an entirely Signals Unit, the airmen there had pretty big opinions of themselves and, with an equal number of Signals Waafs, reckoned that they could bring about a Super-race. The idea of RAFSTUD was born. I don't know if anything came of it but I reckon it was doomed to failure. TPO's were at the bottom of the Signals heap, or at least, very close to RTO's.

In May 1949 I was posted to No 1 Radio School, RAF Cranwell in Lincolnshire to commence Wireless Fitter training. A forty four week, full-time course. I think I had been a very good wireless operator. Certainly far better than I was to prove as a wireless fitter.

Cranwell 1949-50

At Cranwell I was to join a 'special' class. Unlike the usual trainees we were all ex-wireless operators, all held ranks (mostly Leading Aircraftman) and most had seen overseas or wartime service. We were called a 'Conversion Class' Concourse 1, and treated with slightly more respect than the new recruits who were all straight from squarebashing.

Cranwell Camp is a short distance from Cranwell village and about four miles from Sleaford. It is not too far from Lincoln and Grantham. From the latter of course, came the 'Sleaford Flier'. There was also a branch railway line up to the camp but this was not used for passenger services. More's the pity. The Camp was split by a public road. As the home of the RAF College it has a special standing in the Air Force. The RAF's answer to Sandhurst. Most officers started their careers there. Later there came places like Henlow where Technical Officers were trained.

The Wireless Fitters course started off reasonably well for me. The first eight weeks consisted of Direct Current theory, mathematics refresher course, use of measuring instruments etc. I did very well. Always in the top level ... until the eighth week when one of the exam questions was to draw the circuit diagram of a 'Megger'. Doesn't matter what it is, later we were to have fun with them, but for now I hadn't the faintest idea of how to draw the circuit. Consternation on high. One of the star students had suddenly come bottom of the class! It obviously pointed to some defect in the training method which I am sure would have been put right, too late for me.

The course then went through all the rest of the theories involved in what would now be called electronics but was then called wireless. Wireless? There were hundreds of bits of wire in the bloody things. Oh! It was called wireless because there was no wire required between the sender and the receiver. They didn't tell me that! As well we had to become reasonably proficient at workshop procedures. Uses of various metalwork tools, types of patterns on the cutting surfaces of files, smooth, medium, bastard, coarse and of course how to identify them including the shape and length so I learned to say "Pass me that flat, eight inch, hand safe edge bastard" without so much as a blush.

We were all very keen sportsmen and spent every Wednesday afternoon playing either football or cricket. We would also play at week-ends if we weren't going home. We were no fools and knew more about the air force than many of the non-trainee permanent staff. We managed to get hold of a ruined, chuck out, football from the Sports store. On this we did a rough repair and pumped it up. Then we booked out a good ball for the next game. We then returned the repaired ball the following day leaving us with a brand new ball. We did this three times which made us just about the richest football team on the station. That grounding on thieving from apple trees had not been wasted.

We also had a fellow named Joe who had spent time in Malaya. He was an L.A.C. and suffered from nightmares in which he saw snakes. It was not unusual to be awakened at about 1.00 am when Joe suddenly screamed, jumped out of bed, raced up the billet and hit the wall at the far end at full tilt. I don't know how he never hurt himself. At other times he would finish up squatting on his window sill. One day we had to move out into a new billet. As we were carrying our equipment up to the new place everybody was asking Joe "Where you going to sleep Joe?", with the obvious intention of sleeping as far away from him as possible.

My old Achilles Heel came into play again at this time. We had returned from a Bank Holiday 72 hour pass and were at Grantham Railway Station when it was announced that the 'Flier' had broken down. Being a resourceful fellow I immediately said that I was going into town to catch the bus. A couple of Waafs said they would come with me. We reached the bus depot only to find that the bus wasn't running that day. We raced back to the station only to find that the Flier had been repaired and had just gone. We were A.W.O.L. The three of us were duly charged with being late back to camp and appeared before our respective C.O.'s. Things haven't changed much over the 50 years since that occasion. I received 3 days Jankers, the girls received 5 days. For the same offence! When you think about it, we were the only ones who had really tried to get back to camp on time!

Sometimes boredom could make people do the most amazingly stupid things. On a hot summer's week-end, when it was too hot to be outside, we would lay on our 'pits', with the window behind open, and have a spitting competition. This meant spitting backwards, over our heads and out of the window. Could be very mucky. The referees would be outside and judge whose spit landed the further from the hut. Well we weren't doing any harm!

Our Squadron Commander, Sqdn. Ldr. W lived in Brighton so we had an 'in' into the higher strata of the School once he learned that I was also from

Brighton. He used me once to take a Turkey, that he had won in the Officer's Mess Xmas Raffle, home for him. I can't remember the excuse but I do remember delivering it to his Regency home out Kemptown way and not getting past the front door. He had a habit of coming round the workshops whilst we were doing filing, or some such, and peering along the top of the job from the other side. Some of the lads would pretend that they hadn't noticed him arrive and blow the dust off the top straight into his face! Not me. I knew we could use him some time or other. Or perhaps I was too chicken.

At one stage the food in the Airmen's Mess deteriorated to such an extent that our class decided that we would all put in a complaint. This had to be done very carefully. There is a document known as 'The Air Force Act'. This is the Act of Parliament under which the RAF operates and by which discipline is maintained. It is required that at regular intervals Sections 4 to 44 of the Air Force Act be read to all airmen. This was usually done on parade. Sections 4 to 44 cover such crimes as sedition, mutiny, desertion and 'conduct unbecoming' amongst many others and includes the possible penalties for these crimes. Most of the Sections conclude with the words ' ... punishable by xxxx or some such worse punishment as is in this Act mentioned.' This is also used in the case of desertion which concludes something like this ' this act, if committed on active service, is punishable by death, or some such worse punishment as is in this Act mentioned.' As you can see, if we'd decided to go en masse to the C.O. and complain about the food we could be accused of mutiny, and some accused of sedition. We decided to put in individual requests to see the C.O. Wing Commander H, 'reason to be stated at interview'. Twenty odd 'Applications to see the C.O.' dropped on his desk on one day. They knew something was up. I got a summons to see S/Ldr W. I went into his office and he asked me what all the applications were about. I denied any knowledge of any other applications but agreed that I had put one in because I was unhappy about the standard of the food. Next day we were summoned as a group to the Wingco's office. He was flanked by the S/Ldr. and the Catering Officer. The meeting was very interesting. Rather than we all pleading not guilty to mutiny, the Catering Officer was virtually on his knees begging us to give him another chance. Our 'superior' standing as a class and my acquaintance with the S/Ldr. had paid off. The food improved dramatically. I, and two others, only enjoyed the improvement for a short while.

Around August I went to the Church at Cranwell Village and asked if they would read the banns for my marriage. It was pretty safe. No one there would have known either Pat or myself so there was little chance of objections. In October I went on leave and got married.

Before doing this I went to the Radio School Commanding Officer who was a Group Captain and asked for a loan from the 'C.O.'s Fund'. This was a fund of money held by the C.O. of every station to help an airman who was in dire straits. The C.O. kicked me out and said that he was not going to help any airman to start married life in debt. Years later I realised just how right he had been. At the time I had to face a honeymoon with just seventeen shillings in my pocket after paying the Vicar at St. Andrews forty seven shillings for the marriage service.

Prior to the wedding I'd been down to Rye with Mum and Frances' foster son and booked a bed and breakfast place for a week. So that was our honeymoon arranged. I think that that, and the paying of the Vicar were the only contributions I made to the wedding arrangements. All the rest just happened. She'll kill me! The wedding went off fairly well, considering that food was still strictly rationed. You'll have to ask Pat how they managed to put up anything for the guests to eat. Someone in my family must have blabbed because the main wedding group photograph shows Pat, her Mum, Grandmum, her Brother and and her Maid of Honour and one friend plus around twenty seven of my relatives. I doubt that I've seen more than five of them since. They must have come for the free nosh.

I was married in Best Blue uniform with the embellishment of white belt and carried brown leather gloves. Both were illegal but more impressive than the plain Best Blue. The gloves were also very useful in giving me something to do with my hands during all the palava of photo's etc.

After the reception at Pat's place there was a move to get everybody up to the Territorials Drill Hall to carry on. I think that my Uncle George was 'something' in the Territorials. We all said O.K. and started moving off in groups. I heard that Ron was going to try to get me drunk. (I was still teetotal.) Anyway six of us, Pat's brother Ted and her friend Greta, Fooey and his wife Ann and Pat and myself went down the Avenue and got on the bus. Pat and I got on first and the conductor said "Who's getting married then?" so we pointed to the two behind us. The next two did the same so the last two took the honour. Instead of going to the Drill Hall we went to the Princes Hall, near the Brighton Aquarium, and spent the night dancing.

I can't really tell you what followed because that is between Pat and myself. Sufficient to say, next morning we got up and went off to Rye on the bus. We spent an idyllic three days around Rye, Winchelsea and Fairlight drinking many cups of tea until, on the Wednesday, my 17 shillings ran out and we had to go home. I will never forget the couple who ran the B & B. He was ex air force and she had had to manage on her own during the war. They would be telling us stories and he would say "She's 'ad it if anybody 'as, 'aven't you gal?"

I don't think I would recommend such a start to marriage to anybody these days. We had the advantage that both of us had a job, and as a married man my pay was about to be increased by a marriage allowance which nearly doubled it. The Allowance was of course paid directly to Pat. I think it was two pounds two per week paid weekly whilst my pay was now two pounds nine per week paid fortnightly.

A few weeks prior to the marriage a Ministry of Food official noticed that some of our family's Ration Books had the surname 'Common' and others 'Commons'. Rationing had started around 1939. This was in 1949. There had been six years of war and four years of peace. There had been no problem. Suddenly it was all wrong. It seems that Mum thought that on her Marriage Certificate Dad's name had been Common and Dad knew that his name was Commons. If, after one of us was born, Mum went to the Registry Office to register us the Birth Certificate was in the name of Common, if Dad went it was Commons. The MOF man insisted that they must be changed. Eric, in the Navy, refused to do anything about it so his family is still named Common. I wanted as little trouble as possible because Pat was soon going to change her name and I didn't want her Marriage Allowance held up because of some beurocratic stupidity. I had to sign a Declaration under a law passed in the time of, I think it was, James 1st of England. It went through in time and our name became Commons. Recent (2006) family history research has shown that the Common/Commons thing has been going on over a few generations.

Three of we Concourse 1 airmen decided to request permission to live off camp. It was not the sort of thing that a Radio School was used to with its brand new trainees. But again we were different and permission was granted. Paddy Bryant, Chalky White and myself created the precedent. We found rental accommodation in Sleaford and Pat joined me, for the first of her moves to live together. She will tell all about the fun she had with such things as dolly tubs for the weekly wash and various other housekeeping chores. She might even tell you about her first attempt at cooking me a nice suet pudding. She says it was a dumpling, but that's because it looked like a dumpling. Between October '49 and April '69 she was to move twenty nine times!

We did not have anything like a car or even a radio. Our first radio was home-made from a set of three identical valves used as different valves. It was housed in a cardboard box and required earphones to listen in. But this came much later. Our only entertainment was to go up to the camp cinema on pay night and walk back along the railway line. If that railway line could talk! Well, we were young, and I've already said that we had no other entertainment. It's a case of making your own. Which we did. In more ways than one.

I learned the value of careful choice of words during this period at Cranwell. You'd never know it now, would you? Paddy, Chalky and I rode bicycles to and from camp. One evening we were free wheeling down a hill and a tractor and hay-cart were ahead of us. We went to overtake and something happened which left Chalky a bit the worse for wear. I can't remember exactly how he was hurt but next day Mr Plod turned up in the class room to get a statement from me. I told him what had happened and he wrote something down for me to sign. In part it read " ... and we swerved to overtake ... ". I didn't like this and asked him to change it to read " ... and we made to overtake ... ". I was still learning. But not about women!

As Christmas 1949 approached I started dropping hints that I would like a pair of football boots. We went down to The Avenue for Christmas leave and on Christmas Day or, more probably Christmas Eve, we exchanged our first presents as man and wife. Pat never could wait until Christmas Day. I gave her something suited to the occasion, an electric iron and a couple of other things useful for the house. She gave me a … shoebox! Inside, well wrapped up, was a gold signet ring. I must confess that it has lasted a bit longer than the football boots would have but I would be lying if I didn't say that I was a bit disappointed. In those days I was not a ring-wearing type of man. That ring had to be cut off recently for surgical reasons. It was the first time it had ever been removed and I must confess to a lump in my throat as the medics did it. It is back in one piece and firmly esconced again now.

In the meantime the radio engineering course continued. To some trainees radio engineering was just like an open book. To me it was more like 'Via Apian' the first year Latin text book at Varndean. So in the Spring of '50 I just squeaked through with a 40% pass on the finals and emerged from Cranwell as an AC2 again! But now as a Wireless Fitter. It was this moment that settled my career as a mediocre radio man. It also indicated how little thought went into the Air Force's postings system. There was I, a new, barely passed Wireless Fitter and I was posted to No. 3500 Fighter Control Unit, Royal Auxiliary Air Force, Margate. 3500 FCU was the last place that a struggling Wireless Fitter should have been posted to. A terrific posting for a wireless man with lots of experience who had just returned from a heavy overseas posting and deserved a relaxing post for a couple of years. But for me? Barely trained? I think I can honestly say that, any later failure on my part as a Wireless Fitter could be tracked down to that thoughtless posting. All new graduates should be posted to a Unit where there is a constant and varied radio engineering fault diagnosis program to be performed and where there are experienced technicians to advise and assist.

3500 F.C.U. Margate

The FCU had a permanent staff of about twenty, with one officer, one warrant officer, a couple of sergeants and about eighteen airmen and corporals. The job was to train about two hundred Auxiliary Air Force men and women. Most of these were Radar Operators and Fighter Plotters with about half a dozen Wireless Tradesmen. These latter were all mine! (AC2 Alf Commons, brand new). The trouble was that these fellows were all fully qualified radio servicemen in civvy street so my only task would have been to familiarise them with RAF equipments. If I'd had any I might have had a go. In the event, all I had was one part of an aircraft transmitter and an aircraft power generator. Both useless without the rest of the equipment. Even with the equipment they would have been useless for the type of work that was done at the F.C.U. Auxiliary training took place on Tuesday and Thursday evenings and the whole thing was like a big Country Club. The Radar Operating and Fighter Plotting side of the affair was taken very seriously and there was thousands of dollars worth of fully operational radar training equipment for them. They could move into a Radar Station at a moments notice and probably do a good job.

Needless to say my sadly lacking knowledge of radio slowly deteriorated. I took my AC1 exam and managed to pass so again I was an AC1. Before I could take the LAC exam they introduced a 'New Trade Structure', or 'Keep Alf Down'. This was the first of a number. The idea of the New Trade Structure was that Trades should be classified in order of merit with regard to their knowledge requirements. For some reason the Aircraft Engine and Airframes were classified as Class l whilst the Radio Engineering Trades were classified as Class ll. Both were also classified as 'Advanced' trades however and were on the same pay scale. At the same time Air Wireless and Ground Wireless became different trades. I had been trained on both air and ground radio equipments. I was reclassified to a Ground Wireless Fitter. Makes sense. I had that one part of an Air Wireless Transmitter! To make matters worse the powers that be decided that all new Fitter graduates from the Radio Schools would be granted the rank of Junior Technician (a new rank and the lower level of a new, five level, Technician structure). Those, like myself, who had graduated a year before, and had passed another trade test exam since, were reclassified as Senior Aircraftman, another new rank but not a Technician. To become a Technician and reach the rank of today's graduates, we had to sit yet another exam. See what I meant when I said 'Keep Alf Down'? Of course I immediately applied to sit the exam. I'd been awaiting the chance for LAC and Corporal and was now one step further back.

The exam came, I sat it, the Adj. asked me how I felt about it and I told him that I reckoned that I had passed. We waited for the results. Six months later the notice came up on orders for applications for the next Trade Test Board. I saw the Adjutant and asked what could have happened. He suggested that I ring Group Headquarters which I did. They told me that the results had been sent out ages ago. When I told them that I had not received mine they 'searched' the records and said that I had failed. I said that they had lost my result. I sat the next exam. This one was completely different, bringing in all the latest electronic theories being taught in lieu of the wide range of Air and Ground radio equipments that we had studied. At the end I told the Adj. that I had failed. I had.

Again, six months later, two years after passing out of Radio School, I put in for the next test. It was almost identical to the first. I told the Adj. that I had passed. I had. No one will ever convince me that I had not missed out on at least one years seniority because of an administrative failure and two years because of the New Trade Structure. There was nothing I could do. I was now a Junior Technician. The path was opened up the 'Command' ladder for me at last. The new structure allowed an airman to choose between the Technician ladder (Junior Tech, Cpl Tech, Senior Tech, Chief Tech and Master Tech, all achieved after a time and examination process,) and the Command ladder (Junior Tech, Cpl, Sergeant, Flt. Sgt. and Warrant Officer all achieved by time on a waiting list with an Education Test thrown in there) after becoming a Junior Technician. I knew that I was a better Administrator than Technician and chose the Command ladder.

On the home front, at Margate, the Unit was housed in an old Private School building. Nice driveway and gardens in front, big red brick two/three storey building and a big sports field at the rear. There was no airmens' accommodation so we were all billeted out in seaside boarding houses. About eight of us were at Mrs Griffiths. A lady from Birmingham. Pat (who was now pregnant with Andrew though I didn't know it at first) moved in with us, we had a room to ourselves and Pat helped Mrs Griffiths in lieu of rent.

It was indeed a wild boarding house. This was at the dawn of the Goon Show era and we were all avid Goon fans. For some reason it used to come on at breakfast time, I imagine it was a repeat, and we would all be glued to the radio, chortling. Mrs Griffiths who was an oldie (probably 40 -50) couldn't see what we were laughing about. Time has told! There were also other guests living in the boarding house. Summer visitors. We were only a couple of hundred yards from the sea-front of Cliftonville which was the posh part of Margate. One old lady came to stay and made it clear that she had wanted to stay at the sea-front but it was all booked up (and more expensive) so she would make life difficult for Mrs Griffiths. Not if we had our way. That evening we all went out the back-yard and started tossing a golf ball at the wall below her window. Did I forget to mention that Mrs Griffiths had a Corgi which I think may have been called Bunty? Whatever, the Corgi loved this game and yapped incessantly as Corgi's are apt to do. It also happened that Pat was sitting on the back steps mixing up some mock cream for dinner. Well, after the golf ball had been in Bunty's mouth a few times and all over the backyard, it finished up in the bowl of mock cream! That evening neither Pat nor we air force boys ate any cream with our dessert.

There was another young woman there named Grace. Mrs Griffiths had 'picked her up' and given her a job. I'm sure if you read Pat's bio you'll see stories of Grace. I'm too embarrassed to recall them. As we walked to work in the mornings we had to go past a posh Department Store. They had very presentable young lady window dressers who would be fitting 'intimate apparel' to nubile models. We would stop at the window, about six or seven of us in RAF uniforms and tap on it to tell them which clothes should go where. They usually smiled and took it in fun.

As well there was a second hand shop on the same shopping street which had a very nice carving set in the window at 25 shillings. Having served in the Middle East, it went against the grain to pay full price without a haggle, unheard of in England in those days, so haggle I did. I knocked him down to 22/6. We still have the carving set.

I was detached to RAF Sandwich for a short while. Sandwich was a Radar Ground Controlled Intercept (GCI) station. They were obviously short of a wireless fitter and they needed someone to man their transmitter station. I carried on living in Margate and cycled to work, a distance of thirteen miles ... at three o-clock in the morning. I had to have the transmitters on air by 4.30 am when the Dawn Patrol would be on standby. The thirteen miles was all around a country road with links type land around. I was often accompanied by rabbits or hares. Pat heard me blaspheme for the first time during this detachment when the alarm failed to wake me and I woke up late. I yelled "Jesus Christ!" and went like a rocket. No problems.

Once every so often there was a 'do' on at the unit. On these nights we used to go into the Sergeants Mess, (it was the only room with a bar), and enjoy ourselves. A number of the Auxiliaries would also be there. Gin and lemon was a popular drink and cost a shilling. Of course we couldn't always afford the shilling. One day our Medical Orderly came back from the USAF base at Manston with some cough medicine. He asked me to taste it and asked what I thought. I took a sip and responded immediately "Gin and lemon." From then on, if we didn't have a shilling to spare we drank cough medicine. Drinking just a little now! A Gin and Lemon a Day keeps the cough away.

As well as the two main floors of the Unit there was an attic room which was kitted out with a bed for the Duty Airman. All the airmen stood this duty on a roster basis. Our Station Warrant Officer (SWO), the disciplinarian, was a fairly heavy drinker (and Salvation Army hymn lover) and at one of these do's he had a few too many, crawled home, couldn't get the key into the lock so crawled back to the Unit, woke up the Duty Airman, sent him home and slept in his bunk for the night.

This bed was also used by Pat and I … No! No! When there was a Social evening on at the Unit we would bring Andrew up there, fix him somehow to the Duty Airman's bed, and then enjoy ourselves with the others. But that is not chronologically correct. Andrew hasn't been born yet! Just seemed a good place to mention it.

Once each year the Auxiliaries would attend a Summer Camp. This is when they would go into an operational Fighter Control Unit for two weeks and try out their skills. Some of we regulars were sent along for the experience. Me, mainly to march them along the roads as I was a Corporal now and should know about these things. Some while before one of these Summer Camps, some linoleum turned up in the Store. It hung around for some time till eventually Bill Daniels, the Stores Sergeant, decided it was just what he needed for his kitchen at home. So home it went and was cut up to suit his kitchen. Just before we left for camp the Adj. told Bill that he wanted the staircase to the Stores lino'd with the stuff he'd ordered, and it should be done before we came back from camp.

If the staircase to the Store had been a normal staircase it would have been a difficult task with the already chopped up lino. This staircase twisted and turned! When we got back from camp the staircase looked like an ancient Greek mosaic. With copper nails going in all directions holding hundreds of shapes of pieces of lino in position. It truly was a work of art.

Working in the Store there had it's advantages. Paddy Thorman, one of the storemen, never carried his kit up from the boarding house for kit inspections. Everything he laid out was straight from Store and went straight back afterward. As well, Paddy was always wearing smart looking blue poplin shirts. Ours were blue/grey canvas, or felt like it. His habit was to take a new Waaf's shirt out of Store, wear it for a day and then put it back as new and issue it to some unsuspecting new Waaf Auxiliary.

Probably around May or June of 1950 Pat and I went to the cinema, I think it was Dreamland, in Margate on one Saturday afternoon. Part way through I felt very sick. We had to leave and, in fact, took a taxi home. Probably my first ever taxi. Shortly after we learned that Pat was pregnant. Hm!

One day the SWO walked into our 'radio workshop' to see the genius's at work. I now had two young National Service Wireless Mechanics under my command. We'd been playing around with the clockwork motor of a toy car. There was a coil of wire on the bench and a 2 volt lamp fitting. I told the SWO that we were generating electricity with the motor and, turning to one of the airmen, told him to wire it up 'again'. This he did taking the wire from the coil through the motor and onto the lamp. In the background, I had put a battery inside the big coil of wire. I said "Right, wind it up Ray", which the good lad did, then, as the motor started to unwind I touched the battery across the other two ends of the wire. The lamp lit up. The SWO retired in wonderment at the skill that was present in our small unit.

By now Pat had gone back to Brighton to have our first baby. We had tried to get other accommodation at Margate but nobody seemed to want a couple who were shortly expecting to become a triple. One woman said "They are conceived at night and they come at night". I wonder where she got that idea from. Being conceived at night I mean. Andrew was born on December 29th. 1950 at the start of a Smallpox epidemic. Brighton was sealed off. To go into the town you had to have a special permit. I applied and before I could go in I had to be vaccinated again. I did get there and picked out Andrew in a row of cribs because, as I told the nurse, all I had to do was look for the best looking one, he was bound to be mine. Incidentally looking for a good looking baby just a few days/hours old is like looking for a pretty camel.

In September of 1951, I was sent on an Instructional Technique Course. On this there would be about twelve students of different trades ranging from drivers, mechanics, metal bashers, wireless and Medical Photographers. There were others which I cannot recall. The first exercise was for each student to give a ten minute 'lesson' on his own trade. The extent to which the others responded to his questions was a measure of how well he had presented his lesson. The important thing about this was that the RAF insisted that it's instructors gave 'lessons' not 'lectures'. This lesson duration was progressively increased until the final examination which was a lesson from each of one hour duration. There was a specified way in which we laid out the lessons, and all questions were preset. Questions were thrown out to the class in general but nobody could answer until the instructor pointed to one student. This meant that anybody was likely to be asked so everybody had to think. For my first ten minute lesson I thought that the Resistance Colour Code (Bigger Better Resistors Or Your Grid Bias Must Go West – the mnemonic for Black 0, Brown 1, Red 2, Orange 3, Yellow 4, Green 5, Blue 6, Mauve 7, Grey 8 and White 9) was about the easiest thing in radio to learn, so I tried that. After about half an hour the Instructor stopped me and pointed out how difficult it was to judge the right amount of subject matter for a specified lesson time.

Part way through the course, during the critique time which followed each student's piece, (we had been told about tautology), the Medical Photographer pointed out that I had said 'D.C. Current'. Which was tautological. He was quite right but there was no way he was going to get away with that. During his lesson on the preparation of corpses for photography he mentioned that they applied red Rouge to the corpse's face. Needless to say he got his at the end. I very politely pointed out that Rouge was French for red. Tautology! Yesss!

For my final 1 hour lesson I decided to do 'The Development of the Cardioid', you may remember that this was my favourite during my initial W/op training. I just couldn't believe it. What to me had seemed so logically beautiful produced a full class of perplexed and baffled faces. I did pass the board though. Lesson: When teaching, proceed from the known to the unknown.

At 3500 we had a pretty good football team, utilising a couple of the Auxiliaries. As a small Unit we would normally not dream of going into Air Force wide competitions but, without asking anybody, the Accounts Clerk sent the application in for entry to the RAF Junior Cup. I believe the Junior Cup was open to stations of 500 personnel or less. We were (on permanent staff) about 20 strong. As I remember, we beat the Radar Station at Sandwich, then beat the Fighter Station at West Malling and then got knocked out by the Fighter Station at Kenley in extra time. We were pretty proud of ourselves. We also had a pretty good Table Tennis team and played in the Isle of Thanet League. I don't remember winning too many of those matches though.

Later, I think that it was on a Wednesday late in 1952, the King died. Of course Wednesday was our Sports Day. The Adj. didn't think that it would look very proper if a RAF mob were to be seen playing football under such circumstances. What to do? Easy. We held a table tennis tournament in the Recreation Room instead.

We also played a lot of cricket. I remember three special events in cricket. I was umpiring a game between 3500 and the Royal Air Forces Association (RAFA Margate) on our pitch and was at the batting end. They were batting and our bowler bowled a no-ball. The batsman just pushed the ball forward and started to run. Our silly mid-off fielder virtually scooped the ball into the wicket-keepers hands and he smashed the stumps. I gave the man 'Out'. They immediately protested saying that you cannot be stumped on a no-ball. I argued that he was not stumped but was run-out. They did not agree. I would not change my decision and eventually our captain asked me to let the man stay in. Grrr! I wasn't a good umpire. I used to get so interested in the game that I would forget to count the bowls (balls?). Balls bowled! On another occasion I was playing at Mid-on, just about level with the stumps at the bowler's end when I made a good fielding move and threw the stumps down from a lying down position (notice I didn't say prone or supine 'cos I can never remember which is which) when I could only see one stump. I think we won the game because of that action. I was an early Ricky Ponting. The last of the three episodes occurred later when I was fielding in the outfield and went to make a catch. The ball caught the ring finger of my right hand and caused a fracture. I went to the American M.O. at Manston and he made up a plaster cast for it. The plaster cast was fairly loose so I took it off every time I wanted to wash my hands. That finger is still bent!

At this time I came very close to 'going off the rails'. Pat was at home in Brighton. We had all moved out of Mrs. Griffith's to another lady's house, she was a strict Baptist or one of those types of religions. At night we boys used to lay in bed and tell dirty jokes to each other. We were about four or five in the one room. It got so that we would straight-face every joke. Anybody who could produce a laugh was considered to be a great joke teller or at least to have told a great joke. Anyway the Country Club atmosphere of the Unit prevailed. We played mixed table-tennis games with the Auxiliary Waafs and two sisters started partnering another airman and me. The partnerships developed into what could have been a disastrous situation if Pat had not found out about it and turned up one evening at the Unit. That, thank goodness, put an end to it and our Adj. agreed to allow me to find married accommodation outside and live out. The Unit had no married quarters. We found a place at Birchington-on-Sea after a short while at the home of an Auxiliary Corporal in St. Peters near Broadstairs. Pat and Andrew moved in and we lived happily ever after. In my defence, I was still a very young impressionable airman and could still apparently 'draw the birds'. Pat was at home and they were there. As the old song said, 'If I'm not near the girl I love, I love the girl I'm near.' That's my excuse ....and I'm stuck with it.

Oh Yes. One other thing at Margate. We had a very accomplished pianist on our permanent staff and a piano in the 'Rec. Room'. He taught me to play 'Come back to Sorrento' exactly as per the music sheet. Every single note with all the fingers of both hands. I even introduced dramatic pauses. Some time later we were visiting Mum and I sat down at the piano and played it. Mum loved it and asked me to play something else. I told her I didn't feel like it.

Birchington was a challenge. It was a flat above an old stables of what had probably been the Manor House. There was a large corrugated iron front gate and a very large overgrown back garden. We had no tools of our own. I can't remember where we got them from but I got the garden down with a scythe and swophook. Pat has no doubt told you about the railway man and his wife, as seen from our kitchen window. There was a metal plate on the wall by the front gate and I painted it black then painted the words 'Per Ardua' in white. It looked terrible.

I used to catch the bus to work and as we were coming home one evening we had three minor accidents. The third was when a car driver opened his door as the bus was passing alongside. One of our Aux. Officers was on the bus in civvies, he said, very loudly to the whole bus "You can tell that we're getting close to town, we are hitting more cars!"

At some time I had my bike with us because I can remember cycling from Birchington to work. But more so I can remember cycling from Margate to Brighton, a distance of 87 miles to return my bike to Brighton. Riding it was cheaper than putting it on the train. It was only an ordinary bike with a pedal that squeaked each time I pressed down on it too hard. Mrs Griffith's son David, who'd have been about 12 years old pleaded to come with me and his Mum agreed. It took us about twelve hours. We stayed at The Avenue overnight and caught the train back to Margate next day, putting David's bike on the train. Quite an adventure for the lad. And a very hard day for me.

At about this time the RAF introduced a new scheme whereby an airman could sign on to serve to the age of 55 with the option of discharge both ways at age 40. There was a bounty of 100 Pounds. This was a fabulous amount of money at that time so I applied and was accepted. As we used to say, in those days they were needing them not feeding them.

Also, about this time, I was again put on the roster for overseas service. I was to go to Aden. I didn't want to go to Aden. It was known in the RAF as the 'arsehole' of the world. I applied to be put on a Junior Leaders course. This was to teach corporals all the things necessary to be a sergeant. A bit of a bind but much, much better than Aden.

My Aden tour was cancelled and I settled down to wait for the silly course. I think that I can honestly say that that was the only time I did something to avoid a nasty overseas posting. I then decided that I didn't really want to go on the Junior Leader's course so I applied to go into aircrew as an Air Signaller. My application for the Junior Leader's course was duly cancelled and I went before the Aircrew Selection Board at Hornchurch.

This was a very interesting experience with an extensive medical and lots of IQ and manipulative tests. It included measuring your height, whilst sitting on the ground, from your back to your feet. It was presumably because some people would be too long to fit into a cockpit, though the story was that it had to do with the coffin size! One test would have been considered the forerunner of today's computer games. We were seated in a mock cockpit. Facing us was a large Cathode Ray Tube screen on the centre of which was etched a rectangle and in that a cross hairs 'plus' sign. To the side of the console there were two lamps. I think they were red and green. To the side of the 'pilot' there was a short gear lever and on the other side a press button. In front there was a joystick. I believe there may also have been a pair of rudder bars at his feet. A luminous spot appeared in the centre of the screen. After a short time it started moving. The candidate had to keep the spot within the rectangle by use of the joystick and rudder bars. Simultaneously the red or green lights would occasionally flash. If one flashed he had to push the gear lever forward and back again. If the other flashed he had to punch the press button. Unlike today's computer games, we only had one go.

I came through with flying colours (unintended pun) and was told I had qualified for a Pilot, Navigator, Engineer or Signaller. What did I want? I said obviously a Pilot. The interviewing Officer asked why I hadn't applied for pilot in the first place and I told him, quite honestly, that I didn't think that my education had been sufficient. He then went away for a while and when he returned told me that I couldn't be a Pilot or Navigator because they are now automatically commissioned as officers on passing out and, as I was already serving on a pensionable engagement to the age of 55, it would mean awarding me a Permanent Commission. That, they could not do. Again, as an afterthought, one wonders why they could not have offered to revoke my pensionable engagement, reverting back to my original eight years in the colours and four in the reserve. Chances are that they lost an excellent pilot. Future Chief of Air Staff. Probably they just couldn't think of a way of getting back their hundred quid. So I was back to Signaller. As a wireless fitter and ex-wireless operator I should have been a dead cert.

Pat and Andrew moved back to Brighton. She was beginning to get used to it.

Aircrew training, and not

My air crew course assembled at Cranwell in Lincolnshire. We received green disks to put behind our cap badges and a brass albatross to wear somewhere or other. As a corporal, with two or three others, and about 60 brand new recruits, I was given all sorts of responsibilities. These new boys had to be square bashed and we were the boys to do it. Presumably it allowed the proper drill NCO's to have time off. We didn't mind. We had lots of fun. We would be marching three or four squads of airmen all over the square. Doing about turns, right turns, left turns and every other imaginable turn, we would deliberately march our squad straight into the path of our mate's squad or to some intercepting point and at the last minute give an "About Turn!" order. If we got the timing right, and if the squad heard us right, and if the squad knew what to do there would be very neat manoeuvre. Of course, if any of those 'ifs' were wrong, there was chaos.

My big day was Cranwell Sports Day. A very big annual event. I was detailed to take the parade of the whole of the 'Aircrew Cadets Wing' and get them to the Sports Stadium in true military fashion. I had about 270 airmen in three squadrons of three flights of around thirty airmen. I was the 'Wing Commander', my best mates were the 'Squadron Commanders' and the other corporals were 'Flight Commanders'. We did the whole thing as if it were a C in C's inspection and I finished up marching up the main road in front of a 150 metre long column of airmen. We took them to the Stadium, dismissed them, then we vanished to the local coffee shop! There was no point in trying to march them back because the Aircraft Apprentices always won everything that was going and took over the main road after the sports. They would form up in lines about twenty wide, staggered like a racing car grid, then they would march up the road moving from left to right and right to left like a hairdresser's shaver or a hedge cutter. To get in the way was suicidal.

After a few weeks we moved to Compton Basset in Wiltshire for the start of our signalling training. This followed the normal Morse and wireless training in which, again, I was already qualified. We also started to do a bit of navigation training but nothing too serious. A few weeks later we were moved again to Halfpenny Green, which was on the border of Worcestershire and Shropshire, to continue the training. Here I was used as a Morse instructor and began to enjoy the course but again it was not to be and we were moved yet again to Swanton Morely in Norfolk. As we arrived at the camp, in the back of a truck, it was raining and looked absolutely miserable. I turned to my mate and said "I'm not going to like it here". Things at Swanton Morely were lousy. It was probably the worst period of my air force life. I was still going along OK on the course but getting bored because we were still going over stuff that I was already trained on. In all air crew courses there is a very high 'chop' rate. This is the number of trainees who fail to make the grade and get 'chopped' as the course progresses. Our course was no exception and yet I saw all round me idiotic administrative procedures that wasted training time. As well we were now aware that the new boys had only been issued with the minimum of webbing equipment whilst we 'oldies' still had the full kit. As a result of this, the fellows who had been all through it years before were now going all through it again whilst the new boys were sitting back laughing. Blancoing a full kit of webbing and polishing the brass that goes with it on a regular basis can be a bind, and seemed very unfair to us. We stuck with it. Then the RAF decided to issue a new type of blanco. This was applied like shoe polish and came in a tin. It was decided that an initial issue of one tin of this blanco would be made to every cadet one afternoon, in school time. It took some hours. In every course there was somebody like myself who could afford to lose the time to pick up the blanco for his whole course, but this would have been too easy. Seeds of discontent were sown within me.

I was in charge of our room in the barrack block and had the first bed in the room. It was decided that there would be a kit inspection on Friday morning. We all laid out our kit in regulation fashion. Our Flight Commander, an ex-apprentice, came round, inspected and passed my kit then went round the room tearing everybody's kit to pieces. Much of it finished up on the floor. He declared that there would be another Kit Inspection on Sunday morning. We'd all made arrangements to go home for the week-end. These had to be abandoned. Not so easy when you remember that the telephone was not a thing that many ordinary families had. We certainly didn't have one. Over the Saturday I went through my kit with a fine tooth comb knowing that I had been lucky with a few things the day before, so that the kit I put out for inspection on Sunday would have been near perfect. The Flight Commander came in, came to my bed first and my kit finished up all over the floor. I stood by and for the first and probably the only time in my life had to hold myself from hitting somebody. It would have been a court martial offence if I had not controlled my anger. The following morning I put in an application to be taken off the course. This is close to treason!

I was interviewed and told the Wing Commander about all the time wasting that took place. I also suggested that there could easily have been an accelerated course for fully trained wireless operators and fitters. He suggested that I could be moved straight on to flying but I told him that I had to learn the radar and navigation side first. He then told me that I was unfit to be an NCO and dismissed me. I had to wait whilst he wrote up a report about me. As I waited I spoke to the School Adjutant, a Flt. Lt. who seemed to be a nice person. When the report came out he read it and immediately suggested that I should put in a 'redress of grievance'. I told him that I had had enough and would soon get back my reputation on posting to a normal station again. I was moved from the cadet billets to the permanent staff billets and awaited my posting. In the meantime I was marched in front of a board of officers consisting of all the camp's senior officers and given the full treatment. Asked if I had anything to say I just said "No". The sooner I could get out of there the better. The Group Captain in a very nasty tone said "I'll be glad to get you off my station". I was shaking in fear but stood there until I was dismissed, saluted and marched out. It costs hundreds of thousands of pounds to train an air crew cadet and they don't like to be told that they are doing it all wrong!

After a couple of weeks I was posted out again to, of all places, Halfpenny Green. I knew that I was going to be alright again. I was given the post of NCO i/c Transmitters. This was a couple of miles from the main station and I lived there with three or four airmen radio mechanics. We were a happy little group, hardly affected by what went on the main camp. We used to go up there for our main meals but had rations to take care of breakfast. We had a room full of transmitters to maintain and an 'Aerial Farm' which we were also supposed to look after.

The Signals Officer was a Pole who would come down to inspect us every now and again. He would always complain about the length of the grass around the place and suggested that we should start growing vegetables there. I got the boys started on digging a bit but there was a concrete slab directly underneath. When he came down next time he was surprised to see only about one square yard of garden dug. I told him that the soil was only about two inches deep. He replied "Zen Vee Vill grow shallow root plants". One of his favourite expressions when giving 'pep' talks was "Vee British". But he was OK really. As the end of the year approached and time for the annual assessments got closer I went up to see him. I told him that I had come to the camp with a big black mark against my name, and asked how this would affect my annual assessment. He said "Corporal, your assessment Vill be based entirely on the Vork you 'ave done for me." I told him that I was satisfied with that and got a good assessment.

In late '52 Andrew came within 30 yards of being an orphan. We'd left him with his grand-mother whilst we went to the Annual Farnborough Air Show. One of the highlights was to be John Derry breaking through the sound barrier in a dive towards the crowd. His DH 110 aircraft broke up and the flaming engines roared towards the crowd on the hills. Pat and I were there. I realised what had happened and threw her to the ground and myself on top of her. The engines crashed to earth about 30 yards past us killing a number of spectators. I had blood spots on the back of my greatcoat. Near miss!

Around this time I bought a second hand ex Army 350cc Royal Enfield motor bike. I got L plates and drove up and down the road by transmitters for a couple of evenings. On the second day I drove into Bridgenorth and bought a pair of gauntlets. On the way back there was a tractor in front of me. It was going down hill and there was a long sweeping right curve at the bottom. I decided that I was going to have to overtake something sooner or later so I turned the throttles up full and screamed past him hitting God knows what speed and just managed to keep it on the road at the bottom. My first overtake. The next afternoon I set off on the 180 miles journey to Brighton for the week-end. I did my first wheely as I did a right turn at a T junction on to a main road. It wasn't intentional. I was so scared of getting caught by traffic coming from the side that I throttled up and let out the clutch so fast that the front wheel came flying into the air. I don't know how I managed to stay on. I nearly fell asleep at one point and felt the hedge brushing against my left side. It took me 6 hours. 30 mph on a motor bike wasn't exactly speedy but it was cheaper than a bus or train, and faster than hitch-hiking. I remember that shortly after that, it may have been that same week-end, I took off the L plates and put Pat on the pillion seat and drove off to Emsworth to see my parents. Dad now had a fish and chip shop there. On our way back, it might have been in Chichester or Arundel, the coppers, in a car, were the other side of the traffic lights and as the lights went green I stalled the bike. Whew! They hadn't noticed.

The bike wasn't very reliable and I had a lot of trouble with the clutch which would fall to pieces as I went along the road. I had to stop and put it back together again. Didn't know what I was doing. I also had trouble starting it. It was, of course, a kick-start in those days and when you are dressed for a 180 mile drive in an English winter, and the bloody thing won't start, you can bet your sweet bippy that you will be sweating cobs by the time you get going and freezing about two minutes later.

Early in 1953, Princess Elizabeth was crowned Queen of England. London went wild and I have the pictures to prove it. Well, photos of the decorations.

But by now I was on the Preliminary Warning Roster (PWR) for another overseas tour. I drove the motor bike home, leaving Pat to sell it, and went off to Germany.

7. Germany 1953-55

I left Harwich in the 'Parkeston' from Parkeston Quay. It was probably in April or May. It was an overnight crossing arriving at the Hook of Holland in the early morning. From there we went on a military train to the holding centre at Buckeburg which was a very pretty north German city.

Within a couple of days of arriving, there would have been a couple of hundred airmen on the draft, some of the boys started to get their postings. I should point out that unlike the Army which usually moves battalions or whatever around as a single entity, the RAF moves airmen around individually unless a whole squadron is being relocated. So airmen get postings to wherever they are required. These postings went on for a couple of weeks, the place getting more and more empty until there were just two of us Wireless Fitter corporals left without postings. Every morning we would go to the corporal in charge of the postings and every morning he would tell us that there must be something special about us; that we had been trained on some special piece of equipment. He'd had it before with wireless blokes. The other corporal said that he had been trained on some cryptographic stuff but I continually said "No". Not only had I not been trained on anything special, I'd just about forgotten all the ordinary stuff that I had been trained on. The two of us had a great time strolling around Buckeburg each day after the morning report until, after another week or so, we received our postings. I was going to No.68 Squadron at Wahn but would also go down to Schwechat (Vienna) in the Russian Zone of Austria on a few weeks detachment after a couple of weeks at Wahn. 68 Squadron! Night Fighters! I was a Ground Wireless Fitter for Gods sake!

Wahn was the main Cologne airport, later to become Koln-Bonn airport, but for the present it housed three RAF Meteor squadrons. 68 was a night-fighter squadron with Meteor NF11's, 2 Squadron was a Meteor Photographic Reconnaissance unit and I can't remember the number of the third squadron, it may have been 73 which had some other Meteors. Of course of Meteors I knew nothing! I could not have guessed where the radios were housed or indeed what radios they had. 68's squadron emblem was an owl sitting on a crescent moon and were known affectionately as "The cat and banana boys". 2 Squadron's crest was a piece of rope tied into a reef knot. They were known, not so affectionately, as the "Get knotted" squadron. A common expression of disgust in those days was "Ah. Get knotted!" So here I was, corporal in charge of the squadrons' wireless flight who knew less than any of the lads. What a situation! I got stuck in trying to get to know what it was all about but after two weeks I had to go on the detachment to Vienna.

In 1953 Austria, like Germany, was an occupied country divided into three zones. The French, British and Russian. Also, as in Germany, the Capital city, Wein (Vienna) was in the Russian Zone. Vienna was also a 3 Power city. French, Russian and British. However, the RAF base in Vienna was outside the British Sector surrounded by the Russian Sector! My papers took me by train to Munich, from there to Klagenfurt in the British zone and thence through the Russian zone to Vienna. As I said earlier, the RAF generally posted airmen as individuals so there was I, one British serviceman, in uniform, on a train full of Russian soldiery and their 'camp followers'. Uncomfortable would perhaps have been rather too mild a word to describe my feelings. It was going to be a long hard ride. There were two stations between Klagenfurt and Vienna named Moedling and Meidling. I didn't know this until I came to the second. I didn't get off at the first, Moedling, because, although it sounded like the name of the station I'd been told to detrain at, it was earlier than I expected and when I looked out of the window all I saw were Russian soldiers with guns. I took a chance and stayed on the train. Every now and again I guess right. Thank goodness. When I reached the next 'right sounding' station I detrained and was met by a driver from the RAF who took me to RAF Schwechat. It was alongside the Vienna Woods of Johann Strauss fame. No Weiner Blut. Thank goodness!

Of course my job at Schwechat for two months was to maintain the transmitter/receiver in the station communications flight Avro Anson. Another Air Radio job! As it happens it was at least one of the air radio T/R's that I'd been trained on at Cranwell in 1949. We also had a Tiger Moth but that only had a voice tube between the pilot and the passenger.

It was approaching summer and Vienna can get pretty warm and sticky. A few things bring back memories from that detachment. The Russians had MIG 15's at their big air base down the road at Weiner Neustadt and every day they would roar over Schwechat. Very impressive. We had an electrician who had a bee in his bonnet that one day they were going to come for us. Every time they flew over the base he would go spare. Poor devil! As far as I was concerned they were just like the old doodlebugs. If you could hear their engines you were safe.

On one occasion I had to go down to Klagenfurt in the Anson. The air corridor through the Russian zone for us went in a dog-leg, but the station pilot reckoned that it could be flown in a straight line without going over barred Russian occupied territory. About half way down, inside the 'knee' of the dogleg, was the Russian fighter base at Weiner Neustadt where they had the MIG 15's. As we flew over that corner of the dogleg I was looking down directly at MIG 15's. I must confess to wondering at that time if they would come up and get us. They left us alone.

On the way back to Vienna we had to call in at Graz, a small airfield with a radio beacon within the corridor or just short of the Russian zone. I had to check it out. We'd also picked up an airman's wife and child at Klag to go up to Vienna. After we took off again the pilot decided to give them a thrill. As soon as he was airborne he put her in a tight turn, did a shoot-up of the airfield then went hedge-hopping over the pine forests up to Vienna. I could see the tops of the pine trees being bent over by our slipstream. I wasn't sorry to see that trip over either.

By now the mosquitoes were beginning to hit Vienna in plague proportions so our C.O. offered the City Council a DDT spray of the Danube from the air. At that time DDT was the be all and end all of insecticides. I believe that it was later found to be very unhealthy for humans as well. They fitted the Anson with pipes protruding out either side, these were drilled with lots of little holes. 40 gallon drums of DDT with hand pumps were loaded into the Anson along with a couple of airmen. They flew low over the river pumping the insecticide in all directions. When they came back the two poor airmen were greener than the Danube.

One day, as I was walking in front of the hangar, a wasp came down from a nest near the top, stung me on the back of my neck and flew straight back up. Cheeky bastard! What'd I done to him?

Just before my attachment was up we received a new aircraft. It was an Auster. A nice little aeroplane with bungy cords as part of the undercarriage suspension. The CO was to be away for a few days so he gave instructions that the plane wasn't to be touched till he came back. Well, the station pilot got fed up with waiting, so he got the ground staff boys to set it up for him and went on a couple of trips in it without any paperwork being completed. A very serious offence. On around his third trip the CO arrived back unexpectedly just as it was taking off. He went mad, racing out to the airfield screaming "Come back". The pilot took her down to an army strip near Schonbrun and did a circuit and bump. Unfortunately the bump completely dislocated the port undercarriage and he came back with just one wheel hanging downwards. He made a beautiful one wheel landing holding his port wing up until he'd almost stopped. All the airmen were rushing out with fire extinguishers, beating the fire engine to the scene. They weren't needed, thank goodness. I don't know what the outcome of that little escapade was.

The old pre-war hangars at Schwechat were still as they had been left by the Russians after they'd pounded the city a few years earlier, just one tangled mass of iron.

On my last day in Vienna we went down to the city to try to find the Cafe Mozart of "The Third Man" fame. We didn't find it and the boys left me in the city to catch a train back to Klagenfurt leaving at about 3 pm. I was strolling around to waste time when I heard marching feet behind me. I looked around and there saw a platoon of armed Ruskies marching up the road towards me. I suppose it was instinct that made me quicken my pace and get out of their way.

I caught the train and again was surrounded by Russian soldiers and camp-followers. I imagine if it had been RAF men and their women or wives, we would have stood up and given the ladies the seats. As it was, only the women and I were standing. It was an eight hour trip!

I arrived in Klagenfurt near midnight, my train to Munich was not due till about 11 am. so I looked around for somewhere to stay. These are the things which on hindsight make me wonder. There was a lone RAF man, in uniform, travelling on duty through what was effectively enemy territory, or at least partially, with no instructions on where he could gain safe accommodation. One must wonder just when my absence would have been noticed if I'd been 'kidnapped' by the Russians. I eventually came upon a British Army Barracks. I went into the guardroom and they gave me a bed in a hut where I slept and then went to breakfast in the Army mess and had rubber eggs and green bread. It was disgusting. I caught my train on time and travelled all day and through the next night arriving at Cologne around 8 am, next morning. On the train I ate bowls of soup and, though I didn't drink I had bought beer to drink because it was probably clean and cheaper than coffee. When I got back to Wahn I submitted my travelling expense report, expecting to get about thirty or forty Deutsch Marks. I got around eight Marks. The reason was that I'd had the accommodation in the Army camp to break my journey. I argued that, though I didn't drink, the beer I'd drunk to prevent myself dying from thirst had cost more than that. My pleas fell on deaf ears. I wuz robbed!

Back on the squadron I started to get more involved with the aircraft and the sporting activities. However two weeks after my return to Wahn I was on my way, with the rest of the Squadron, on detachment to RAF Coltishall in Norfolk. Gets around this boy don't he? It was a two weeks exercise. The RAF in Germany was 2nd Tactical Air Force (2TAF) and, as such, should be able to pack up and move on very short notice. We were moving on the Monday. The Squadron was flying out straight to Coltishall whilst the ground crews were going by train to the Hook of Holland, boat to Harwich, and trains to Norwich to arrive next day. On the Sunday before the move the hangar looked like a normal working day. I wasn't used to this sort of thing so I wasn't involved but what was happening was that in every aircraft except the Squadron Commander's, radar and wireless equipment was being stripped of big valves and filled with cigarettes and bottles of spirits. They were then closed up, pumped up to normal pressure and sealed with stickers stating that the equipment was pressurised and must not be opened. The Squadron Commander's was the only plane to fly with radar! Of course, this is purely hearsay because as I said, this was all new to me. Certainly part of it was true because when we arrived the next day the planes had been 'recrystallised' (retuned to the UK radio frequencies) by the Coltishall ground staff. All the fags were missing! In the squadron workshops the Colt boys were offering the Wahn boys a cigarette from a 'Duty Free' packet and there was nothing they could do about it ... officially!

Late that first afternoon we were told that our aircraft were going to fly on exercise operations that evening. I was to take over one of the aircraft. The Flight Sergeant told me to watch what one of the other corporals did then to take 'S' Sugar as my own. The other corporal went through the engine start-up and using a pair of illuminated wands waved the pilot out of the 'pans' on to the peri-track. My turn! A couple of mechanics were standing by the chocks, and the starter accumulator was plugged in. Both could have done this with their eyes shut but it was me instead. I managed to get through the engine start-up OK. Disconnected the trolley acc. and I waved the mechanics with the chocks away and started to bring the kite forward with my wands. I then spotted another chock under the plane dead in line with the ventral fuel tank which reached to about a foot above the ground. The tank caught the chock and rolled it over. I was horrified and stared at the thing to see if any fuel started to pour out. I couldn't see anything and waved the plane away. I did get better at it. I wonder if that pilot had any idea that the corporal waving him away had just controlled his first aeroplane after just five minutes training! I managed to get home that week-end for a 48 hour pass. I think that it may have been Pat's twenty fifth birthday.

On completion of the exercise and our return to Wahn I applied for a posting on the grounds that I was misemployed. In the meantime I got stuck into both the work and the sport. We played a lot of football and I was in the Squadron team. One of the SAC radio mechs, Garvey, was the self-appointed team manager. He was good fun and was exactly right as team manager. One day we had an a new airman posted in. The first question was always "Do you play football?" It was always called 'football' in England because that was the only big ball game except Rugby that was played, and that was called 'rugby'. Anyway this airman said "Yes". The 'manager' asked him who he'd played for, to which he answered "Bomber Command". A Command player! They were just about professional! All our birthdays had come at once. He agreed to play for the Squadron on the following Saturday. The big day arrived. In the warm-up kick about the ball was passed to him a couple of times and he seemed to have some difficulty. The game started. Within a few minutes it was obvious that this fellow had never kicked a football in his life! We were passing it anywhere rather than to him. I saw one of our team turn away from him and try to dribble through three of the opposition rather than push the ball to him. We lost, heavily. As we walked back to the barracks our 'manager' said

"Hey Bomber, you played for Bomber Command?",

"Yes."

"Did they ever drop you?"

"No."

"Well they should have done, from forty thousand f ... g feet".

It was a classic comment. One of the best I ever heard. A case where the obscenity was absolutely appropriate.

Obscene language was of course part of the way of life in any of the services. I was as good at it as anybody. However there was a time and place for it. Just before I left the squadron, one of my mechanics had wired a new 'Press to talk' microphone switch into one of the Meteors. I agreed to go out to one of the spare aircraft out on the airfield and do a two way test with him.

I gave him a call. Got no answer. I heard a bit of banging about and gave him another call. Again got no answer and then heard him say, "Come on Alf, get with it" or something like that. I called again and still got no response. Then again I heard him saying "Come on Alf, where the F ... are you?". I started to get a bit worried. If I was hearing this, half of the Air Force in Germany could be hearing it. Now there was a lot of banging and swearing along the same lines so I dropped out of the aircraft that I was in and raced back to the hangar. I had already guessed what was wrong. He had wired the switch in the wrong way. When he pressed to talk, he was receiving and when he thought he was receiving he was transmitting all of the language. As I got back to the hangar the line Flt. Sergeant came out of the office and asked if anybody was using obscene language on any of the radios, the Waaf fighter plotters at 83 Group Headquarters were complaining. I declared that nobody in our squadron had been on the air then gave the airman a dose of my own obscene language.

During my short stay at Wahn Konrad Adenaur, the first Chancellor of the Federal Republic of Germany (West Germany), arrived to a guard of honour of the new German Navy. I believe the occasion was the proclamation of the F.R.G. but have found no evidence for that. Could be that only he and I knew it.

The most memorable happening on the squadron was when the aircraft had just returned from an air firing exercise. The pans at Wahn were in two rows and each in the second row was immediately behind one in the first row. Normally they are staggered. The rule at Wahn was that kites returning from air firing should be parked in the front row. One of ours wasn't. The armament mechanic, fairly new I believe, went out to do his 'after flight' inspection, pressed the firing button and half a dozen cannon shells went tearing into the ventral tank of the kite in front. Flaming Avtur (jet fuel) started to pour from the tank whilst radio and electrical mechanics poured out of the hatch, just behind the tank, where the radio and electrical equipment was housed. The fire started to spread outwards. The fire section were quickly on the scene and an airman with a hose started directing foam onto the fire. However the fire started to get at the fire engine so the driver jumped in, drove it away pulling the poor bugger on the hose base over apex. My mate was a corporal Armament Fitter. We were in the hangar. He grabbed a fire extinguisher and yelled "Come on Alf!" to which I responded, "Not me Matt, I've got a wife and a kid!". He carried on out to the airfield where he passed a couple of our mechanics nonchalantly walking back to the hangar, throwing their screwdrivers into the earth like knives. As Matt passed them they said "Don't worry Matt, it's not one of ours."

Learning to speak German, or pretending that you didn't understand German was useful. We used to catch the train from Wahn into Cologne and return. They had first and third class carriages. We used to get third class tickets and go into the first class carriage. When a ticket inspector came round and started to scream about Erste Klasse and Dritte Klasse we just answered "Nicht Verstehen" (I don't understand) until we reached Wahn when we'd say "Ah! Wahneheide. Gut Tag."

Just as I was beginning to enjoy squadron life and become a useful member of the Squadron my posting came through. I went to 2TAF FRU at Butzweilerhof, the other side of Cologne. FRU stands for Forward Repair Unit. The Unit was the RAF's major maintenance depot for all types of equipment, except aircraft, for the whole of Germany. The place that I should have been posted to in 1950. We had hundreds of new, used and thoroughly squashed vehicles stored around the place, heaps of PSP (Pressed Steel Plate) runway sheets for laying runways on quickly cleared strips and a very big radio and radar servicing hangar in which I was to work. I also received notice that I was going to attend a NATO UHF Ground Maintenance course with the USAF in Munich in February '54. But first I managed to get some leave in UK approved. I think we used to get three weeks a year. I again went on the train and boat through the Hook and Harwich and down to Brighton where I quickly managed to get Susan conceived. Well, I was hungry wasn't I? After about a week I received a telegram ... You don't know what a telegram is? It was like an email but it went through the Post Office and was delivered by little boys, with pill box hats, on bicycles. Much faster than ordinary mail and much dreaded in wartime. This ordered me to return to Butz immediately. I went back, again on the boat and train, I was getting to know that route by now.

The Cold War hadn't ended with the Berlin Airlift. It was intense at this time and the Americans were pschycotic regarding all things Communist. It seemed that before the Yanks would let me nose into their Hi-tech equipment they wanted assurance that I, my family, their families and anybody who knew me were not associated with the communists. I had to be cleared by the FBI. I filled in the forms and asked if I could return to complete my leave. The Wing Commander agreed and even agreed to make me a compassionate case so that I could get off the ship at Harwich first and get the first train to London. It was more of a passionate case than a compassionate one! I wonder if the FBI still has that check of me on their records? After a few days I was again recalled and returned on the ship and train, but this time the North Sea was scattered with dozens of mini ice bergs. I was in a berth at the front and right against the skin of the ship. All night I could hear the lumps of ice crashing against the hull (not skin!). On the train journey through Holland and Germany I saw a man cycling down the Rhine River! As well the Dutch people used to flood some of their parks and when they froze use them as big open-air ice rinks. It was a beautiful sight.

Within a few days I was again on the train to Munich and from there to Freising where I joined the 7490th Tech. Training Squadron, USAF. As it happened, the day that we arrived was George Washington's birthday and a US National Holiday, so we needn't have rushed. I could have finished my leave. The RAF gave us an allowance for the U.S. Zone so that we wouldn't need to be as poor as the church mice that we imitated. It was needed because everything in the Yank PX (Post Exchange) down there was a lot dearer than it was in the NAAFI in the British Zone. Imagine our delight when the Yanks announced that we were to receive a special NATO allowance for the same purpose.

We worked very hard on that course. It lasted eight weeks. All the instructors were U.S. civilians, employees of the big U.S. military radio suppliers such as Collins, Philco and RCA. A lot of them and the U.S. airmen who were students on the course had their own cars. They were very generous and we got on remarkably well with them. On our course there were eight USAF men from corporal up to staff sergeant, four Greeks headed by Warrant Officer Angelides and including three sergeants, and four of us RAF, myself and another corporal and two senior aircraftmen.

The method of teaching was excellent, and sensibly, you could refer to manuals when taking exams. About half way through the course I was called out of the class to see a staff sergeant who, it turned out was the editor of the Newsletter. I had been selected as 'Student of the Week' and they wanted a short bio on me. So I'm not entirely new to this game!

Fasching, the big Munich Beer Festival takes place in March and we went into the Augustinerhof Bierhalle in Munich one night. I think I probably got drunk. We sat at long tables with about thirty others, the beer was served in two litre jugs which were passed around and drunk from by all and sundry.

Each time the jug (or Stein) was refilled the barmaid marked another line (five bar gate style) on a label stuck to it. I've no idea who paid for it. I'm pretty certain that none of us RAF blokes put our hands in our pockets. The hall holds hundreds of people and they are all out for a good time. A good night out, yet I still thought of myself as essentially teetotal!

As well, one of the instructors took us up to Oberammergau where the Passion Play is held every fifth year. To get there we had to pass the Etaler Monastery where the monks make the most amazing liqueur. It is at Unterammergau and there is a bit of local double Dutch that says something like Unterammergau ist unter Oberammergau aber Oberammegau ist uber Unterammergau.

About half way through the course we got word that one of Pat's American Pen Friend's was working with the U.S. Special Services at Ludwigsburg. One of my Yank friends immediately offered to drive me up there at the week-end, to visit her. She was a very charming lady and she agreed to come down to Freising the following week-end to attend a ball that had been organised by the Yanks. On the evening of the ball I picked her up at the home of a friend of hers and somehow or other we got to the ball. She was extremely popular with all the RAF and USAF boys and then it came time to go home. I walked her to her friend's home. She asked why we walked and didn't get a taxi and I told her, truthfully, that we always walked everywhere because we couldn't afford to do otherwise. I dropped her off and went back to our barracks. The boys were waiting for me. "Did you?" "Of course not, she is my wife's friend." "What a bloody waste!"

At about this time I was feeling very sick one night. I wrote to Pat and told her that I had been sick. She replied telling me that she was pregnant. It may have been a coincidence but you may remember that four years earlier, in Margate, we had gone to the pictures and I was suddenly very sick. We'd had to catch a taxi home. Shortly after she announced that she was pregnant! I don't think Pat ever suffered from Morning Sickness, I did all the suffering for her.

On a more sombre note we went one Sunday to visit the ex Nazi Concentration Camp at Dachau, near Munich. It was very cold and the whole atmosphere of the place made it seem even colder. We went through the gas chambers, the gallows, the pistol walls, it was horrible. I think that it should be compulsory for any would be neo-nazis to be incarcerated there for a month or so.

A couple of days before we completed the course I got a phone call from the RAF Liaison Officer at the Wiesbaden USAF base, a Wing Commander. The RAF had heard that we were getting the NATO allowance and therefore we must pay back the RAF Zone allowance! I argued that we probably didn't have it. He remarked that we must have been having a good time down there to which I replied that we had gone out last Friday night for the first time since we arrived, that everything was very dear down here and that our NAAFI breaks cost two or three times as much as in the British Zone. He said "You don't expect the Queen to pay for your NAAFI breaks do you?" to which I replied "No Sir, but I do expect her to pay for the difference!" Anyway, we were told that we were to break our return journey at Wiesbaden and repay the allowances to him.

We took our final exams, and, because of the system with manuals and the superb index that I had built up, I came equal top with W/O Angelides and, I think, a Yank Staff Sergeant. I didn't know the Yanks could be so diplomatic. They then showed their ignorance by making the Certificate of Training out to Cpl. Alfred W. Commons, (R.B.A.F) Royal British Air Force! There's no such thing! Everybody knows that the Brits don't need to put their country in their titles. Its the Royal Navy, The Royal Air Force. Even in Golf where you have the U.S. Open, the French Open, the Australian Open, and you have the Open. Everybody know that means the original. We duly called in at Wiesbaden and paid our money to the Wingco. I've often wondered what would have happened if we hadn't got it. Would he have kept us in the U.S. Zone?

Back to FRU Butz where I arrived to find that there was a stores shed full of the American UHF equipment that I had just been trained on. I was the RAF's American UHF expert in Germany. The other trainees had just gone back to their ordinary units to do their ordinary jobs. This stack in stores included a Direction Finding Equipment that I had not been trained on. CRD 6. I quickly trained another FRU corporal up and we set about installing the stuff all over Germany. We should have communicated with each other more frequently because it turned out that we had both come across the same problem in one piece of equipment which we each overcame in different ways. The big power supply unit had a fan operated switch. If the fan was blowing it blew a thin brass 'blade' downward and actuated the switch. The equipment was designed for American 110 Volt 60 Cycles per second (cps) mains operation. We were using something like 220 Volt 50cps. The blade would not be moved down. No blade, no power! I decided to make the blade a little heavier by coating it with solder. The other corporal solved the same problem by flattenning out the blade (it had a bend in it). As it was a safety problem I think his method may have been the safer.

I was now at the top of the list for a married quarter and took possession of a house in Rehorste Strasse. Koln. This process is known as 'Marching In' for the new occupant and 'Marching Out' for the one vacating the quarter. The process is supervised by the Families Officer and attended by both parties and a Senior Stores person. All bedding, cooking utensils, crockery, furniture etc is counted and handed over officially. I was pretty new to this sort of thing and when I was asked by the airman who was 'marching out' if his wife and kids could hang on there until the transport came for them, I agreed. Seemed the decent thing to do. I then went back to work. The quarter was now mine and it was just a matter of arranging for the family to travel out to join me when I would start 'Living Out'. I can't recall exactly what was wrong after that, I believe that some stuff went missing, but I know that I had learned a lesson. I do recall that when Pat and Andrew joined me and we went to reposition a sideboard that was obviously out of place, it was found to be covering a big hole in the wall.

I don't recall too much of married quarters life, that's womens' business, but two incidents I have vague memories of. The first was a massive fight between the feller next door and his wife, late one night. Pat was all agog, holding her ear to the wall whilst I refused to be quiet so that she could hear. The second was about rations. We were still allotted rations from RAF catering supplies for a number of essential items that were best not bought from German shops at that time. The rations were delivered in a big metal box once a week by the Corporal in the Ration Store who also happened to live a couple of doors along from us, and who, I believe, also came from Brighton, from Picton Street which I mentioned earlier. On this particular occasion we had a very large extra leg of lamb in our box. It wasn't on our bill. I suspect we didn't say a word about it believing that it had been illegally intended for the Corporal's box.

In November '54 Susan was born in RAF Hospital Wegberg. This was about 40 miles from Koln and required a dash in an Opel Kapitan at night. On the following day or thereabout, our neighbours (not the fighting ones), were due to return to England and Pat had told them that they could come in and have lunch with us after they had 'marched out', whilst they awaited their transport. On that day I attained the heights of my culinary expertise. They said that of course they could not expect me to do it and I said of course I would. I cooked roast beef, roast potatoes, peas and Yorkshire pudding, a real British Sunday dinner for them. All by the book! It was a great success. If you ask Andrew about my culinary skills he will tell of my superior handling of Smiths Crisps and Heinz tomato soup.

I was now offered a brand new flat (Unit) in Iltis Strasse at the end of the tram line. I think it was in Bickendorf or Ossendorf. The Belgian Army had a Club nearby. There were six units and we had a beautiful piece of grassy land surrounding the place. Six families moved in and we all started to enjoy life. Parties became quite a regular occurrence. We cycled up to work each day and home for lunch (dinner). One day, as we came through the gate, Doreen Simmons was hanging over her balcony saying, "I hope you enjoy your dinner Alf." Strange! I went in and Pat put up a plate of pigs trotters cooked in red cabbage. Today I would probably try it, and possibly even enjoy it, but then it was far too avant garde for me. I'd never seen a pink dinner before. I refused to eat it. I suppose I must have had something else. Can't remember, but it was unlikely that Pat would have sent me back to work on an empty stomach.

By now of course, Andrew was attending a British Forces School in Koln and learning bad habits. He was standing on the balcony one day when a fat bald headed man walked up the road. Andrew called out "Oy! Skinhead!" Luckily the skinhead was either German or Belgian and didn't understand.

One of the education officers advertised a car for sale for £25. I decided that we needed a car. He lived up in the mountains so, as I couldn't yet drive, Vinnie Simmons and I went home with him one night after work to pick it up. Vinnie was to drive it home. When we got up to the Ed. Off.'s place, there was snow all around the place and the Ed. Officer said "There it is." All we could see was a big heap of snow. We brushed it off and underneath it all was a big Opel Super Six. We started back in terrible conditions. Nothing worked. I was hanging out of the windows wiping the windscreen with some rags. We managed to get it home, through the city of Koln, and with a bit of work partially serviceable.

As a Tactical Air Force everybody was expected to be able to drive so I now applied to go on a driving course. This was done in a 4 ½ ton Magirus Deutz diesel truck. They were big and heavy. I had a German ex-submariner as my instructor. On the first day we drove around the camp a few times then went out of camp towards Cologne (Koln). He stopped me at the Ring Road and took over driving through the city himself. On the second day, after just once around the camp, we went out through the gates again on the Cologne Road. I stopped again at the Ring Road. He asked why and I told him that it was for him to take over. Oh No, not today. Today I drive into Cologne! I didn't hit anything. On our way back we stopped in at our house and had a cup of coffee whilst he told Pat all about the German submariners. Seems sailors are the same the world over. We left to go back to camp and at the top of our street I had to do a very acute right turn. An old German was riding a bike along the road we were joining and I could just see the red width indicator ball slide by his head. The instructor looked at me in horror and I said "Well I missed him didn't I?" I got my license after the first week. The rest of the training was 'convoy driving' by day and finished with 'convoy driving' by night. Not as easy as it sounds.

We started to drive around a bit in our 'car'. Mainly up to the camp to the NAAFI shop for our shopping. It was too dangerous to take it any further. I seem to remember that every now and again the back seat would topple backwards and the passengers would finish up in the boot. As well, the universal joint on the connecting shaft to the rear axle would come loose and create a terrible wobble. The main value of the car was as a source of petrol coupons which we bought on camp every Friday. The coupon allowance was set according to the size of the engine. Mine was a big six cylinder. These coupons were bought for about one third of the price of petrol in the German filling stations. We would deposit the coupons with a local German garage and be credited with the full petrol cost. Thus we made two hundred per cent profit on every coupon. When we had enough in credit we bought a small car from the garage. We bought a Ford Eiffel. It was in better condition than the Super Six but every time you slammed the door, if the windows weren't wound up tightly, they smashed. Vinnie Simmons was again useful here as he worked in the vehicle workshops so he replaced them for me ... for the first few times.

I was on leave in '55 when I got a message saying that I had been promoted to sergeant. I was to go up to the camp, collect my stripes and have them sewn on when I returned to work after my leave. On the last day of my leave I got another message asking, or rather telling, me that someone had gone sick and I was to do Orderly Sergeant on my first day back. First day on camp as a sergeant and doing O.S.! It is probably impossible, for anyone who has not experienced it, to understand how big and white new stripes appear on one's arms. It seems that even as you walk they flash into view with every swing of the arms. As well, I had to wear an arm band with O.S. and when doing O.S. duties I had to wear my webbing belt. As an airman I had seen the O.S. do his bit in the airmens' mess and the NAAFI and as Orderly Corporal I had had to do some of the duties with him, such as closing up the NAAFI and corporals bar on time, so I thought that I would probably be O.K. What I had not reckoned on was that the Sergeants Mess is an entirely different kettle of fish to the Airmen's and Corporals. I settled myself in the O.S. room in the Mess. Went about doing the "Any complaints?" bit with the Orderly Officer at mealtimes, closed the NAAFI, then the Corporals Bar in the evening. Then I went back to the Sergeants Mess. On all the previous duties the O.S. wears all his regalia of office as mentioned earlier. I walked into the Sergeants Mess attired so! The place went deadly silent. Then "Get that cap off in the Mess!", "Remove that belt in the Mess!". Whew! OK I could live with that. I sat around until just before 11.00 pm then went to the barman to tell him to close the bar. That's what it said on the orders for the O.S. It seems that whoever wrote those orders had never actually been in a Sergeants Mess. Once the obnoxious types had had their bit of malevolent fun with me a couple of the decent ones advised me to go to bed. The bar would get closed and all the doors and windows would get locked O.K. I'd arrived! I'd joined the senior ranks and it was indeed a different air force. I then understood why, along with the many versions of the Internationale that I'd heard, there was now a new one to learn. The last two lines went 'The other ranks can kiss my arse, I'm in the Sergeants Mess at last'. I had also walked the rocky path because it was a very rare occasion for a sergeant to be put on the O.S. job on his first day.

We eventually got rid of the Eiffel and bought a 1938 Mercedes Benz 170S. Of course it was another wreck. I think I paid Twenty five Pounds for it from a Warrant Officer. It had its petrol tank running along the back of the dash board above the engine. It also had some problems which caused it to overheat. We had to take a bottle everywhere we went, and every so often find the river and fill the radiator with river water. Susan was still a babe in arms and Pat was scared to sit in the front seat with her. I suppose things haven't changed, you gets what you pay for. I should mention that, at a later stage, we needed to buy a new push chair for Susan, too big now for the pram. Easy! We sold the Mercedes and bought the push chair with the proceeds. No change!

We had a lot of Germans working for us in the radio workshops. They were members of the German Service Organisation (GSO). We got on very well with them and they were very fine tradesmen. On New Years Day they used to have a lot of fun. It was not a holiday for the RAF so they also worked. It was however a special day for the GSO and they got up to all sorts of antics. One of them crawled under a bench at one end of the workshop with a pot of white paint and a brush, crawled under all the benches until he came to where one of his mates was working, carefully painted the back of his shoes white and crawled away again. Hell to pay! Another did a similar trick but tied the fellow's feet together, loosely, so that he couldn't feel it being done. Like a hobbled camel! Yet another was working on a big transmitter, rather like a big metal wardrobe. He had the back door open and was sitting on a small stool with his head in the back. As I walked past he called to me. I went over and he gave me a glass of Schnapps. He had a full bottle in the transmitter.

I was still playing a lot of football and on Mondays it was not uncommon for me to walk into the workshop with a distinct limp. At Xmas the GSO's had a party in their club room. They invited me and one of my Officers. We had a great time and I came away with a certificate acknowledging the great battles I fought each week-end which resulted in leg wounds. My boss, a Flying Officer, received one for his battle with a bee. I had let slip the story one day of when he and I had been to another camp and I was driving us back when he started to scratch his crotch. This went on for a bit then he asked me to stop. He undid his trousers and there was a big bee in a very awkward place. They had a great sense of humour.

Most of our radio fitters and mechanics at that time were national service men, doing their two years. They were usually ex civvy apprentices and were good fellows. Most of them accepted that they had to do their time and made the best of it. University students had their National Service deferred until they got their degrees. I had three of them posted in. All B.Sc.s in electrical or radio engineering. They regarded me as an ignorant bloody regular. They had to do as they were told but they made it quite clear that they considered themselves superior to me. I did get the three of them one day on a disciplinary matter but the most satisfying event with one of them was when I was walking up the workshop, passing his bench. He was obviously having some difficulty. Seeing me he said that he just couldn't work out what was wrong. I think that he reckoned that his piece of test equipment was kaput. I stood at the end of the bench, leaned over, switched on the mains switch to the test equipment and said "Try it now". I walked away without another word. That taught the bastard who the ignorant one was.

I spent many days and nights travelling up and down the Autobahn doing UHF installations. On one particular job, we installed the American D.F equipment at Gutersloh. When we had finished the installation it kept on varying on the bearings from a test transmitter. Using a compass I would place the transmitter to the north, set up the equipment to read 360 deg., test it all round and it would be OK. Next morning I would switch on, plonk the transmitter at 360 deg. and the CRD 6 would read 040 deg. or some other stupid thing. Eventually I took the receiver back to the workshop at Butz. to go over it. I checked it out, seemed OK. Next morning at 7 am I left Butz in a van, drove 100 miles or so, put the receiver back into the equipment, switch on and it would swing another thirty or forty or sixty degrees off. Back into the van with it. Drive back to base arriving at about 11 pm. Wash the vehicle down! This was compulsory. Bike down to home and get to bed around midnight. Back to the workshop next morning, put in another full day's testing. Next morning on the road again and a repeat of the 17 hour day. This went on for a week or so until I brought the actual rotating aerial down for checking out. I'd tried everything else assuming an electronic fault. When I took it to pieces I found that the part that was rotated by an electric motor was floating loose. The manufacturers had failed to put a locking pin through the shaft. Every time I switched on, the shaft started rotating whilst the antenna skidded until it got rotating. It skidded for about 40 degrees (or perhaps 320 degrees) every time. That was hard work. A very hard week or so.

Driving at night on the Autobahn in bad weather could be very frightening. There was no speed limit at that time. There were hundreds of trucks with trailers which swayed side to side. Red rear lights looked like turning indicators as they were covered and uncovered by the trailer. It really was a nightmare. In fact it was a nightmare. Pat still tells the story of one night, after a particularly nasty drive back, how I jumped out of bed, rushed to the foot of the bed and lifted the blankets to find out what had gone wrong with the truck.

In December we left Germany and travelled on the same old train and boat back to Harwich. I think it was on this journey that we had been stopped at Oberhausen for quite a long time waiting for the military train from Northern Germany to join us. Andrew had to go to the loo. Just as he had pushed the lever to flush the lav the other train coupled onto us. The train jerked, as they do, and Andrew came running out claiming that he had only flushed the toilet. A real Giles Grandma cartoon situation. Of course he was only coming up to six years old then.

At Harwich, the Customs people gave us a going over. We usually took home cigarettes and whisky for the family, and as it was so close to Xmas we also had the Xmas presents for Andrew and Sue with us. The Customs man was going through it all saying 30 bob for this, another 25 bob for that and it was building up. I said to him that he had better take away the cigarettes and whisky but we had to keep the toys for the kids. I couldn't afford to pay for it all. He just said, "Go on." Marked all the stuff and didn't charge me a penny. I suppose he could have just been having me on.

When we got back to Brighton we took Andrew around the shops in London Road and Western Road, the two main shopping streets of the town. He said "Where are the Xmas things?" The difference between the German approach to Xmas and the English approach at that time was unbelievable. We had, mostly, enjoyed Germany. So that was the end of the Germany tour. My next posting, after some leave in Brighton, was to be to the Radio Engineering Unit at RAF Henlow in Bedfordshire, not too far away from that sloth of despond place, Cardington.

8. REU Henlow 1956-59

I arrived at Henlow leaving the family in Brighton, and was told that I would be joining the Radio Installation Squadron (RIS). The duties of RIS were to carry out all major radio installations for the RAF all round the world. Most overseas commands had small Radio Installation groups for routine installations such as my experiences with the UHF equipment in 2 TAF, but RIS was the big'un. As a sergeant I would be in charge of a Fitting Party which would normally consist of five or six airmen in the wireless and electrical trade groups. At that time the UHF equipments (British and American) were beginning to proliferate and much of the installation work was introducing these on to RAF airfields and radar stations throughout the U.K.

I can't remember all of the stations to which I went on the job but they included St.Athan in Wales, Buchan, 45 miles north of Aberdeen, in Scotland, Boulmer up in the north-east near Newcastle, Kelvedon Hatch in the London area, Benson which housed the Queens Flight, Linton-on-Ouse, Patrington, Trimmingham, and Lindholme in Yorkshire, Valley on the Isle of Anglesey, Fairlight Glen and Wartling in Sussex, Middle Wallop between Salisbury and Winchester. Oh Yes! I should also have gone to Gailes near Prestwick in Scotland but that story will appear later in this section. I've probably missed half of them out. Small wonder that my kids thought that I was a visiting Uncle. Working memories of the time include the very big job at St.Athan, at which we were to fit the brand new air traffic control tower out with all the updated equipment. St Athan was one of the, then, new type of Control Tower with the big, all glass, cupola atop the main building for Local Airfield Control. The job was originally expected to take about eight weeks. About half way through I got a call to halt. The job was to be changed to the installation of a Master Diversion Airfield (MDA). Big! A whole new pile of installation diagrams arrived and lots of other equipment. We had to do a lot of changes to the stuff we had already fitted then install all the extras that a MDA required.

We had finished most of the job and were starting to apply power to the equipment one bit at a time, proving each item before moving onto the next. Power was applied to one of the racks (all equipment used to be mounted in 6 foot high, 19 inches wide racks). Bang! The fuses blew. We carefully checked it out, tried again. Bang! There was a lot of equipment in these racks so we did this for a couple of days and still we only got Bang! On the third day we came back from tea (about 5 pm) and instead of going over to the rack that we had been working on I turned left and walked up to a rack that housed the battery standby equipment (This was the radio equipment that the tower would use in the event of a complete mains power failure) we hadn't started installing or testing that. I just lifted a bundle of copper braided cables off of the rack and then went to the trouble spot. Perfect! The braid had been touching the common line which received power when I switched on the 'trouble' rack. I'll never know what made me do that. It hadn't been in my mind as we walked into the radio room. Some instinct took over. I was bloody glad, believe me.

On the last day of the installation, we'd worked continuously through two nights and a day with only meal breaks, I had to wait for some Works Services inspectors to come at mid-day. I sent the lads to bed but wouldn't go myself in case I overslept and didn't make the appointment. My corporal had a little car so he suggested that I take a ride to the beach at Southerndown on the south coast of Wales. I went there, fell asleep on the rocks but woke in time to go back for the appointment. The job had taken 16 weeks. That is important because the next big job I did was at Lindholme. Another full, brand new Air Traffic Control tower.

On arrival at the job the Senior Air Traffic Control Officer, a Squadron Leader, told me that they had the Chief of Air Staff coming to the station for the Battle of Britain flying display, and they were currently operating out of a caravan. He wasn't going to control an air show from a caravan. How long will it take? I told him that it wasn't possible to give him a finishing date. It depended on time availability for many aspects where we may want to use equipment and facilities at the same time as their staff. He asked me how long the last one had taken and I told him 16 weeks. He was gone like a shot from a gun. Within minutes my boss was on the phone from Henlow, "What's all this about you taking 16 weeks to do that job?" I put him straight.

About half way through the job I sent my boys off for the week-end. The SATCO was immediately onto me. I told him that if he wanted the job done on time it had to be done on my choice of hours. I pointed out to him that my lads worked all through the night for a couple of weeks at a time with no time off. We were going fairly well. We got the job done with time to spare. He was delighted. When I got back to Henlow my boss told me that there was a Commanding Officer's letter of commendation from the Lindholme Station Commander for the job we'd done.

The Benson job was a bit of a struggle. My party consisted of the usual set of wireless mechanics, an electrical mechanic and a Junior Technician Ground Wireless Fitter on his first installation. Remember them? Junior Techs? They're the ones that put me back a couple of years in 51/52. The job was an updating job, increasing the number of radio channels. We had to fit a number of new multi channel control units and refit the existing single channel units into different locations. Compared with most of the jobs it should have been a piece of cake. But I had a Junior Tech. with me! It was his first job. We'd gone quite well and by the middle of the week I told the SATCO that if he could close the airfield for the week-end, I could give him a new system at 8 am Monday. At 4 pm Friday the airfield was mine. I started the lads working. "You do this", "You do that", etc. and the Junior Tech I told to "Disconnect the CU 315s." These were the control units that we were to use again. All he had to do was unsolder the wires to the units (they weren't plug-ins). At about 9 pm he came to me to say that he'd finished the first one. Four hours to unsolder about ten connections? He should have done the lot by now! I came over all funny and went to where he had been working. He had taken the leads off of the inputs, removed the control unit's cover and unsoldered every bit of wire inside! 9 pm. Friday evening. Henlow had packed up for the week-end. Where the hell was I going to get a new control unit from? It was my own fault of course. I was the supervisor, I hadn't supervised. I quietly told the lads to go back to their billets and to turn up again at 8 am. Luckily, it was common practise in those days to have a circuit diagram stuck to the inside of a cabinet. I sat down and carefully rewired the unit.

Next morning, when the boys turned up, we went ahead with the job and by 8 am on Monday we had done ground tests of every channel. The SATCO sent up a plane to do air tests and all was well. Funny thing was that the old control unit that I had rewired produced the most beautifully clear output compared with the other grotty old ones.

The RAF has a group of Senior NCO's of each trade who work under the title of the Aeronautical Inspection Service (AIS). These people come round various jobs and inspect the quality of the work. We had one particular AIS sergeant at REU who was renowned for his sheer bloody stupidity. He came to the Benson job and called me over to where a group of cables were held by cleats to a timber cabling board. The cleats were fixed by ½ inch 6's wood screws. The term ½ inch 6's was a byword to all fitting parties. We would have used a couple of gross (288) on every big job. Two to each cleat. The idiot pointed out that the screwdriver slots on the heads of the screws weren't all lying in the same direction. I couldn't believe what I was hearing. I took him over to the window, where some carpenters had been working, pointed to the woodscrews that they had put in. Obviously the slots were all over the place. I then pointed out that these screws had been put in by carpenters to whom wood screws were their bread and butter. My lads were wireless tradesmen. Should they be any better than chippies? I then told him, in no uncertain terms, where to go. Of course, back at Henlow, Herbie Lowes, my boss, asked me what I had done wrong that AIS would complain about. I told him. I wasn't in on the conversation that he would have had with the AIS boss but I could imagine. Flight Lt. Herbie Lowes was a down to earth, north of England born, ex wireless fitter. A good bloke. He later tried to get me to take a commission but I said "Thanks, but no thanks".

Herbie and I had a good laugh on the Kelvedon Hatch survey. I was driving in a RAF Mini. I can't remember why he decided to come along. We had no idea where the radar station was. In the middle of the village we saw a bobby on a bike. I stopped to ask him where the place was and it took ages for him to tell us 'because it was secret'. He eventually allowed the fact that we were both in uniform with identity cards and a RAF vehicle to sway him.

At some point during this time I was on a round trip, probably doing surveys, driving myself and doing it in a relaxed style. Imagine my surprise when, on arriving back at Henlow, I saw Andrew with his arm in plaster. It seems that he had been doing something that little boys do and fallen, with the resultant broken arm. Pat had asked the Flt/Sgt. who was our neighbour, to get a message to me. She was told that no-one knew where I was. I still don't know the reason for that. Whilst some of the places I was visiting may have had a very high security status, they were known to REU and were in the list of scheduled jobs, else why would I be visiting them?

I believe it was whilst I was visiting Linton-on-Ouse, doing a survey accompanied by an AIS Flt/Sgt. that, as we got out of the car at the tower, something in the distance caught my eye and I was treated to the spectacle of a Vulcan Bomber looping the loop. I believe they weigh 70 tons! Later that year the Vulcan did it at the Farnborough Air Display.

One of the civvy drivers who took me up to Buchan, up past Aberdeen, turned out to be an old friend of my father, "Are you really Chris Lock's son?" he'd asked. Dad's uncle, a fishmonger, had been named Lock and Dad had worked for him many years before. People knew him as Chris Lock. The driver made me laugh about the service habit of using torn up blankets as pads to prevent scratching polished lino on the floor. He had asked the Service Police (SP) sergeant if he could use the phone. He went into the guardroom and walked over to the phone and the SP yelled at him to put some pads on. He turned round and said "Sergeant, if the Air Ministry hadn't wanted this lino to be walked on, they would have put it on the ceiling." You can say that sort of thing as a civvy!

Gailes was an interesting job that I wouldn't want to repeat. It was to be a survey and for some reason there were three of us SNCO's on the job. Chunky L, a Flt/Sgt. was driving in a Standard Vanguard saloon. It was mid-winter and we were going along the top end of England towards Carlisle. There was thick snow and ice on the roads, the sort of weather in which, if you had to drive, you would choose to drive very carefully. Chunky was not renowned for his modesty and this included his opinion of himself as a driver.

He had once told me that he had been failed on his first driving test because he'd wanted to light up a cigarette, so he'd held the steering wheel between his knees ... Anyway there was a car in front of us which wasn't going fast enough for Chunky so he pulled out to overtake. We started to slide slowly across the road, luckily nothing was coming in the opposite direction. We mounted the grass verge and slowly overturned. I was sitting in the back seat and in those days we still didn't have seat belts. The Vanguard was a pretty roomy car and, as she rolled I walked on the part that was on the ground. I stayed upright the whole time!

Once we'd stopped I pushed the back door open and, before I could start to move out, the other sergeant had bolted, from the front seat, through the gap. I followed in a more dignified manner. We then opened the front door and started to pull Chunky out. He was yelling away, it turned out that his foot was the other side of the pedals and we were trying to pull his foot off. None of us were hurt, and we looked pretty stupid standing there with an upside down car. We felt even more stupid when a policeman came along, looked at the situation and suggested that what we should be doing was turning it back up the right way, which proved to be very easy. We then waited for an Army tow truck to come and tow us to Carlisle. They dropped us off at a boarding house and went off to fix the car. The trip to Gailes was abandoned and we started back to Henlow the next day stopping for the night at a hotel at Chester. I recall that the other two signed in, with our address at Henlow, Beds. (abbreviation for Bedfordshire) I must have been tired because where I saw they'd written 'Beds' I wrote 'bed and breakfast'!

One of Chunky's other claims to fame was supposedly a Direction Finding station on Mount Troodos in Cyprus which couldn't be used in one direction because he had sited it in the shadow of the mountain peak! It was known as 'L's Folly'. He later earned yet another claim to fame when he got booted off of the Officer's Training Course. According to him it was his London accent, but the rumour was much more interesting!

I was still playing football and at this time was playing for the Sergeants Mess team. One day I was shocked to get a call from the coach of the Station Team asking me if I would like to play for the station on the following Wednesday. We are now talking of a big station. Probably over a thousand personnel. No RAF Junior Cup team here. I agreed. I can't remember who it was that we played against, it could have been Stanbridge, but I do remember that the left back that I was opposing (I was on the right wing) was an ex Scottish Schoolboy International player. I didn't stand a chance, but I did get the only shot at goal that we achieved during the whole of the game. It was saved of course. I never got another call.

After about 18 months of travelling the U.K. the chance came to take over the RIS Tool Store. It had been run by a Flt/Sgt so they were quite happy for me to go in. The Tool Store held the tools and test equipment for over 100 installation personnel. Typical stock figures would have been 1,000 screwdrivers of different types and sizes, a similar number of spanners, dozens of test meters and the consumable stores for all the installations. It was a very big store. I had a Stores Clerk corporal as my assistant.

Things went well, I had a good arrangement with most of the airmen. If a man had been doing the job for a year or so and then came in to report that he'd lost a screwdriver I could manipulate a replacement without him paying. If on the other hand a fellow was obviously spiriting off tools he got the chop very quick smart.

We were all at home one night when we heard strange noises outside. Obviously we had to have a peek and there, to our surprise, was the biggest bonfire we'd ever seen. I believe it was at the time of the Suez crisis, one of the big storage hangars was stuffed full of radio and radar vehicles ready for deployment to the Suez Canal Zone. That hangar was burning merrily away. That fire was big. One of the stories which I remember from it was some brave airman who jumped into a vehicle to save it, screamed backwards out of the hangar and crashed straight into the next hangar. The Flt/Sgt in charge of the Fire Section was awarded the British Empire Medal (BEM) for letting it burn the hangar completely out. I always thought his job was to put them out.

From my point of view though, the funniest part was the number of tool-kits and test equipment that I had to replace with the reason stated as 'Destroyed by fire'. I reckon every airman on camp had two tool kits in that hangar.

On the other side of the road from RIS, the Aerial Installation Section also had a store. Occasionally the corporal in that store would look after my store when neither I nor my corporal could be available. The arrangement seemed to work well.

One day two SPs (Service Police) turned up in my store with 4 foolscap (before A4) typed sheets of RAF stores items. They asked me if these items could have come from my store. I read the list and said that I stocked most of the items but doubt that they would have come out of my store. It seemed that two of the Aerial Erectors had been pinching motor bikes, doing them up and changing engines then flogging them. When the police raided their home they had found all these items in their shed.

My store was immediately put on an Inventory Check by two Officers. Our Squadron Leader asked me how accurate my stocks were likely to be and I told him within around 5%. Imagine my surprise when he sent for me and asked how one item was hundreds in surplus. I was amazed and asked him what the item was. "File Handles" he said. I burst out laughing and explained that whenever someone came in for a new file handle, I took the old one off him and threw it into a box. If anybody wanted some kindling wood for their fire I would give them a bag of file handles. Better than throwing in the rubbish bin. He also laughed.

The only thing I was worried about was the fact that I also had a couple of test meters surplus. Again I regarded these as for replacement against any genuine loss. Our parties travelled thousands of miles with lots of equipment. There were bound to be losses sometimes. They'd been there when I'd taken over the Store from the Flight Sergeant. Against the rules, but not for any personal gain on his or my part. I don't recall the Store being Inventory counted by anybody before so they hadn't been of any concern. I would have great difficulty explaining them away. That night as I went home I slipped the two extras into my bike saddlebag. At home I put them on the fire and burned them into unrecognisable bits of wire. After dark I went for a ride around the countryside and scattered the bits and pieces over the fields. As always, on hindsight, what a stupid thing to do. The outcome of the Inventory check was that it was deemed that the RIS Tool Store was much too big for a mere sergeant to control. I was replaced by a Warrant Officer and a sergeant whilst my corporal also remained plus another airman.

I went back on the road. Some of the job experiences that I have mentioned earlier would have occurred during this second spell of installations. Timing is hard to remember. I recall at some time an astrological type Comet passed over our house and we took Andrew out to see it.

We did get involved with aero modelling during our stay at Henlow and we had a lot of fun. We were members of the Aero Modelling Club. We built and flew gliders with 4 foot wing span (Swiss Miss) and powered free flight models which had to have a timed engine run and a fuse to change the shape of the tailplane after so much time so that the aircraft floated back to earth. We also built control line models. Andrew and Pat love to remember the time when I had the engine running on the free-flight model. I was standing ready to release it, Andrew was yelling "Don't forget the timer Dad." I couldn't hear what he was saying so I sent the thing off with about two minutes of fuel in the tank.... and no timer: it was usual to set the timer for a 15 second engine run. We chased it and got it back thanks to the tailplane characteristics change device after the two minute fuse actuated it. One that we didn't get back was during a leave at Brighton. Andrew begged me to make a glider so we bought a small two feet wingspan Mercury kit model. We went up the hill at Bevendean and slowly started to adjust its balance with B.A. nuts as ballast. Eventually it got going, doing little dips then up, a little dip then up and each time the up was more than the little dip. The last we saw of that one was in the beautiful woolly clouds travelling in small circles, ever Northwards. Andrew and I followed it for quite a way. A man with a bicycle was walking the other way. He suggested that we should write to the Manchester Guardian for it. We gave up the chase. The big event was when the Russians launched their first Sputnik. There was an Aero Modelling rally the following Sunday and someone had built a Sputnik with a Jetex engine and flew it.

We also bought another second hand car during our stay at Henlow. It was a 1939 Hillman Minx. Yet another wreck but not as bad as the previous wrecks. I remember filling up rust holes in the panels with Polifiller and hand painting it. Susan called it "We Car." Since then, until recently, every car we had was given a name. We used to go over the airfield in the mornings picking mushrooms. The car had a folding down boot lid upon which I sat Andrew and his job was to look for mushies. Poor kid, going along very slowly used to build up deposits and every now and again I kicked the throttle and a black cloud of smoke was emitted.

Eventually my time at Henlow came to an end. We sold our, hopefully last ever, second hand wreck. I swore that we would never again buy a second hand car which meant that we would never again own a car.

I was at Henlow for three years. This was the longest time I was ever posted to one station, even though I was rarely there! I was off overseas again. This time to Cyprus where the EOKA problems were, hopefully, coming to an end.

9. Cyprus 1959-61

I took snow to Cyprus. The EOKA emergency was drawing to a close. I arrived at Nicosia on 18th or 19th February, 1959 as the Zurich agreement was being signed. Archbishop Makarios (Black Mac) was to be exiled to the Seychelles and General Grivas the EOKA leader, was to be returned to Rhodes. However all was not well. Feelings don't change because some high-ups sign bits of paper a thousand miles away. But first, my arrival.

We spent our first night in Cyprus at Nicosia in tented accommodation. It snowed! Cyprus, at the eastern end of the Mediterranean Sea, snowed on me. Next day some of us were moved down to H.Q. Middle East Air Force (MEAF) at Episcopi on the South coast, not far from Limassol. Again we were put into tented accommodation but this time near to the sea, on the cliff tops in fact. It snowed! Welcome to Cyprus! The next day I was posted to 103 Maintenance Unit (MU) at Akrotiri. This was on the Akrotiri peninsular, which stuck out from the coast between Limassol and Episcopi. This was to be my work place for the next two and a half years.

A little history would probably not be amiss here. Cyprus had been owned by the Turks (or the Greeks) who were very lazy, so to save the bother of having to work for a living they started selling it off to the Greeks (or the Turks) until the Greeks (definitely!) owned 70% and the Turks only 30%. The British had been given protection powers and it was a very important base strategically. A number of Greeks decided that they wanted the Brits out and to have Union with Greece. ENOSIS. A guerrilla war broke out and lasted for several years. The pro-ENOSIS Greeks forces were known as the EOKA. It was a terrible and bloody war. I came in at the end of it, luckily, but tensions were still very high. As well, the Greeks and Turks 'disliked' each other so that was a continuation of the struggle.

I arrived at 103 MU with a few others. One of the others was also a Sergeant Wireless Fitter so we both reported to the Ground Radio Installation Flight together. I didn't like the sound of this. If I was to go back on to installations it meant that I would again be travelling all over the place and once again Pat and the kids would have to manage without me. I wrote to tell her that it might not be worth their joining me. She blew up and went to the M.O. and complained. I seem to remember that I had a letter from someone recommending that I be used in a static position. It was in my pocket but, in the mean time Flt.Lt. Jack Lamey, the boss, had given us the choice of (a) Installations including a big starter at El Adem near Tobruk in Libya or (b)

Cryptographic Maintenance at Akrotiri. The other Sergeant had done his share of Crypto work and was fed up with it, me likewise with the installations so we had a very convenient swap of jobs. The letter was never used.

About a year later Pat and I visited the other Sergeant in the Military Hospital at Dhekelia. He was awaiting casevac to England having had a nervous breakdown on the installation job.

I got stuck into the crypto machines and gradually got to understand them. They were, of course, Secret equipment. This meant that our Section was also Secret. Locked doors, with a bell at the front. No one allowed in without we escorted them. Very convenient. When the boys had finished any outstanding servicing they settled down to games of cards, until the front door-bell rang.

By now, anybody who has read anything about WW2 has heard about the British Code Breakers cracking the German 'Enigma' cypher machine's code. It is sometime's considered to be the single greatest event to ensure that we won the war. The machines that I was now servicing were the British versions on the same principle. There were also some American equivalents.

My boss was a Warrant Officer, Bill Bevan. He spent most of his time in the office, just inside the front door. I think that the machines were probably too much for him. I reckoned that we had to put a guide on for him if ever he ventured into the workshop. But he was alright most of the time. The Section was mine.

The State of Emergency wasn't concluded until July so we were still on active service (about 150 days) until then. In those days it was quite common to dump scrap equipment out in the deep sea. One day I had to dump half a dozen sacks of bits and pieces from our machines. I contacted the Air/Sea Rescue people at Famagusta and arranged for a trip well out into the Med with them. I had a driver and a big truck and off we went. I had to wear a gun belt and a revolver. I wasn't too happy about this, so I wore it under my greatcoat. We stopped at what was known to all servicemen in Cyprus as the halfway house. This was where the road split, left to Nicosia and right to Larnaka and Famagusta. I went in for a cuppa wearing my greatcoat and didn't dare take it off. I was most uncomfortable. We had no problems though and had an enjoyable trip in a high speed launch. Nice day out and, apart from standing guards, the only time I carried a weapon in anger in twenty two years of service.

We used to stand guard duties every four or five nights and some of them were a bit nervy. The most lonely was at Fishermans Cove. It was on a bit of coastline which was absolutely pitch black. The Sgt. had a tent with a Tilley Lamp and the airmen slept in another tent. The Sgt. had to stay awake all night to send out the patrols every two hours. I remember that every so often through the night there would be the noise of a small marine engine chugging along the coast and wondering who it was and, even more important, where it was. In the blackness it was just a noise. I suppose that they were just fishermen because we never had any problems whilst I was on guard. I was on one of the airfield guards the night that they took General Grivas the EOKA leader through Akrotiri to deport him back to his home at Rhodes. Good riddance!

Our Crypto Servicing Section had a couple of 'run-ins' with HQ MEAF about our servicing standards. On the first of these my corporal had issued five machines in the middle of the night and had taken them from the Unserviceable stack by mistake. Bill Bevan didn't want to admit that we had made a mistake and wanted to suggest that storage in a hot climate had made the contacts less springy. I eventually got him to agree that it was better to admit to a simple mistake than to admit that our machines could not be relied upon after they had been serviced. We swapped them and accepted the shame of an error.

The second was of a similar nature when AHQ insisted that two of their machines which were recently serviced were unserviceable. I didn't believe them so got permission to go across to Episcopi and into the cypher section. Our Squadron Leader accompanied me, he had to go there for some other matter. I was driving. We approached a peasant on a bike riding in the same direction as us with a scythe strung over his shoulders. As I approached I gave him a very wide berth and he swung round to see what was coming. The scythe swung round as well, and I just missed him. The Squadron Leader commented on the fact that I'd swung out so far and I told him that I just knew that that scythe was going to swing out. The cypher Section at HQMEAF was even more secret than our workshop and the Cypher Clerks, all Senior NCO's, were horrified that I should be permitted to observe them at work. It didn't take me long to see where the fault was. The system was that the machines were set up initially to a series of letters. (The decoding machine at the receiving end would be set up to the identical set of letters) Then the messages were typed in, being encoded as they went. Each operator would set up the letters for his next message, call to his mate say, "E F J A O", his mate would lean across and glance at the machine and repeat the letters. This was supposed to check that the settings were correct as called. I spotted at least two occasions when the checker was merely repeating what he had heard and, in fact, it was not what was set up. I suggested that, as they couldn't trust each other, every time they went to start a new message they should set up the group, grab the next airman that walked by outside, get him to check. It would be a more reliable system. They weren't impressed, but I wasn't worried, I had proved our equipment was serviceable.

Pat and the kids arrived at Nicosia a few months later. An old friend of mine from Cranwell days had a rental house down in Limassol owned by a clerk at the city council. The friend was moving up to camp into a Married Quarter so I took over the rental. The owner Andreas Thermostocleus, his wife Lespoula (I think) two little daughters and the grandmother (YaYa) were very nice Greek Cypriots. They introduced me to the local taxi driver who took me up to Nicosia to pick up my family. Pat was very pleased to have a private taxi for the 50 or so miles trip and to receive a big bunch of flowers, when an officer's wife on the same plane only got a kiss. She got an even nicer surprise later when she discovered a beautiful night dress and negligee that she had admired in the window of a big Brighton store and mentioned in a letter to me, sitting on the bed waiting for her.

We settled down quite quickly and started to enjoy our first tour on which, with overseas allowances and a sergeant's pay, we were able to live and have money left over, probably for the first time in our married life. The climate was very good, sunny from April to November and rain from December to March. You could almost bet on it. It was so reliable that they would seal up the drains at the start of April and unseal them again in November. There was a beautiful beach, known as Ladies Mile, in which the sand sloped very slowly into the sea. It was probably as safe a beach as could be found except for a period in the evenings when the offshore winds would come up. This was the time to keep your eyes on the kids if they were lazing on a Lilo mattress in the water. It wasn't long before we had face masks and flippers and could study the fish from under the water. These were followed by a spear gun with which I caught fish anything up to nine inches long, on a good day!

British Forces in Cyprus could buy cars with no taxes, which brought the price of a Hillman Husky down to £490. We took a chance and ordered a brand new car. A Husky, two tone, antelope and foam. The first brand new car of a continuous line which (apart from a second hand Camry) we still maintain. What a difference to our life style that tour made. But first I had to get used to the car. Mr. Solomonides' Rootes Group Agency was on St. Andrews Street, the main shopping street of Limassol. Busy, busy! I had to reverse my first brand new car into the traffic of that street. I managed that, made straight for the bypass and drove home.

Hillmans were the most popular cars on the island, probably because the price was so good and they were pretty reliable. We joined The Hillman Drivers Club (Cyprus S.W.) and got involved in their activities. These included Rallies, Skilled Driving Tests, a monthly magazine and Quiz nights. They were good fun and we thoroughly enjoyed them. I joined the Committee as Trade Liaison Member. My job was to go round various suppliers of items that our members were likely to use, and try to get a discount for mentioning the supplier in our magazine. That magazine was the first instance of us using 'lowerhouse' as our non de plume. One month, everybody seemed to be on leave, leaving just Pat and me to produce the mag. Pat did all the typing onto thin metal plates. This was more difficult than it sounds because the plates were typed in 'landscape' format. Thus on one plate might be Page 1 on the left and 8 on the right, whilst the next would contain page 2 on the right and 7 on the left. Took a bit of working out. More about that later. In this particular edition I had included an article taken from the British Advanced Motoring Assn.'s newsletter, discussing the mathematics involved in the half inch of slack that was allowed in fan belts. About three full pages of maths! I only put it in for fun. On the last page, instead of putting 'Printed by Flamingo Press, RAF Akrotiri' we put 'Printed by The Lower House Press'.

The following month I took our Wing Commander's copy of that month's mag to his office and he told me firstly, that he had spotted the Lower House Press bit on the previous month's mag. and furthermore, the mathematics were wrong. He had been a Maths Master before joining the Air Force. I told him that I hadn't checked it because I didn't expect anybody to read past the first half page or so. Fact is of course that I couldn't have got past the first couple of lines anyway.

The Rallies, or treasure hunts were great fun. Everybody reckoned that Pat and I had a zip fastener down the middle of our car because every time they saw us at a T junction she was pointing one way and I was pointing the other. On one treasure hunt we had to find all sorts of clues and pick up odd things. One of these was a piece of coal. Where on earth were we going to find a piece of coal on Cyprus? Well it so happened that the route took us past a power station and it was coal fired. Coal was imported into the country especially for it. The entrance way had lots of pieces that had fallen off the lorries. No worries! But what about the next item? A goose feather! We drove on, searching for a goose feather on the road. As we drove into a small village there was a goose waddling up the side of the road. I cut off his escape by driving the car towards the wall whilst Pat jumped out, grabbed the goose, tore out one of his feathers and we were away before he could say 'hisssssss' (it takes longer in Greek!). Mad dogs and English women!

On another occasion our route took us through a mountain village. We had to approach the village from the rear and come down one of the streets. It would not normally be used by traffic on a Sunday and probably very little on any other day. The villagers had their tables and chairs set up in the middle of the road when the first Hillman came tearing down the street. They hurriedly moved their tables and chairs to let him by then resumed their places. Drinking out in the street on Sundays was traditional. The second Brit. turned into the street! Must be an unusually busy day. They again moved their bits and pieces! I don't remember how many of us drove down that street but I do suspect that we changed their Sunday habits.

I agreed to take on the planning of one of the rallies. We planned the course. Went over it half a dozen times. Worked out the best places for marshals. Measured and timed it. It was a beauty. Come the day, and we started the competitors off. I then drove around the course checking that the marshals were all in place. One group were in the wrong position! "What the hell are you lot up to?" They pointed up the road. The Cyprus Dept. of Works had decided to close off the road that I'd been checking for the last month! I gave up organising and decided it was easier to compete. We also had rallies which didn't go on the road. One held at Episcopi airstrip was good fun and we came away with a couple of prizes. Our first was in the Concours de Elegance. Our little Husky was pretty as a picture and everything, as bought, was in place and shiny as a new pin. My corporal, to whom we'd offered a lift nearly sabotaged it for us. He'd had the temerity to flick some cigarette ash into the ash tray. He got a flea in his ear!

The next event we won was the skilled driving tests. The Husky had a very slight advantage on vehicle length and turning circle over the Minx. Red Witches Hats were placed to form various obstacle courses and one small 'garage'. We had to manoeuvre the car through all these without touching any of the Witches Hats. Everybody was just about even going through all the 'in and out the windows' courses but when it came to the 'garage' we had to go through the 'doorway' then come out of it going forward each way. That is, we had to turn the car around, in the garage, without knocking over any of the Witches Hats. That tiny advantage of the Husky allowed me to go in, do a neat three point turn and come out again. The others were getting themselves stuck in all directions. Another win for the Commons'.

The most interesting part of the day was the blindfold driving tests. Yes! I said blindfold driving. In the first test we had to line the car 'rear to kerb' against one edge of the run-way, and, one car at a time, with the driver blindfolded, drive the car until we considered we were close to the other side, without going over the other edge of the runway. That was hard and frightening. The second of these blindfold test included a 'navigator'. A set of Witches Hats were lined up in the typical 'in and out the windows' set-up. Each driver in turn was lined up then blindfolded. He then had to drive, under his navigator's instructions, to do in and out on the way out and a straight run on the way back. The run was timed!

The conversation in our car (we'd left the zip at home) went something like this "Go left". "Go left". "GO LEFT!" "I'm going left" "GO MORE LEFT!" "Right, now go right", "Right". "RIGHT!" "I'M GOING BLOODY RIGHT", "YOU AREN'T GOING RIGHT". "YOU'VE GOT TO GO TOWARDS THOSE PYLONS!" "WHAT PYLONS?" THOSE PYLONS

OVER THERE?" "OVER WHERE!" "OVER THERE!" " I CAN'T SEE ANY PYLONS!" "WHAT? ARE YOU BLIND OR SOMETHING? OVER THERE!" It was a good day! Needless to say I didn't win any of the blind driving tests.

We sometimes had Trivia nights at which I was the question master, and we had bells and horns for wrong and right answers. All the questions were about motoring and, as most of the wives did not drive at that time, they were included in the highly technical questions like, "Where do you put the water for the radiator?" They were hilarious and very noisy. Years later our Hillman Drivers Club Badge was to attract attention. In Holland! At the Annual Dinner which was held at the Curium Palace Hotel we were sitting down just taking bites out of the first course which I took to be mushroom pie, but not quite. We asked the waiter what it was and he told us it was Octopus. Pat had two portions! Changed our lifestyle may have been but my palate was, I am now ashamed to say, still very English.

I now encountered another duty that Sergeants are expected to take in their stride. It was known as Sergeants' Mess Caterer. This involved spending two weeks as assistant barman in the Mess then a second two weeks as senior barman. You were expected to perform your normal work duties as well! It should be remembered that I was still essentially teetotal. I had still never spent an evening in the Mess bar. Two events occurred during my period of duty. The first was when I'd poured out two French Brandies from an optic for a Warrant Officer. I placed them on the bar and one was filled to about a quarter of an inch below the other. "I'm not going to pay for them." he said. "Why not?" "Look" he said, "would you pay for them?" I replied "I wouldn't drink the muck." I took them back, emptied the glasses back into the bottle and gave him two more. They were level. A little later he asked for two more. I used the original glasses and one was a quarter of an inch down. I sat on the cupboard at the back of the bar with my feet upon on the bar shelf and smirked. There were some more comments but he refused to apologise to me. The second occasion was on a Sunday lunch time. It was customary to serve drinks out of the back door before the official bar opening time of mid-day. We'd done this and, with the cleaning up from the Saturday nights work, were a little late in going for our lunch and opening the bar officially. When we opened the place was crowded with discontented SNCO's and W.O's. and I was reported to the W.O. i/c Sgts Mess. The Chairman of the Messing Committee. CMC. Who duly reminded me of the bar times. The following Sunday I arrived and opened the bar exactly at mid-day. The crowd that were usually served with drinks before time were all muttering and calling me a 'black enamelled bastard'. I merely told them that the CMC had told me that I must open the bar at mid-day.

Before we moved up to the Married Quarters on camp, Andreas decided to extend his house. It was on the same block as the one we lived in. He was going to add a room coming out through our 'garage' and into the front garden. It would mean moving our garage. The garage was a wooden framed corrugated iron affair. A couple of afternoons later I arrived home from work to see half a dozen of Andreas' mates bodily lifting the garage out onto the road (we lived on a corner block), around the corner, (that's where I arrived home). This had to be recorded. I got Pat to take the picture, got in amongst them in my RAF Sergeants uniform, and helped to finish carrying the garage to its new location. The picture is in one of the albums.

Andreas's brother-in-law was a builder. "A very lazy man" says Andreas. "He is going to build the extension but first we must make up the plans". I imagined tape measures, theodolites and spirit levels would appear. Andreas walks up to one corner of his house, paces out a number of steps and says "To here Mr Alf?" I agreed and in went a spike. He then paces towards our house to another point and says "To here Mr. Alf?". In went another spike and that was it. In a little while the building commences with 'here' and 'here' as the approved extremities.

Andreas's family and their friends and neighbours were very friendly to us. From Lambros (I believe translates to 'brilliant') the taxi driver to the people who ran the shop round the corner. At first Andreas said to let his family get stuff from the shop for us as we would be charged more than them. I think we may have overcome the problem before we left there. There was also a Turkish shop down the bottom of the street. "Ossy" was quite popular with the English families and seemed to live quite comfortably amongst his Greek neighbours. I wonder what happened to him in later years when the Turks invaded northern Cyprus.

We would sometimes sit out in the garden with the family and drink Turkish coffee and eat their foods. I wasn't keen on Greek food but the stuff we had in the garden was usually within my ability to cope. As we sat there just about every car, taxi or truck that went down the street would toot and Andreas would wave and say "My best man." I was puzzled by this until I found that all the best men would pin paper currency on to the brides wedding dress, or something like that, so the more 'best men' he could muster up, the richer they would be.

We were also invited up to the family home in the mountains at a village named Anoyira. It was via a very steep winding road with, I think it was, 14 hairpin bends in about one mile. Hairy! Andreas pointed out the carob trees and olive trees in which he had 'part shares'. The house was built around a courtyard with a big, outside, mud brick oven. In one corner of the courtyard was the year's harvest of carobs or locust beans. I remember that we used to chew on them when we were kids. Our kids had the time of their lives running up the pile and sliding down. Again they were extremely hospitable but I didn't eat much of the meat. I still think it was goats meat.

Marriages were still arranged and the brides father had to be able to come up with a dowry. Andreas had two daughters! I think that is why he had two houses. Unfortunately he had a niece, Bobby, who was a very attractive girl but who had no father nor any dowry. In England she would have been married, no problem. In Cyprus the poor girl was left on the shelf. They were trying to get her a husband in Australia who did not require a dowry. Sad. Soon after Pat had arrived and quite a while before things had really settled down, we went for a ride into the mountains and found the village, I think it may have been Lethkara, which was famous for its lace. It seems that we were taking a bit of a chance as the area had been EOKA territory. As it happens we were again treated with the utmost respect and Pat bought some lace.

On the road up to Mount Troodos was a typical piece of British vandalism. On a rock was painted 'Home Rule for Wales'.

We experienced our first big earth tremor in that house. It was in the middle of the night and I thought that a big lorry with loose shovels and other tools was going down the street. I woke up immediately. I think Pat slept through it.

Andrew got in the wars about this time. He was playing football with the school at a field in Limassol. The ball was kicked off the pitch and went bouncing over a big ditch surrounding the pitch. Andrew rushed after it and went to jump the ditch. He didn't see a broken toilet bowl that had been dumped there and tore his knee open. The M.O. sewed him up and gave him an anti-tetanus injection. That night and all next day he was crying in pain. We thought that it was the injection. Eventually Pat got the M.O. out to him and he was rushed into hospital with appendicitis. More stitches. We felt very bad about that, but we really could not have guessed. He was later to be very proud of those stitches. He later went into the hospital again for a rather more personal operation. Whilst he was in there I bought our first tape recorder. A Grundig portable which recorded and played three inch tapes. We took it to the hospital to show him and he decided that he wanted to be recorded singing a song about a cuckoo. I think that we may still have the tape but no means of playing it back.

A few of us used to take it in turn to drive up to camp each day. Early car pooling. Don Lamble, an armourer, of which more later, invariably came running out of his house clutching his breakfast. He was on a 'Cooks Tour'. He knew that he would not be doing a full two and a half years because he had been specially selected for Officer training and was expecting to go back to the U.K. any time. He argued that it was the RAF's fault so why shouldn't he and his family enjoy a short Cypriot holiday. He was well over six foot, his wife nearly six foot and two of his kids, though very young were extremely tall for their age. He bought a tiny Fiat 500 car with a sliding sun-roof. When the family were all aboard it was packed full and he would drive everywhere with his head apparently sitting on the roof. The 'specially selected' came into being when, as an instructor at the Officers Technical College at Henlow there was an inspection by, I think, the Chief of Air Staff. In the foyer of the College there was a model of a machine gun. The CAS saw this and asked who had made it and was told Snr. Tech. Lamble. He immediately sent for Don and asked him how he had come to build it. Don replied that he had seen various items in armament magazines from around the world concerning the latest Russian machine guns and had built up enough data to construct one. The CAS then said that this machine gun was still on the Russians' Secret List and we'd love to be able to get to know it. He then said that Don should be sent to Officer Training. Don was awaiting this when his posting to Cyprus came through so he said nothing to stop the posting.

There were two routes from Limassol to Akrotiri, both with some interest. The first was by the main road to Episcopi then turn off at Kolossi. There stood Kolossi Castle. The walls were reputed to be ten foot thick. As with much of Cyprus it was built at the time of the Crusades. If you buy a bottle of 'Commandaria St. John' (not the KEO brew) you will see a picture of the castle on the label. On the left of this road were the Akrotiri Salt Flats. A large dried lake covered in Salt. Every year the Flamingos would migrate to the lake. It was a beautiful sight. One day we drove out onto the salt pans to get closer and the car dug in. We were stuck! The first thing Andrew thought of when I told them was that he was hungry! By a great stroke of luck we saw a Volkswagen tearing at speed across the flats towards the road. We waved wildly to it and they saw us. In it were a couple of very strong looking Englishmen. They got their shoulders to the back of the Husky and I got behind the wheel. We soon had it free but never did that trip again.

The second route was shorter and went through the Phassouri Plantations. This was always beautifully green. I have pictures of these and the castle. On this route there was always a big dog that hid behind a parked car, he would jump out barking at approaching cars. The first few times it scared the living s ... ts out of us (the family) then one day, as we sped along the road, I told Pat and the kids to wind down the windows and just as the dog jumped, to yell "Woof Woof' as loudly as possible. The dog was in mid-air with nowhere to go! He had the living s ... ts scared out of him that day.

At about this time Pat spent the afternoon in the Limassol Police Station! She had been riding as a passenger with our friend, Pat Wilson, who collided with a motorcycle. Pat's husband Clive was in England (I think) on a course so I got the phone call. I raced down to Limassol and after lots of questioning we were allowed to leave. Of course, after you fall off a horse you have to get back on again, so I had to take Pat out for a 'get my nerve back' drive. Me!

The greatest passenger coward in the world! We drove out through Limassol to the western end of the town to one of the beaches, strolled up the beach and back and she drove home to our place. That was to be her home for the next few days! I learned in that week that having a 'menage a trois' is less fun than you would imagine. I wasn't too unhappy when Clive returned. Oh yes. Clive was one of these car owners who wiped off every speck and touched up every chip immediately. His Pat was more terrified of his reaction than of the Police! I have another good picture of the damage.

Eventually we were allotted a married quarter on camp. They were all prefabricated wooden bungalows known as Caywoods. Ours was very conveniently placed opposite the school, (it only took Sue 45 minutes to get home), near to the shops and we were the Commanding Officer's (later CAS) nearest neighbours. I don't recall him ever dropping in for a cup of sugar or anything like that but Andrew certainly knocked at their door during the Wolf Cubs' Bob-a-job week.

Andrew was a 'sixer' in the Cubs and I have a beaut picture of him with a shield for being the best six. We also have pictures of the cubs marching to church. Andrew reckons that he is the only one in step! There was also a Boy Scouts/Wolf Cubs/Girl Guides field day in which much of the airmens' focus was on two of the young birds who were daughters of some poor airmen who were one day going to have lots of problems.

In the Cypriot political situation things were straightening themselves out and Black Mac was returned from exile to be the first President of the Republic of Cyprus. One night the Queen dropped in. She rode in a big car with the C in C. Even she didn't come round for a cup of sugar! I was on call in case anything went wrong with the cypher world, and Susan wanted to see the Queen. I took a chance and took Sue down. We have a good photo of the occasion. Thank goodness nothing went wrong because I suppose I'd have been in deep s..t if it had. The chances one take's for one's family!

Cyprus is steeped in ancient history and the country is littered with ancient artifacts. It was a perfect place for people like Pat and Andrew (Sue who was rather young, still joined in enthusiastically). We would go to various areas fossicking for ancient coins and medallions. One of my lads, Peter, would sometimes baby-sit for us and we would invite him to join us in these fossicking expeditions to give him a bit of family life. Sue was going to marry Peter! Andrew's favourite fossicking area was the football field. It would be graded every so often and Andrew would go along behind the grader to see if it turned anything up. I believe that now, 45 years later, he still has a box of all the items he found.

There were also a large number of ancient sites controlled by the Cyprus Government Department of Antiquities. Curium and the Temple of Apollo were close to hand and we spent many days around them. There were wonderful mosaics and an amphitheatre where the lions were supposed to have fought with the gladiators. There was also a stone bath-like construction with a blackish mark about a foot from the top. I told the kids it was a bath and the black line was the tide-mark. I believe the former may have been true.

We were now involved with the production of the Camp newsletter. Pat was again doing the plates and I was getting involved with the printing side. This led to two occurrences worth recording. The first concerned Pat. It was in the early days of the move to associate smoking with lung cancer. Our Senior Education Officer, S/Ldr. Rice, had written an article on the matter. Probably for most of us the first inkling that there was a relationship. Of course we all knew about the 'smokers' cawf', but that was just a cough, not cancer. We thought! Well as I said earlier, typing the plates was a particularly difficult operation. Pat had to work out just where each page started and finished and on which plate, and indeed on which side of the plate the next words should be typed. I don't know how she managed it. Again on hindsight I realise that she first typed it onto sheets of paper which were the same size as the plates, then retyped it from them. Well, that's how I would have done it. The article used the expression, not so common in those days, 'a causal relationship'. Pat on the first appearance of it, remember it was hand written when she got it, typed it in as 'a casual relationship', and on every other occasion that it appeared! The newsletter was printed and distributed. I received a summons from S/Ldr. Rice. Wow! Was he upset! He screamed that the error had completely altered the intent of the article. No doubt he was right, but he wasn't going to scream at me about my wife! I told him just how lucky he was to have somebody who was willing to devote many hours freely to help the passage of information (or in this case mis-information) on the camp. It was an unfortunate error, but it was just that. An error. Well, a number of errors. Ah well.

I think that he got his own back on me a little later. I'd been studying for 3 GCE 'O' levels. Trying to make up just a little for my school failures. I was doing Maths, English and Geography and was quite happy with my progress. The Ed. Off. told me one day that I would have to give up my work on the magazine or one of the 'O' levels. I stopped Geography and managed to get passes in the other two. Those, with my RAF. Education Test Pt. ll passes (for Senior NCO) are the only educational certificates that I have ever acquired

The second, even worse incident was down to me. The permanent staff member on the magazine was on leave and some other people were doing it. Pat was out with her friend Pat Wilson at the keep fit class over in the school. I was at home with the kids. We'd had deep fried chips with our dinner. The oil was in the pan and I was to do the washing-up. Andrew was about ten and Susan about six. Archie Andrews was a very popular show on the radio. Andrew loved it. I thought that it would make the cleaning of the pan easier if

I were to warm it up first, so I put it on to the cooker. There was a knock on the door. Somebody was having trouble with the printing machine, could I go and fix it? I promptly went out leaving the fat on the cooker. It seems that after a while Susan noticed some black smoke around the place so she called to Andrew. Andrew was listening to Archie Andrews on the radio and wasn't going to miss a bit. He told Sue to go away! I don't know the exact sequence of the events that followed. I only know that when I got home Pat was there trying to clean the place up, and I wasn't the flavour of the month. There were millions of specks of soot flying all through the house and I was lucky that the place hadn't gone up in flames. Remember that it was a timber house. We worked through the night scrubbing and polishing. I was very lucky to get away with it. I deserved some serious punishment for my carelessness. Someone up there just might love me.

We were still doing the occasional tourist bit. Frequently driving up to Mt. Troodos though we never did find L's Folly. It was very comfortable up there in summer. Similar in height to the Blue Mountains. We enjoyed a few picnics under the casuarinas at altitude. We also went up to the Northern part of the Island, which is now occupied by the Turks, to the town of Kyrenia. A very pleasant port with some very pretty scenery. On the way we went up the mountainside to St. Hillarion which was reputed to be the castle used by Walt Disney in his Snow-white movie. St. Hillarion was a very steep climb after parking the car but the views from the 'penthouse suite' were fantastic. We also visited Ayos Nicolias (St. Nicholas) monastery. Where we were met by the old priest in charge. It was said that he had lots and lots of nuns to look after him and though he looked 80 he was only really 26. I wonder what they meant? I don't know why we never got to Paphos where Aphrodite was supposed to have arisen from the water though we did get to the spot known as Aphrodite's Rock which I suppose is where it actually happened ... if you believe all that sort of thing.

Back at work I dropped a big bloomer and Bill Bevan earned his keep one day. Again it was the old foul language that nearly did me wrong.

The Officer in charge of 'Ground Equipment' the generic term for all electrically operated and some other tools etc. that are subject to regular safety checks, decided to check up on the items I held on my inventory. Truth probably was that he was dying to know what went on in there and couldn't think of a better way of getting in. I'd never known a Ground Equipment check in any previous workshop. Bill Bevan decided to take care of it whilst I carried on with my work. Soldering irons were 'ground equipment' and came under the Stores category of Section 1B. Sledge hammers were also in one of the Section 1 stores categories.

These two 'old' men went through the various Section 1B items, we probably had about 10 soldering irons on charge, and called out to me to find

1B/nnn. I was puzzled by this and, looking over their shoulders at the inventory sheets, pointed out to them that this was a sledge hammer not a soldering iron. Didn't have to be checked. OK. They carried on and after a while called to me again to find 1B/nnn, I looked again and again politely told them that it was the sledge hammer. OK. They went on and after another while called to me again to show them 1B/nnn. I looked again. Same item! I then said "I've already told you twice, that is a F ... g Sledge Hammer!" and stormed away. As soon as I turned my back on them I realised what I'd done. I'd screamed an obscenity at a commissioned officer. I was deeply in the soft stuff! Bill Bevan, God bless him, immediately turned and said "Don't take that attitude with me Sergeant!" at which I apologised and the matter was closed. Phew!

We had a party in our house one night. We had invited the boys from the Section, 'Pop' Stapleton with his wife and Bill and Mrs Bevan. Bill was known for being very fond of his booze. Everybody except Bill and missus had turned up, the lads wearing ties and looking very uncomfortable. There was a knock on the door and Bill's son stood there announcing that Bill was unwell and could not come. This meant that he'd had a couple too many already. We went in and told the assembled crowd. The lads all heaved a sigh of relief then removed their ties. Just as they got set the doorbell went again and there stood Bill and wife. Massive scramble to get dressed again. Again we had a great time, with Bill Bevan and Mrs Stapleton, can't remember her name, doing a delightful rendition of the love duet which just uses the words:

"Jim"

"Marcia"

"Jim"

"Marcia"

Getting steadily more urgent and more passionate. Bill earned a new respect from the lads that night.

Not long after this, on a Monday morning, Bill came into work and told me that he had had some terrible chest pains whilst driving back from Paphos on Sunday. He looked terrible and I told him that he should go and see the M.O. He never came back to work. He was admitted into hospital and diagnosed as having suffered a heart attack. Of course this was before transplants, bypasses or pacemakers. We visited him in hospital and he was eventually casevac'd back to England. I took over the section.

By this time Jack Lamey our Flight Commander had suggested that I should put in for a commission and again I turned it down. It just wasn't me.

It was now decided that our section was nothing to do with installations and more correctly part of the Radio Servicing Flight so we were taken over by a Flt. Lt. from the big hangar over the road. It was just a paper job. He never had anything to do with us and we just carried on as if nothing had happened. We had no problems. Then came the Air Officer Commanding in Chief's Annual Inspection.

I was used to these. Just a matter of getting everything right up to scratch. Stores neat and tidy, airmen all properly dressed, floors polished and security correct. Unlike other sections, no-one stood outside our Section when the AOC was in the area, the bell had to be rung before we let him in. So, on the morning that he was due two things happened. Firstly, a Turkish-Cypriot who was working in the ceiling of our shed crashed through the asbestos roofing and sat astride some girder which prevented him from falling into the workshop. We hastily got rid of him and had to sweep and polish the floor and clear the Stores racks of all the rubbish that he'd brought down. As we were doing this my new boss rung the doorbell and asked to look at the place. I let him in and showed him around. He didn't like the position of the storage racks and suggested that we should move them to a different position. I pointed out to him that if we did that there would be big scratch marks all over the floor, and a big patch of lino which we would never get up to bullshit standard before the AOC turned up. There was a nose to nose confrontation and he told me to come outside! I thought I was in for a scrap but it seems he didn't want the lads to see us arguing. Pity, they were lapping it up. He had a go at me and I told him that if he wanted to start controlling the section he should have come across yesterday or the day before, not half an hour before the AOC was due. I didn't move the racks and I seem to remember that he agreed that he had left his inspection too late. Seems I always got on tremendously with my officers or had fights with them. Of course it was always their fault.

Working hours in Cyprus for day workers were designed to allow a rest during the heat of the day. Shops closed from around mid-day to 4 p.m. It was our habit at home to close the wooden shutters, lie on the bed with the ceiling fans going and have a doze. A couple of months before we were due to go home we were lying thus when one of us suggested going home overland. I'm sure the thought had never crossed either mind until that moment. It suddenly seemed the obvious thing to do. For the next two months we raced through all the necessary preparations for such a trip. Hallweg, (I think) which was a big touring book covering Europe. Camping equipment (two pup tents without fly sheets) and some ex military camp beds, sleeping bags, bookings on a Roll-on, Roll-off ship from Famagusta to Venice, Camp site details for Italy, Austria, Germany and France. Tickets for the Silver City Air Freighters for flying us and the car from France to England. Passports, Insurance Green Cards, International Driving Licence. We'd got everything covered, except for one thing.

We farewelled our friends at Akrotiri and drove to Famagusta where the TV Hermes was awaiting our pleasure. The next few days were a beautiful

Mediterranean cruise calling in at Rhodes, through the Aegean Islands to Pyraeus, the very impressive Corinth Canal and on to Venice. On disembarkation in Venice we shot straight out of the city to a camping site at Vittorio Veneto in the mountains. We were now driving a right hand drive car on the right side of the road. Had to be extra careful. We set up the tents that night and enjoyed our first night in Europe. Every car that screamed down the mountainside sounded as if it was going to land on top of us

Next morning we were up early, cleared up, loaded the Husky and turned left out of the Camp-site up the mountain ... on the left side of the road. A stupid Italian car was coming down straight at us. Sue was screaming at me about driving on the right? Oh Dear! We got away with that OK but it was scary. That day we drove through the Dolomites, having a picnic lunch at Pieve di Coniere, not far from Cortina which had once been the scene of a Winter Olympics. The mountain scenery was very impressive and the green grass, that only European countries seem to have as a natural part of the scenery, was again prominent.

Just before we left Italy we filled up with petrol with our tourists' cheap petrol dockets. As we approached the Brenner Pass into Austria I could smell petrol so I stopped and found that petrol was overflowing out of the filler cap. I'd been greedy and overfilled with the cheap stuff. I immediately did a trick that I'd seen somewhere. I lifted the rear corner of the car by the bumper bar to force the petrol down the filler pipe and into the top of the tank, then resumed our ride into Austria and on to Innsbruck. The weather at Innsbruck was absolutely appalling so we pressed on into Germany to Garmisch Partenkirchen in Bavaria, arriving there very late at night and found the camp site a quagmire and still raining. We decided to erect just the one tent for ourselves and let the kids sleep in the car. A couple of hours later (about 1.00 am) the moonlight broke through the clouds so we then erected the second tent for Andrew and Susan. At about this time Sue started to show signs of a severe asthma attack. We then realised the one thing we hadn't covered for the trip was medical cover in Europe. We had very little choice but to aim straight for the English Channel coast.

We crossed the French border near Strasbourg but had no time for sight-seeing and stopped the night in a 'routierre', probably similar to a transport cafe. They had rooms so we stopped for bed and breakfast. I made the mistake of not asking "How much?" before we agreed to stop. In France that is recognised as being a very expensive mistake. The toilets were an experience for us all. A hole in the ground with two dirty tiled 'footprints' on which to squat whilst doing whatever you needed to do. Believe me, under those conditions it is very easy to convince yourself that you don't 'need' to do anything. Next morning I asked for the bill and at the same time got my wallet out of my pocket. It was bulging with New and Old Francs (the former being worth 10 of the latter). The lady hotelier or whatever took one look at my hands and said "Ah! Capitalist" and charged like a wounded bull.

We got out of there and drove through the WW1 battlefields towards the coast at Le Torquet. We were booked to fly out of there on a Silver Cities car freighter in a few days. We asked if we could bring our bookings forward by three days and get away on the next flight. Unfortunately there were no more vehicle spaces available that night and they suggested that if we drove up the coast to Calais we might be lucky. We shot off up the coast road, upon which we'd never driven before, making for a place we'd only heard of in Geography. We made Calais and found the airport in very short time. Again we were unlucky but the British Automobile Association people there rang Bologne and got assurances that if we could reach there in time there was a flight for us. Again we hit that coast road and literally flew towards Bologne. That car was later to be nick-named the 'Hillman Lightning' by a civilian radio technician and he never even knew about this ride. We made Bologne and relaxed for the first time in quite a few days. Within an hour we were on the ground at Lydd in Kent. Home again.

English customs officers! We'd arrived somewhere between 12.30am and 1.00am. He assured me that he didn't want to do the wrong thing by us. On the roof-rack was all my dark-room equipment including the Durst enlarger. That, he could find in the book but, he said, overseas they are usually sold with such and such a lens. Mine had a Schneider lens. A much better quality, that's why I had bought it. I told him that in all the English photographic magazines it was advertised with the Schneider lens. He was very kind and again assured me that he didn't want to do the wrong thing by me. Meanwhile the family waited. Every twenty minutes another Silver City Bristol Freighter with another three or four cars and twenty or thirty passengers came in, cleared customs and left. We eventually got away and made for Brighton and, I felt, some well deserved leave. Left side. Left side. Must drive on the left side. So I went the wrong way around a small roundabout in Kent! It was in the early hours so there was no other traffic about. The end of the beginning of a new era in our lives. I was to be posted to RAF Coltishall, where, in 1953, I thought I'd damaged the night fighter.

Pat and the kids were to be staying in Brighton.

10. Coltishall 1961-63

I may have taken snow to Cyprus but I brought some beautiful days back to England with me. Unfortunately the leave didn't prove as nice as the weather. It started out alright. There's pictures of Pat and I lazing in the front garden of her mother's house in The Avenue, Lower Bevendean. I'd done a bit of gardening round the back, digging into rock hard ground, but felt good. Then suddenly I yelped. I'd had a back spasm. Never had one before. I couldn't sit, I couldn't stand. We immediately went to a doctor (I think it was down by The Level). She diagnosed a slipped disk. Rest on my back for at least three days. The lifting of the back of the car in Italy was almost certainly telling me that I'd been too greedy.

However, things at the Avenue had taken a turn for the worse. Pat's father had returned with the packet of fags that he'd gone out to buy about twenty years earlier and, to put it mildly, Pat and he didn't hit it off. Things got really bad. There was going to be no way that I could go off on my next posting leaving her and the children there. We were very lucky in that oldest brother Eric, now out of the Navy, offered us accommodation for a few days. On the second day I drove with Pat up to Norfolk to try to arrange some living-out accommodation for us. 360 miles in one day with a slipped disk. I don't think my back benefitted much from that trip. At least we had a good car to do it in. I hate to think what we might have done if we'd still been on our old wrecks.

We called in to the Headquarters at Coltishall to see what the Married Quarters situation was and to pick their local knowledge for somewhere to live to bridge the gap. An officer happened to be in the Orderly Room and he said "Are you Sgt. Commons?" There was no point in denying it. He said that he was F/Off. Cunningham, the Off. i/c Ground Radio Servicing Section and they were desperate for a Senior NCO and to get my butt in there as soon as possible. I told him that I was supposed to be flat on my back and he said not to worry they'd put a bed in my office. They needed me.

We found a beautiful home at Bacton-on-Sea on the Norfolk coast close to Happisburgh (pronounced Haysborough) where now the North Sea Oil or Gas comes ashore. In 1961 it was an idyllic spot. About ten miles from camp. The home was some farm worker's cottages made into one with an overall thatched roof. At the back there was a lovely big lawn. It was probably as near to perfection as we could have hoped for given all that had happened over the last week or so. We moved in as soon as possible though not before setting a false trail by marking our boxes in The Avenue with an address of a RAF Signals Liaison Unit in Wellington N.Z.

Andrew was now going on 11 years old and we had to think seriously about his (and of course Susan's) education. We'd earlier attended an interview at the Brighton Education Office where the Education officer that we saw happened to have been a former Headmaster at the school in Cyprus that Andrew had attended, so he knew of Andrew. It would have been nice to get him into Varndean but our subsequent moves eliminated that option. As soon as he was old enough we took the decision to send him to The Paston School at North Walsham. It had a Boarding House, a good reputation for quality and was not too far away for a start until he got used to the idea. I believe we received some assistance with the costs. Its main claim to fame was that Lord Nelson had been a pupil there and it was also probably something to do with the Paston Family. I remember that as we left him there for the first time, to try to give him some encouragement, I told him to see if he could do what Lord Nelson had done. Some time later he reported that he had done it.

"What?"

"I've done the same as Lord Nelson."

"And what was that?"

"Scratched his name into the brickwork."

We had a comic in the family!

Meanwhile Sue was showing promise at each of the primary schools that she attended. She was only 7 and was on her 4th or 5th school already.

Pat loved the days at Bacton. She would watch the 'longshore' anglers catching herring from the shoreline. We got used to having fresh fish soused for tea. I think that though we were both born as 'townies' we are both 'village' people at heart. There were some very pretty places around the area and we did our fair share of touring. As well it was safe to go walking on the long summer evenings. There's a few pictures of us at the Bacton home. Mainly playing football in the back garden. If I'd been a golfer then I'd have perfected my pitching and saved myself years of difficulty later in life. It was almost with regret that we moved up into married quarters on camp.

Apart from the normal corporals and airmen in the radio section I had three civilian technicians. Mr Fred Fisher, 'Nick' Nichols and Horrie (whose surname I forget). They were good techo's and were essential to the continuity of the section where the Senior NCO's i/c such as I were continually being posted. Nick did most of the paperwork and still had a good knowledge of the radio installations. Fred Fisher took care of the transmitter station and that was one big problem that I didn't have to worry about, and Horrie was very good at the airfield navigational aids. I should perhaps point out that although I was in charge of the servicing of all the wireless and non-radar navigational aids on the airfield, I had not been trained on most of them. I was working in the dark and was glad of people that I could rely on.

At about this time the RAF introduced a couple of new mobile equipments. The first was a bird scarer and the second was a new PYE radio equipment for the Air Traffic Control vehicles and Fire engines. We installed these and I then suggested to the Signals Officer that it would be a good idea to produce a map of the area showing expected signal strengths at various locations. If an aircraft should crash in the vicinity, the ATC people would have an idea whether they were going to have good communications with the emergency vehicles or, if necessary, where to locate a relay vehicle. He agreed and I set it up for the following Sunday. We stationed a couple of my lads in the ATC tower and then we shot off around the countryside calling in, marking maps and generally having a great deal of fun. If you've never driven a fire Landrover around the countryside you'll not understand the feeling of power that comes with that fire engine red vehicle complete with radio. In those days, of course, radio equipped vehicles were a rarity! It made a change from the normal day's work and was intended as a really useful exercise. I've no idea whether it has ever been used. Luckily RAF aircraft don't crash all over the countryside.

The bird scarer was a different matter altogether. It used a loudspeaker horn on the roof of a fire engine and a tape recorder inside the vehicle. The tapes that came with it were of the warning cries of various birds. It was not a great success and most of us still believed that the best way to keep birds off of a runway was to have a tractor continually ploughing a field next to the airfield. The birds would follow it day in, day out.

I often used my own car for trips out to the transmitter station, receiver station and the middle and outer markers of the Instrument Landing System. I was still reasonably young and liked a bit of speed and on the country roads surrounding the airfield. Speeding was great fun ... for the driver. Horrie, it was, that christened the car 'The Hillman Lightning'. The main squadron at Coltishall at that time was the English Electric Lightnings of 74 (Tiger) Squadron. It wasn't unusual for me to stop off at home on our way back from one of the outstations for a cup of coffee.

We were sitting at home one night when at about 9 of the clock there was a knock on the front door. When I opened it who should be standing there but Andrew. His first words were "What's the time?" When I told him he said "I made it." It seems that he had made a bet with his schoolmates that he could break out of school and run home by 9 pm. It was four and a half miles and he had to come through a really creepy part called Captains Pond. The road at this point dropped down to the level of a pond that was surrounded by big, dark trees. I wouldn't have fancied going through there alone at night. We rang the school and told the headmaster that he was with us and that we'd keep him overnight and return him in the morning.

In 1962 I took some leave and we decided that it had been a while since we'd done any travelling. We went over to Holland and stayed a couple of weeks in a B & B at Arnhem. Pat still has a lovely letter from the lady who owned it in which she refers to 'hot and cold streaming water' in the rooms. It gave the kids some insights into places that they had heard about in war stories and movies. They clambered over a tank outside of the Castle Dorn that General Urquart used as his HQ and saw a number of war memorials and Commonwealth War Grave Commission cemeteries. The war memorials were of special interest because the Dutch had made them up from battlefield remnants. Shell casings, steel helmets and the like.

I did three more training courses during my 18 months at Coltishall. The first was the 'Commutated Antenna Direction Finding' (CAD/F) equipment course on which I managed 75.5%. I never could understand much of it. This was the point at which being a 'wireless fitter' became a misnomer. CAD/F was, apart from the UHF radio receiver part, entirely electronics. I was already getting too old for that sort of thing.

The next course was 'Senior Trade and Management' (S,T & M). This was a very interesting course where, besides having a bit of radio updating, (I learned about Transistors some thirteen years after they were invented) we also studied management principles. These included such things as man management, time and motion study and method study. We had a very interesting trip to the Clark's Shoe Factory at Street in Somerset. Clark's were leaders in motion study in the UK at that time. There, in the middle of the factory, sat a man doing everything differently to how we had learned. Our studies had told us that he should be picking up a shoe with his right hand, going through the motions of his part of the process on the machine moving from right to left, passing the shoe to his left hand, putting the shoe down on the belt to the left of him whilst picking up the next one from the right. Bill was picking up from the right, doing the motion and then putting it back down on the right. definitely a wasted motion. In the Q & A session at the end of the visit we asked how come 'Old Bill' was sitting there doing it all wrong. The answer was that Clarks was a family business which had employed local labour from day one. 'Old Bill' had been there all his working life. He hadn't got long to go and rather than make him change his ways they were prepared to wait until he retired and change the procedure on that bench at that time. Very nice. I managed 77.2% on that one.

The last of the three courses was on Super High Frequency Radio Relays and Multi-voice Channelling Equipment. The sort of stuff they used on Post Office telephone relay stations and radio links. During this course, Pat received a call from my Warrant Officer to tell me that I was again on the

Preliminary Warning Roster for overseas. I should have known that this one would be different. I'd always told her in the past, now she was telling me! I got 84% on that course plus a rocket from one of the civilian instructors for swearing all the time. Nobody had told me that he was a F ... Sunday School Teacher!

Back at Coltishall I was told that I was posted to Gan, a RAF staging post in the middle of the Indian Ocean.

In early January I went to the Personnel Disposal Unit at RAF Innsworth in Gloucestershire. RAF Innsworth was the home of RAF Records Office. The place was filled with old Warrant Officers, Flt. Sergeants and Sergeants (Clerks, General Duties) who managed promotions records and postings. Whenever their own card came up for posting it went to the back of the queue, as did my card for promotions. It was like being in an Old Peoples' Home (Retirement Village). The Sergeants' mess was so quiet you would have heard a spider running across the floor. They had waiter service for the actual meals plus a big aluminium teapot on each table. This was refilled by the poor individual who picked it up when it was empty. Me!

I went to the big tea urn right in the centre of the dining hall took the lid off of the pot and refilled it. As I went to put the lid back on it slipped out of my hand crashed to the floor and rolled steadily over the floor until, running out of puff, it did that trick where it runs round and round on its rim in ever decreasing and ever faster rotations. It made a hell of a noise. It would be wrong to say there was a deathly hush as that was the normal state but everybody sat bolt upright and looked for the culprit. I did the only thing possible. I also stood perfectly still and looked around the hall accusingly at everybody. Of course on my table, where we were all on the Gan draft, it created great mirth.

It was mid-winter and there was snow on the ground when we went to stores to get our tropical clothing. They asked each person his rank so that they could issue stripes or whatever then kept the parts that had to have the stripes sewn on so that the tailor could do his bit. As we trod warily on our way back to our billet with a new, extra kit bag on our shoulders I was the one who went base over apex, or arse over breakfast time as it was known, onto the ground. No damage other than to my pride.

On retrieving our shirts and jackets, with red stripes attached, mine had to be the one that had been done wrongly. They'd sewn the stripes on upside down making me a Senior Technician instead of a Sergeant. Why me? By this time the other SNCOs in the draft all swore that there was no way that they would fly in the same aircraft as me.

We took off from RAF Lyneham in Wiltshire in a D.H. Comet 4C at 4 pm on a Thursday afternoon and as we climbed through the cloud into clear sky we saw the sun for the first time in about six weeks and flew to Khormaksar in Aden. There we rested in a transit billet and took off again for Gan later in the morning. Aden is everything that everybody has ever said about it. At 6 a.m. it was like being in a stinking pressure cooker.

On the trip over, there was a selection of books handed round by a WAAF stewardess. I picked up a detective novel. Not my usual cup of tea but I got into it. It was fascinating. I couldn't put it down. I read all through the night and day, I had to finish it before I got to Gan or I'd never know 'who dun it'. As we approached the runway at Gan I got to the last page. The murderer and the detective inspector were alone, no tape recorder, no second copper. I knew that the suspect was guilty but couldn't see how he had done it, and the murderer says to the Inspector, "Yes, I done it, but I'm not going to tell you how". The End. Things weren't getting any better, were they.

11. Gan (Maldive Islands) 1963-64

We landed on Gan, one of the islands of Addu Atoll, in the early afternoon. The temperature on the tarmac was 117deg F. Quite a change from U.K. On the tarmac there was a group of airmen standing to greet the newcomers. Among them were a few old mates of mine. We shook hands and they immediately told me that I was going up to Male. Where the bloody hell was Male? Anyway by now the Comet was taking off for Singapore. We turned to watch it then went into the Air Movements section to pick up our baggage. Mine wasn't there! The bloody thing had taken off for Singapore with my bags still on board! Things were still going wrong. When was it going to stop? I had to wait three days before the plane (396) came back with my kit, during which time I went through the usual arrival procedure. The roofs of the billets at Gan were all aluminium to reflect the sun and keep the inside of the huts cool. Unfortunately they reflected the sun at me and I got very unhealthily sunburned.

We had a very interesting interview with the Padre, a Wing Commander, during our arrival procedure. He had evidently dropped a rank in order to go to Gan. He had us all in the church and asked us if we were confirmed. Most of us were not. He said that to be a C of E and not be confirmed was sitting on the fence. He didn't want anybody who wasn't confirmed to be in his congregation. So that was the last time we went to church on Gan. I suppose that I should mention here that I now regard myself as an agnostic. Over the years I have been a Christian and have gone voluntarily to church. But I have seen so much hypocrisy and so many wars fought in the name of religions that I gradually drifted away. I don't know whether there is or is not a God. I do think that if there is a God then there is only one God. I have no way of knowing if that one God is the one that my place of birth decreed should be mine. It is unlikely that 'God the Creator' only created some parts of the world. So my feeling is that all this could be solved if everybody in the world agreed that there was only one God and called him/her 'It'. Simplistic? Of course. But then, I am just a simple man.

On the Friday afternoon the Station Commander sent for me and told me that he wanted me to go up to Male and "Get that bloody corporal back to here as soon as possible before he starts a bloody war." There started the most courses I'd ever done ... in one morning. On that Saturday I was 'trained' in Air Traffic Control, Meteorological reporting, Enciphering and Deciphering signals using the Enigma style crypto machines and Fire fighting. At lunch time I was put on a launch to HMS Cavendish which was standing in the lagoon, and that afternoon we set sail northwards for Male Atoll. Actually we went north-east because it was very dangerous to navigate through the hundreds of coral Islands that make up the Maldive Islands. Shortly after leaving Addu Atoll the ship's company went through the 'Crossing the Line Ceremony'. All those who had not previously crossed the Equator are put through the mill of having whitewash and other yuck liberally plastered all over under the direction of King Neptune. I pleaded having no cleaning facilities so got out of the drubbing but still received a Certificate from Neptune signed by the ship's captain. 'Sgt. A. W. Commons of H.M.S. Cavendish'. I have thought about this over the intervening years. Assuming that the Royal Navy crews are mainly British, and that they all either sailed with the ship from a British port or flew to somewhere to join the ship at a location south of the equator as I had, they must have all, as had I, crossed the equator at least once before. It's just another excuse for a piss up.

We arrived in Male Atoll at noon the next day and took over from HMS Whitby as the 'Guard ship'. I went ashore with the ship's senior officers to meet the man who was to be my boss for the next three months, Mr Humphrey Arthington-Davie of the Commonwealth Relations Office. United Kingdom Representative to the Maldives. Ex- Indian Army Colonel. As well I met '..that bloody corporal' who was about to start a war. He was big enough too. We were to spend a couple of days together until the re-supply aircraft came up. He would go back to Gan on it and I would stay.

The set-up at Male Atoll was that the Maldivian Government had its offices on the capital island of Male. The U.K. Representative had his residence on another island named Dunidu and there was an 800 yard airstrip on a third island, Hulule. The painted sign on the doors of the shed, which was the airstrip's only building, read 'Hulele International Airstrip'. There would have been another dozen islands forming the atoll but these three were the ones with which I would be concerned.

On Dunidu we had the Residence complete with Union Jack and the coat of arms with the lion and the unicorn known in the RAF as the Tate and Lyles. There was another hut in which lived three Maldivian boys who were servants for sweeping and washing etc., a tennis court and a big shed which housed two massive diesel-electric generators. There was a small 'stand-by' generator just outside the residence which, in the event of main generator failure, fed essentials such as refrigeration. Within the residence we had a Wireless Cabin, the boss's quarters, my room, a wireless operator's room and quarters for three Indian servants who were the boss's personal servants. One of these, Cookie, cooked for all the residents of the house. My duties were to control the supply of goods for the residence, maintain the power supplies, inspect the airstrip runway and control aircraft movements, supervise the

Wireless Cabin and act as courier between the British Government and the Maldivian Government. Diplomatic relations were 'elastic' to say the least. I have recently re-read Hammond Innes novel "The Strode Venturer" which describes in some detail the political situation in the Maldives at that time. I must confess that I had no idea that the situation was so critical. It certainly explains why 'that bloody corporal' may have started a war. They had forgotten to include 'Current Affairs' in my Saturday morning training programme. There was virtual war between the southern Islands around Addu Atoll (Gan) my home base and the majority of the rest of the Maldives which was a Sultanate, based on Male, where I was now to work!

Drinking water was collected in tanks built into the corners of the residence from rain water run-off, whilst water for toilets was pumped up from the ocean with a hand pump feeding into a 45 gallon drum built up on a trestle to give it some oomph. The metering of the main drinking water tanks was achieved by having cork floats in the tanks with string attached, going through pulleys to the wall outside and, at the end of the string, beer cans filled with enough sand to maintain a tension. If the tanks were full the cans reached the ground, if they were empty the cans were near the top of the wall. Very technical. During the next three months I discovered that normal soap and toothpaste are useless for use with sea-water. Of course it should be understood from the outset that I knew nothing about plumbing, mechanical engineering or anything much. They'd also been missed on my Saturday mornings training.

For travelling between islands we had a copper bottomed launch 'Victoria' with a Maldivian skipper. It was in this that we went across to Hulele after a couple of days to meet the RAF's Varsity aircraft bringing up mail and supplies. It was due every second week but evidently was not very reliable. The only communication we had with the aircraft, after leaving Dunidu, was a Verey Pistol. Even whilst on Dunidu we had no communication with the aircraft, only with the base at Gan. They advised us of its departure, we went across in the launch, got the Maldivian airfield fire fighters ready, inspected the pressed steel planking (PSP) runway and awaited the plane's arrival. If it had to turn back we would have to wait for the wireless operator to receive a message from Gan then the launch would be returned to Hulele with the news. If and when the aircraft arrived overhead it would do a low sweep up the run-way and I would fire off a green Verey flare (ensuring that I missed the aircraft) to let him know it was safe to land. We would unload the supplies, cross over to Dunidu for the pilot to have a cuppa with the boss, return to Hulele and see him off. Then on returning again to Dunidu I could open and distribute the mail and supplies.

On the first occasion all had gone well, I'd got that 'bloody corporal' into the air on his way back to Gan and settled down to look at the mail. There was a largish letter from Pat. We had opened a Barclays Bank Account in Brighton for her before I'd left two or three weeks earlier. Now the Bank had advised her that we hadn't both signed all the forms and she couldn't access any funds until my signature was on the form. The voodoo continued. The Varsity wouldn't be back for another two weeks minimum, Pat had two kids and no money. What could I do? I couldn't get the signed form back to her for at least three weeks. I couldn't leave her without money. I did know that, because there was nothing to spend my money on at Male, I did not get any pay. It would all be credited to my pay account at Gan. I sent a signal to the Flt/Sgt in charge of the Signals Section at Gan worded something like this. "Please take all funds due to me and send them as a Money Order to Mrs P. Commons, 19 The Avenue, Lower Bevendean, Brighton, Sussex. Also send a telegram to the same address to read 'Money Order to the value of X Pounds in the mail'."

The Flt/Sgt did just that. Pat got a telegram telling her that a Money Order for X Pounds was on its way. I'd used the X because I didn't know the amount, he'd used it because he was too dumb to know what I meant. She eventually got the money and after another three weeks or so the signed forms. Thinking back, there was probably a service organisation that could have helped her such as SSAFFA, the Soldiers, Sailors and Air Force Families Association. We just didn't think of it.

Those Maldivian Firies I mentioned earlier were, presumably, paid by someone to man the 'mobile' fire extinguishers. These were a dry powder extinguisher which depended on a big bottle of some gas on wheels to operate. I hadn't the faintest idea of whether they knew how to operate the things and as I knew nothing about them myself, couldn't test them. A couple of months later, the boss of the RAF Regiment at Gan, who also ran the Fire Section, came up on a visit and checked them out. It seemed that the cylinders still had the plugs, that are inserted into the nozzles when they are shipped, firmly fitted. If we'd needed them they would not have worked! They'd missed that on the fire-fighting lecture.

When we received the word that the aircraft was to come up I went, on the launch, to Hulele, carrying my trusty Verey Pistol and some green and red flares. The launch would then return to Dunidu whilst I went to the airstrip to carry out my inspection. I had to walk up to one end on one side, down to the other end on the other side, then back to the middle on the first side again. I was looking for any loose items, unhooked sheets of metal planking and anything else that might be hazardous to a landing aircraft. It is amazing that, before I arrived the Maldivian Firies would be out there with the fire extinguishers. I never found out how they knew the aircraft was coming. A crowd of the Hulele natives would usually assemble at the hut and set up a show of turtle and other reef shells. These they would exchange for British Duty Free cigarettes.

On one inspection I saw some natives at the southern (touch-down) end of the run-way. I quickly walked up to them to tell them that they would have to move. They turned out to be two young Maldivian men and two beautiful girls. I took a not very good picture of them, then dispatched them on their way. When I got back to the hut the Maldive gang chief had a big grin on his face when I asked who the people were. It seemed that they were Male 'girls of the night'. No good to me, I was only allowed over there in day time!

On Hulele there was also a boat building yard run by an English Naval Architect named Bob Saunders. Bob had a nice house there and the boss and I sometimes went across for a cup of tea with him. In the boatyard he had a number of fishing vessels under construction. The labour included political prisoners from the south (Gan area). They were controlled by soldiers of the Maldivian Military. It all seemed pretty friendly, though I think it was deadly serious. As well sometimes high officials of the Maldivian Government would come across to see the plane land. This was usually when some people from Ceylon (Sri Lanka) were arriving, (most of the school teachers were Sri Lankan). On these occasions it was not unusual for me to be offered a leaf with some lime paste (I think) to eat and to have a chat with the Maldivian Foreign Minister.

Meanwhile on Dunidu I still had my regular daily duties to perform. These included ensuring the radio was in working order for the routine contacts with Gan, deciphering and enciphering any classified diplomatic signals and keeping the thirsty 20 KVA Lister diesel generators supplied with fuel. This entailed moving 40 gallon drums around on my own, heaving them onto a stand and pumping the oil into the main tanks. Only one of the generators was working and I hadn't the faintest idea of how to get the other one going, so the good'n had to run for 24 hours a day, 7 days a week.

I also sent a daily weather report to Gan. Well I'd had an hours training hadn't I! The method was the wet finger test for wind direction. I knew that the Hulele runway ran approximately North/South so I would stand where I could see Hulele, wet my finger and hold it in the air and feel which side got cold (300 miles north of the equator at sea level!). I'd then compare that side with Hulele and guess at the direction. Wind speed was rather harder. Definitely by guess and by God. Cloud cover was interesting. '8/8ths' or 'Clear' were easy but the more vertical you looked the less the cloud cover appeared to be. I suppose there was a fair bit of guesswork in that as well. Cloud type was easy. I had a wall chart covered with cloud photos to compare my cloud with.

One day, it must have been at a time when we were talking to them, the Boss said we were going across to see the Postmaster General. The Maldives did a roaring trade in 'foreign' stamps. 1963 was the International Year of something or other and special stamps had been issued by the Maldivian Government. The Boss wanted a set of First Day Covers. We landed on the jetty and made towards the Post Office. "Ah! Good!" said the Boss, "He's in." I asked how he knew and he told me that the bike leaning against the Post Office wall belonged to the PMG! He was right. I went in with him and have photographs of the Ceylon page of the Maldivian Government's official stamp album. The PMG held the album up for me. I tried to get him to sell me the page, but no go.

By this time I was becoming a very useful bow man, leaping ashore as the launch approached the jetty and tying up.

Every so often the Captain of HMS Cavendish (he was a full Captain) would come ashore to have a cuppa with the Boss, he'd be accompanied by his First Officer and perhaps the Lt/Cdr Eng. The naval launch would set him ashore then either return to the ship or wait at the jetty. I would take my rightful place in the group as, I suppose you could say, the Aide de Camp, to the Boss. This would upset the First Officer, a very snotty Lt/Cdr who hadn't liked me from the moment I accepted the offer from the Captain to join him on the bridge on our journey north from Gan. No way would a naval Petty Officer be allowed to join in such august company, yet there was this cheeky RAF sergeant sitting there drinking tea as if it was his birthright.

I also had a run-in with the Sergeants in the Cipher Room at Gan. I was encrypting and decrypting messages as per the 'training' I'd received but every so often things would go wrong. A lot of these problems could be tracked down to a group, or a whole line of groups being missed by the sending wireless operator. This could be detected by shoving one or five groups of random letters in at the point where the signal went wrong and if the signal came back good again after the added groups you knew what was wrong. Sometimes however, none of these tricks worked. It was usually when I was encrypting messages to send. I noticed a common factor in the problem messages which concerned the system used. I could not tell them in plain language because the system was secret and I couldn't tell them in code because it wouldn't work. Eventually I managed to get the message across to them that they were doing it wrong. These were the people who had been working in crypto offices for ten years and had given me my one hours training. Who the bloody hell does this Sgt. Commons think he is? Later, on my return to Gan, we became great friends and it seems that the instruction that I was adhering to was never used by normal Crypto people. They told me that, at the time, they hated my guts!

Every day we would go to the beach and swim and sun-bathe in the nuddy. All the places that had never been brown were now going positively black. This came to a halt one day when the natives started rowing around the island in their dhonis. As it happened it wasn't serious so we were able to continue. Swimming in our small harbour, which was partially enclosed by the coral jetty, was fairly safe. Outside the jetty was the Indian Ocean and that was full of sharks. But what was the use of being in such a beautiful place if you couldn't explore the edge of the reef? We soon found the answer. If we wanted to go swimming outside the reef we would call one of the Maldivian boys to the jetty and throw him into the ocean outside. If he came up and swam back with all his limbs we reckoned there weren't any sharks around. They would get their revenge on us by picking up Sea Cucumbers (Sea Slugs) and throwing them at us. These would excrete a long string of horrible sticky stuff that was very difficult to remove. Swimming over the edge of the reef was the most beautiful and somehow terrifying experience. The face of the reef dropped immediately possibly thousands of feet. The reef surface just disappeared to be replaced by a black hole. You felt as if you could fall straight down into it. I would dive down a few feet and study the reef face as I ascended. There was whole new sea world down there. I'd never seen anything like it.

Within the jetty we were fairly safe. I do recall one day though, there were some navy boys swimming there and I was nearer the beach looking seaward when I saw a large shark going to and fro past the entrance. I had to make a big decision. Actually it was very easy. I was a married man with two kids and the others were single. I carefully worked my way backward on to dry land then shouted a warning to the others. They all got ashore OK.

Some of the RAF people who had been there before me must have been very heavy drinkers. There was a 'garbage storage area' around the back of the residence, probably about three metres square. This was piled up to about one metre high with empty beer cans. I had to call on the navy to assist me in clearing up the mess. The ship sent a couple of sailors ashore who sat there for a couple of days plunging their knives into the cans and filling up countless sacks with these cans. They then took them out to sea and dumped the lot. One of my wireless operators was also very much drink inclined and tended to get nasty with a few in him. This was not a very good situation so I quietly got rid of him. What I mean is that I had him replaced. The next one, Peter, was pretty good and we got on very well.

All this time the ship, HMS Cavendish was in the lagoon, formally as the protection ship for the Maldives which had been placed under British Protection by the United Nations. The Maldivian Government didn't see it this way. As I explained earlier, there was trouble between them and the Maldivian islands to the south who were very gainfully employed by the RAF. The Male Government regarded the ship as the Gunboat. There to suppress them.

One day I noticed that there seemed to be a large ship near the tip of Male. It never moved. I asked the Boss what it was and he told me that the Maldivis had built it on the island. It was made of plywood. He called it Her Majesty's Cardboard Ship, HMCS. It seemed that as the RN ship was changed the Maldivis changed their ship. HMS Whitby was met by HMCS White Lie, HMS Owen was faced by HMCS Oven whilst my ship, HMS Cavendish was menaced by HMCS Cabbage Dish. Jolly good. At least they had a sense of humour. The humour went even further though. Ships at sea have to 'blow' their smoke stacks at regular intervals. I believe this is to clear their funnels of soot. When our ships did this so did HMCS. I commented on this and again the Boss had an explanation. They were burning an effigy of him behind their ship. I rolled up laughing at this but he was not amused. Of course, it wasn't my effigy that they were burning!

At some time someone had imported a chicken and a cat onto Dunidu. The chicken had managed to fly up into the trees to avoid the cat. One day I was standing on the shoreline when I witnessed an amazing sight. The chook and the cat were both within my vision and at that moment a small shark swam in close to the shore. I could see a chook, a cat and a shark simultaneously in mid-Indian Ocean.

I haven't mentioned how big, or rather small, Dunidu was. I would walk around the island a few times every evening. If I took the hardest route, that is, clambering over the coral rocks, it would take me ten minutes per circuit! Needless to say any noises on the island could be heard all over the place. The constant roar of the diesel generator was so natural after a few days that you just didn't hear it. Thus it was that one night, or early morning, I was awakened by absolute silence. I lay there for a while wondering what I couldn't hear. It suddenly dawned on me. The generator had packed up. All our food was now in danger of thawing out rapidly and rotting at a similar pace. I jumped out of bed and had my first go at the 5KVA Nunn Cub standby generator. Thank goodness it started first time and fed the essential circuits. Next morning we had the Navy send in some of their engineers and fixed both of the big gennies.

One day when I was refuelling one of the gennies and was going to start it up, one of the Maldivian boys, I think it was Sweepie, wanted to try his hand at starting. It required that you held open a valve thing with one hand whilst turning a bloody great wheel attached to a flywheel with the other. He tried it, it kicked back at him and the handle caught him on the shin. There developed a very big bump by the time he came to me later in the day. In the residence there was a big cupboard full of medical stuff. They hadn't remembered to give me a full doctors training course that Saturday morning at Gan so I looked in the cupboard and pulled out a tube of white cream. God only knows what it was. I carefully rubbed some on his shin and gave him the tube to continue the treatment. The next morning he asked if he could go over to the doctor in Male. Just as he was getting into the launch I noticed that he had the tube of ointment in his top pocket. I told him that I needed that and removed it. I shall never know what I did that day.

Once again diplomatic relations between us and Male cooled off or warmed up whichever way you want to look at it. They weren't talking to us. They weren't talking to us enough for the Boss to get a bit worried. He decided that he and I should have a serious talk. It went something like this. "Alf, if they decide to invade, this is what we must do. You send Peter down to the jetty to fight them off" (I still only had a Verey pistol, Peter had nothing). "I will go into my rooms and change into full diplomatic regalia, cocked hat, tail coat and ceremonial sword. You go to the flag pole. When Peter is killed, you lower the flag whilst I come down, crack my sword over my knee and surrender, because half of my force has been killed." Real Indian Army stuff. Needless to say, I never told Peter of this bold action plan. Thank goodness they never did invade us ... at Dunidu. Again, on hindsight, I don't think that I could have sent Peter down on his own. My actions would more probably have been to try to talk to whoever came ashore. I'd have been terrified of course.

The navy would by now send some of their lads ashore for a game on the beach. Being sailors they would have their game then wash off liberally in my drinking water. We had no rain for seventeen days! The tanks were getting very low. Early one morning I was awakened by the sound of rain thundering on the roof. I rushed out with soap and flannel, stood under the eaves and washed in the overflow. It was beautiful, but not enough.

On one of these football game days one of the sailors sustained a broken arm. It could not be fixed aboard the ship so we had to ask Gan to make a special Varsity trip to collect him and take him back to Gan. The Varsity was notoriously unreliable and for days on end we got word that it was coming. I would go over to Hulele with the sailor and some of his mates, the trip was aborted! This happened for a few days and towards the end I felt most uncomfortable knowing that there were a group of hairy arsed sailors behind me thirsting for my blood. They could not see the difference in a ship losing power whilst at sea and an aircraft losing power at ten thousand feet. We got him away eventually. This was when I learned of the Navy description of the RAF as 'Penguins'. All flap, no fly!

On other occasions when the Varsity was unserviceable they would utilise a Shackleton to drop supplies to us. The Shack would make a number of runs over the sea close to the island and drop a series of Lindholme Containers attached to small parachutes with our food and mail. Of course when this happened we could not send any mail out. It was an interesting exercise though and I have a number of pictures of the Shack doing these runs.

I was never overly fond of the Boss. I did my job because that is what I was there for, but I didn't have to like him. I, and a number of other RAF people before me, had served him very well over a number of years so it was not surprising that a remark he made one day annoyed me very much. The ship was sending a launch to take him out to join the Captain for lunch aboard. I was not invited! The launch was to arrive at the jetty at mid-day. It did that at precisely mid-day. He turned to me and commented that next to the Indian Army you couldn't beat the Royal Navy. I bit back my response.

I think I mentioned that our toilet cistern water was taken from a big drum outside the loo window. To fill the drum I had to pump with a hand pump. Sometimes this would take anything up to two hundred pumps just for enough for a pee. Of course I didn't know why. Eventually the sailors showed me that there were small rust holes in the pipeline just below high water mark. Unless the tide was high I was pumping mainly air! I said that I knew nothing about plumbing.

In order to ease relations with the Maldivis it was decided that the ship should sail out over the horizon one night. During that day the Navy converted thousands of gallons of seawater into drinking water, by desalination, and filled up our wall tanks. In the dead of night they landed a Sub/Lt, two Petty Officers and about half a dozen seamen, then sailed off. The Sub/Lt. told me that, as the Senior British Officer ashore, he was now in command of the island and that I was under his command. I immediately told him that he could do what he liked with the island but that the radio room and the airstrip remained under my command. I then sent a message to the Commanding Officer at Gan to the effect that I had been 'invaded by the Royal Navy' and I needed some muscle. The C.O flew up almost immediately. Another point of contention was that the RAF had ceased compulsory Church Parades a long time previous to this. The Navy still had 'Divisions' on Sundays. I objected to this. As well the Navy had an inspection every night at about six pm when everything had to be 'squared' away. They brought this habit ashore with them. When I asked what it was for they said that if the ship were to sink at night you'd know where to find things. I assured them that the Island was not going to sink at night but that was a stupid argument. I did not know of Tsunami at the time. Again I said "OK. Have your inspection but I decide what happens in the Radio Cabin." My CO asked me to humour them regarding the Church Service business. Another habit they carried on with was the 'splicing of the mainbrace'. Each sailor receives a tot of rum every night. It was very powerful rum. I was still essentially teetotal and I could smell it from the other side of the room from the moment the cork was removed from the big stone jar. One night I was sitting with the sailors when one, a South African sub-mariner, offered me 'sippers'. I said no thanks I didn't drink. They all insisted that I should accept his 'sippers'. I knew that I would not like it so I took his mug, turned my head upwards and swallowed the whole lot in a single gulp. There was immediate uproar! What had I done? They all yelled in a single voice. "He said sippers not gulpers!" I was only supposed to take a tiny sip!

From talking to these sailors I discovered that they had been on the long boats in the rivers of Borneo when there had been a call for sailors for 'hazardous duties'. They were a load of tearaways and had volunteered. The job that I had been doing quietly for three months was to them 'hazardous duties'!

They were housed in the storage shed. It was just an open fronted nissen hut. In it were the personal belongings of two spinster lady English school teachers who had been evacuated from Male when things had got a bit naughty. It didn't take the sailors long to go through their possessions and decorate the shed with items of ladies underwear. There were two R.N. cooks among them and they set about cleaning up the kitchen in the residence. Poor Cookie was most upset. Curries never tasted the same after that. They also made a fish trap in which we caught a massive fish. There's a photo of me holding it somewhere. When that was curried it was something else again!

When diplomatic relations were bad we had no Maldivis on the Island. The Maldivian servant boys and the launch skipper were withdrawn to Male. The coconuts didn't stop growing though, so I decided that I should get some down and send them home to Pat and Andrew. I found a large brick, tied a long length of rope to it and started to twirl it round and round then releasing it at great speed up the tree to land on the back of my selected coconut. I then pulled and tugged and shook and everything you could do until the brick dropped to the ground when I started the whole procedure again. After numerous throws and some exceedingly blistered hands I had the two coconuts on the ground. Each the size of a big football, I painted the husks with RAF Blue/Grey paint and then painted their addresses in white paint. I got the aircrew boys to take them back to Gan and put a tu'ppeny ha'penny stamp on each and post them off. Andrew said that it caused much amusement at the school. One of the teachers had to open it once they realised what it was.

When relations were good, the Maldivis would come over in a long boat with some dustbins and sweep the island using palm fronds. I didn't realise how dirty it had got until after a clean-up. Of course whilst they were with us they would just about clean out the coconuts.

With just a few weeks to go for my spell at Male to end I received a letter from our friend from Cyprus days, Clive Wilson, who was a sergeant engine fitter in the U.K. In it he told me that in future all sergeants had to take and pass a Chief/Technician board before they could be promoted to Flt/Sgt. I was currently (or at least on my last enquiry) just 55th off promotion to Flt/Sgt.

No word of this new structure (Keep Alf down 2) had come from Gan and the board was due shortly after I was to return to Gan. I was very annoyed and sent a signal to the Signals Officer 'demanding' that I be entered for this board and be given the opportunity to study for it. Having got that off my chest I suddenly shivered knowing that I hadn't a snowball's chance in hell of passing it, and would just make a fool of myself. It was too late. On the next Varsity they sent up another Sergeant who was an old mate of mine and who'd been an instructor at Radio School. He brought some old Radio School exam papers up with him because he also was going to sit the exam.

I saw the Varsity touch down and, to my horror, saw it run off the end of the runway and slew round about sixty degrees. I ran down to the end and saw that he was just about down to his axles in coral dust. His brakes had failed, he had been unable to stop and had tried to turn before going into the ocean. He had done what is known as a 'ground loop' which puts tremendous strain on the undercarriage legs. Of course it was my job to get him out! What the hell did I know about aeroplanes? Especially aeroplanes that were stuck in coral dust. The pilot said that if we could get some strips of the runway metal planks pushed under the wheels, he could rev up his engines and try to pull himself onto the strips. I got in there with a shovel, dug away in front of the wheels with props spinning just behind my ears and slowly managed to get the strips into position. I then had to hold them there whilst he revved up to pull himself out. It was terrifying to say the least. Suffice to say that we managed it and got the aircraft back to the middle of the runway just before nightfall. All on board had to stay the night. They included a couple of 'works and bricks' civilians who really had just come up for the trip.

The overnight stay allowed me to go through the old exam papers with my mate and argue over all the questions that I knew nothing about. Next morning we went over to Hulele for take-off. As I understood it, the aircraft needed to build up a certain level of 'boost' before letting off the brakes in order to have enough speed for take-off on a short runway. This was a big aircraft on an 800 yard short runway! The brakes would slip at less than half the required boost so, as soon as the pilot felt the brakes start to slip he had to release them and give the engines total gun. Then pray. The two civvies were in the seat behind me and I heard one of them tell the other that He was not very happy about the situation. He wasn't very happy! He wasn't Robinson Crusoe there! I decided that I would point my camera out of the window and downwards. I would click the button as soon as I could see water. If the water was all round me it didn't really matter too much, the shot would be spoiled anyway. If the water was below me ... I would treasure that shot for the rest of my life. It may not look a very interesting picture, until you know the story behind it.

The flight down to Gan was fascinating. There are reputed to be between 1,200 and 2,000 coral islands in the Maldives, I suppose we must have flown over 600 or so. Many were just beginning to break through the surface of the sea whilst others were well established with palm trees growing. It is a trip worth taking.

We landed at Gan on what was to be the Varsity's last landing. We knew that, as long as the undercarriage didn't collapse, there was enough runway (about 6000 feet or more) for us to come to a halt (all flaps down!) with or without brakes. This we did and the excitement was all over for another day. The Varsity was checked and it was decided that it was beyond economical repair. Such aircraft are excellent training material for the airfield fire fighters, but that is a short way off now.

A few days later I sat the exam, my mate had been sent back specially to sit it, I passed and he failed. He must have believed the arguments I had put up that night at Dunidu.

I now had to settle in for another nine months on Gan. An entirely different kettle of fish. I was to be a shift supervisor in the Circuit Control Section. This housed the receivers and multi-channelling equipment for the RAF's world wide communications network (the other end of the Stanbridge network), and controlled the Transmitter frequencies at the sending end. Most of the communication was in the high frequency range and was very much affected by the movement of the atmospheric layers around the earth. These rise and fall over each twenty four hour period. To maintain 24 hour communication the operating frequencies had to be continually lowered as the night came on and raised as morning approached. We had to monitor the received signal and if it appeared to show signs of starting to fail, we would send the signal QSY, say, 4575. This interprets as "Change the transmitter frequency to 4575Kcs". This would have been the next lower channel to that which we were currently working on. We'd then immediately retune our receiver to that frequency and hope to catch the transmitter as it came on line. This would continue throughout the night. Doing the right thing at the right time to maintain contact was quite an art. I'd never done it before but was lucky enough to have a corporal with me who knew what he was doing. I remember one night when the layers were moving much faster than usual. We were leapfrogging the channels downwards until I suddenly dived under the control desk. My corporal looked at me in amazement until I told him I thought that the layer would come through the roof at any time now. At around 3am. the layers would start to rise again and the channel hopping process reversed.

One of my first jobs in CCS was to install a lot of new equipment. It happened to be the stuff upon which I'd been trained before being posted from England. I unpacked it all, got out the manufacturer's equipment manuals from the boxes and started to work out how I should install it. I got through the job, doing literally thousands of acceptance checks before declaring that it was operational. When I'd finished it one of the younger sergeants, who'd been in CCS some time before I came down from Dunidoo, produced a complete set of installation diagrams. I asked him why he hadn't given them to me when I was about to start the job and he replied that I hadn't asked! As I still hadn't done the practical part of my Chief Tech. board I asked that my major exam equipment be changed to this new stuff. It was agreed that it could be so.

I went over to Singapore for the second part of the board. The Sergeant in the Signals Section was another ex-Radio School Instructor whom I had known years before. He told me that he had set up five or six faults on the equipment and I was to find them and write them up as I corrected them. After I had done at least five of the faults and the equipment was nowhere near serviceable I asked him to confirm that he had only put on six faults. He read my report and only found about one that he had put on. The others were faults that would have materialised in a very short time anyway. I made a deal with him that I would do the equivalent of a six monthly servicing on the stuff and give it back to him better than a shop bought one. So I passed my board. Once he confirmed that I'd passed I took him out to dinner. It would have been improper otherwise.

Back at Gan I continued to work in CCS but now that I was 'pretender to the crown' as one sergeant put it, I was second in command. A Warrant Officer was the boss of the Section.

The CCS was over the far side of the island from all of the other installations and we had a bus to take us to and from work. The drivers would go madly around the perimeter track and across the end of the runway. I used to warn them that one morning there would be a sheet of ice across there and we would end up in the oggin. This was 35 miles south of the equator at six feet above sea level!

We had a big emergency water tank outside CCS which was controlled by the Fire Section. In it we had a fair selection of fish including groper and small sharks. With only a few aircraft flying through each week we didn't have a lot of aircraft fires and as there was no need for any room heating, domestic fires were not an everyday event either. Imagine my surprise then, when I asked the Warrant Officer fireman if he could get some of his boys across to clean up and top up our tank, and he responded that he'd get it done when he could get around to it. Not surprising that I responded "What, in between fires Henry?"

Although the 'invasion' did not eventuate at Dunidu, there was an invasion at Gan. It was in the late afternoon. Most of us were resting in our billets when we heard an unusual chanting. A bit like the war chants in 'Mau Mau'.

We stirred ourselves and walked out towards the beach where we were met with the sight of dozens of Dhonis coming ashore. They were full of Maldivian men and at the head of most of them were young men wielding sticks and rope. They came ashore around the hospital where they were met by the RAF Regiment Flight with riot shields and truncheons. We knew a lot of the 'invaders' as local workers in our sections. One of our Section cleaners jumped ashore with a big grin on his face and shouted "Hello Sergeant." to which I responded with a "Hello Ibrahim." Nothing like knowing your enemy. The Regiment boys then started to advance, one row at a time, poking their truncheons ahead of them at the Maldivian men's tummies. Within half an hour or so they were all back in their boats rowing home. Invasion over.

The great hobby at Gan was the collecting of shells and coral. This was long before it was realised that reefs could be killed. We would spend hours out on the reef, treading around the coral, having Moray Eels poking their heads out of holes at us and finding some beautiful shells, all live of course. The shells we would bury in the sand near our billets for a week or so and when they were exhumed the ants would have eaten all the insides leaving them absolutely clean. A polish with some oil would put the finishing touches. The coral would be soaked in a bucket of detergent water for a few days then rinsed under a tap to come up snow white. The reef was generally considered safe in daylight. The sea level varied but was rarely above hip level. Few people would chance it at night.

One day my Signals Officer asked me if I would take a visiting Group Captain (Medic) from Singapore out onto the reef. He was a keen shell man. I agreed. We arranged to meet just after lunch. It started well enough but I noticed from the beginning that this man was a fanatic. Every single thing on the reef interested him. We didn't make the edge of the reef till well on into the afternoon. We were still only about half way along to where we would normally have turned in. He was still examining everything. At about half past four I suggested that we should be turning shorewards, and pushed on ahead of him to try to suggest that the time had come to be clearing off the reef. We were going in across a point that I hadn't normally crossed. It started to get dark and as it did so the depth of water started to rise. We were obviously walking into a depression in the reef that I knew nothing about. I tried to skirt around the depression keeping the lights of CCS in view. I knew that was where I wanted to make my landfall. By this time he was also aware that we were treading on dangerous ground and started to speed up. We managed to keep our shoulders above water and eventually came up the other side of the depression and ashore. I took him straight into CCS for a cup of coffee. He said that it had been a very exciting afternoon, (he could say that again!) and, a few weeks later, I received a parcel from Singapore with a cigar box of small Singaporean shells and a 'Thank you' letter from him.

RAF Gan had its own radio station from which various airmen would play request records, read news items and all the other things that what is now called Community Radio does. My first association with it was when Pat sent in a request for Ray Charles to sing "I'm Busted", reminding me of the banking incident. The old lady who ran the YWCA book shop, Sweaty Betty, 70 years of age and the only female on camp, hadn't got that record so she played Ray Charles singing "You are my sunshine". This became my nickname for some time! I then started to do a series of one hour programs on Sunday evenings playing popular tunes from the ballet and opera, about which I knew nothing! I chose the Overture from "The Thieving Magpie" as my signature tune. I would go to the studio after it closed down on Saturday night, play dozens of records till I heard something that I liked, and record it as one of my selections. The details that I announced were straight from the record sleeve. I decided to do a series of ten shows. On the night I was due to record the ninth programme one of our sergeants was having his farewell 'do' in the Sgts. Mess. I still didn't drink so I joined them drinking orange juice. At about eleven pm I left and made my way to the studio to start my recording. I decided to say something about it being my penultimate programme but, as often as I tried, I could not enunciate 'penultimate' correctly. I changed it to something else. The next day I found that the lads had spiked my orange juice with Vodka. There's a lesson in there somewhere.

At Gan we were probably one of the first Radio Broadcasting stations in the world outside of Moscow to announce that Valentina Tereshkova had become the first woman in space. In CCS we always had a receiver tuned to Reuters International teleprinter broadcasts. I happened to be on watch when Reuters broke the news and immediately rang our Studio who immediately announced it. Sadly we received the news of President Kennedy's assassination the same way.

Fruit bats were the main form of animal life on Gan. There were also a few pairs of Terns. It was a common saying when a couple of them flew by that 'he' was taking a Tern round the Island. There were masses of the Fruit Bats though. They would start flying around 4pm and nest again next morning with much squawking. They have an unfortunate habit of urinating on the wing, so you never looked up at a Fruit Bat. There was an island nearby, Willingilli, which was a penal island, and every afternoon at 4.00, as we were watching whatever football game was being played, a Fruit Bat would fly over the football pitch and off to Willingilli. It was known as the 'Four-o-clock to Willingilli'.

The Varsity had by now been assigned to the scrap heap which was on the CCS side of the island. The engineering boys attached a tractor and started towing it round through the paths that were used mainly by bicycles. Half way round it got one wheel into a ditch and there it stayed for quite some time. Seemed a sad end for such a well worn aircraft.

Most of us had RAF, sit up and beg, bikes, and cycling round the island every afternoon was very popular. I used to ride round with a Welsh Warrant Officer Telegraphist. We used to have a lot of laughs on the way round. One day we passed one of the Education Officers of whom certain tales were told. Taff told me that one day the Ed. Off. had asked him if a certain airman worked in his section. There were two airman of the same name on the island at the time. Taff said that the Ed. Off. had described the airman as "the tall, willowy one with hazel eyes'. Case closed!

The Sergeant's Mess on Gan was a constant source of laughs for us. A popular one was for someone to stand up during dinner and shout out "Any Senior NCO on Gan that can't Ice Skate is a Poofter!". Immediately twenty or thirty chairs would scrape back from the tables and their occupants would start 'ice-skating' around the Mess. Hands behind backs, heads up and whistling. An alternate shout was "Any Senior NCO on Gan that can't Tap Dance is a Poofter!" The response was equally as mad.

The way from the Mess dining room back to the billets went through a covered 'breezeway' in which were a number of wicker arm chairs. A door to the left led to the 'Music Room'. My mate (a Crypto Sergeant) and I, both still reasonably young, would put a Strauss Waltz L.P. record on the radiogram turn up the volume a bit and sit watching the 'oldies' come from the mess. They invariably carried a mug of tea and, as they entered the breezeway, would change step into a waltz, dancing their way through. Shades of the Cox's Pill Factory Clock trick of my school days. Another trick was to sit either side of the breezeway and, when all the chairs were occupied, one of us would scratch the top of our legs where it contacted the edge of the wicker chair. (We were usually in Khaki shorts). A few seconds later the other would do the same. We'd repeat this for a few times until others started doing it. Then one of us would get off our chair, lift it, slam it to the ground again and stamp on an imaginary insect. We'd then both get up and walk out leaving everybody scratching.

Gan was where I first learned that a good way to maintain a friendship was to be insulting to each other from the start. With two hundred airmen on the camp, and only Sweaty Betty, it would be very easy to have arguments. Not over Sweaty Betty, she was reserved for the Officers. If all your conversations were abusive you never knew when the other really meant it. Everywhere we went, and in everything we did, we never paid a single compliment to each other. Of course I didn't expect compliments one day when, representing the Sgt. Mess in a five a side football game played on a full sized pitch, I was playing as a forward and the ball was lobbed over the heads of everybody straight to my feet. I had to run about 70 yards with it. Not a soul in front of me. I raced down to the other end, open goal and was so shattered that I couldn't kick it properly and put it wide. When I looked back nobody had followed me. I could have walked it in. One of my greatest sporting moments. My current best mate, John, has had to put up with this abuse for more than twenty years and it still works.

At around this time the Warrant Officer i/c CCS was Tour Expired. I was made i/c, no new Warrant Officer was expected. Of course, I was not going to get any promotion. I was still a sergeant. My board results having not yet been promulgated.

There was a small inhabited island very close to Gan. I think it was Midu. Some of the Maldivian workers would walk across from Midu to work. They would be up to their chests in the ocean. If it was raining it was not unusual to see these people holding umbrellas over their heads! I imagine that it had been intended to join the two islands with a causeway sometime because there were very big concrete piers between the islands but no road.. These piers were about ten feet apart. It was said that lads had seen Manta Rays swim between the piers and had to fold their wings upwards to clear them! It was also alleged at Gan that the well known underwater explorer team of Hans and Lotte Hass anchored their yacht in the Addu Lagoon, took one dive and left hastily. What did they see?

Annual leave at Gan was normally taken either on the Island or in Singapore. However, with Comets and Britannias flying through in each direction around twice a week, there were frequently spare seats. Arrangements were made that allowed us to scrounge a flight to Lyneham on the understanding that it was our responsibility to ensure our own return if no free seat was available for the return. Many of us took the chance. There was a Mr. 'Somebody' at Air Ministry Movements Section who had a soft spot for the Gan personnel. His phone number was available to all of us and the idea was to ring him about a week before you were due to start back. I applied and got a flight in October just in time for our wedding anniversary. We had a good couple of weeks and we had Andrew home for one week-end. I was driving him back to North Walsham and talking about music. This was the era of the guitar. Everything that was recorded was played on guitars. It was the time of the Beatles. Andrew was going on about them so I thought that I would just put in a word for real music, so I mentioned Chopin and Tchaikovsky. "Yeah I know Dad, Tchaikovsky is good but the Beatles are Fab!" I gave in. I got my flight back to Gan thanks to Mr. 'Somebody' and RAF life resumed. As it happens, I now agree with him. The Beatles were Fab!

My experience as a Wireless Operator came in useful around now. Some research was being carried out into lightning. Some civilians required a Wireless Fitter who knew how to handle a Morse key. I was their man. I spent a number of hours in a radar vehicle sending a signal every time a lightning flash was recorded. These flashes were way out over the ocean and could not be seen by us. It was amazing how many lightning flashes are going on all day and every day in the world.

We were getting towards Christmas and that is the time when the 'big boys' at U.K. Transport Command bases decide it is time that they did a refresher flight to Singapore. Shopping at Singapore was so much cheaper. One day a Brittania, on its way back from Singers landing in very heavy rain, aquaplaned off of the runway into the coral sand. It is a big aeroplane and dug in deep. The boys from the Aircraft Engineering Flight started the recovery. They tried everything! They had jacks, air bags, you name it. A couple of the legendary skyhooks would have come in useful, but they still hadn't been invented. I couldn't resist it. Section rivalry was a feature of Gan. I put a request on Radio Gan from the 'CCS boys' to The Engineering Flight for the tune "Rule Britannia". I was very popular with the CCS boys but not so with the Engineers.

Meanwhile, in the Section, the place in which packaging was beginning to rear its ugly head, in all areas of life, began to manifest itself. A Store's van came round one day with 2 big crates for us. I looked at the Issue Voucher which said they were 2 valves. I refused them and said that we didn't use valves that big, they must be a Radar device or something of that nature. Twice they came back and twice I returned them. Eventually I looked up the part number in the catalogue and to my surprise it was one of ours. I unpacked one. I hope that I can include pics in this because the valve, which was about six inches long and three inches in diameter, was wrapped in multi-layered tissue paper, this was packed into a cardboard carton which had a webbing frame around it which in turn was attached by webbing straps, springs and dog clips to a wooden frame. All of this was inside a cardboard carton which was in a wooden crate. It would have been possible to pack eighty of the valves in the same volume! If sixty had been broken it would probably still have been cheaper.

At home in Brighton Pat and her father were not getting on very well again, and around Christmas things got very bad. She contacted me and I arranged for her to talk with the people at SSAFFA. In January the SSAFFA people managed to arrange for me to end my tour a month early. This was not before I had had some talks with one of the sergeants who'd been to New Zealand for his leave and was full of praise for the place. Thoughts of emigration were planted.

I flew home to Lyneham, then by train to Hednesford in the Midlands. It was still snowing! If I hadn't been home in October I'd have been prepared to swear that it had never stopped.

12. Stradishall and Abingdon 1964-65

I must have known of my home posting to RAF Stradishall and advised Pat before leaving Gan because she assures me that she and Susan drove up to Suffolk, with Sue, now 9 years old, doing the navigating. They found some accommodation near to the RAF Station and we moved into Top Cottage near the village of Cowlinge (pronounced Coolinj) in the county of Suffolk on my arrival home. The cottage was a charming little place with a 'tin roof'. It was owned by a very nice Doctor and his lovely wife. He was the Editor of "Family Doctor" and smoked like a chimney regardless of the warnings that he was publishing every month. They lived in the village of Helions Bumpstead which, though it sounds like something from 'Much Binding in the Marsh', actually does exist. Cowlinge was in a very pretty rural setting in Suffolk and we went for lots of walks in the twilight evenings. Nearby towns were Newmarket and Bury St. Edmonds. As well, not too far away was the County town of Ipswich, the best shopping town in the area. The RAF camp was not too far away from the house and we had our Hillman Husky 'station wagon', known to the family as 'Hilary'. In the cottage I had to bend my head as I walked through the kitchen door.

Stradishall was in Flying Training Command and was responsible for the training of Aircrew Navigators. I seem to remember that I met up with Varsities again. These were kitted out as flying navigational classrooms. My job on Strad. was in charge of airfield radio and non-radar navigational aids again. It was the first time that I had been dealt a handful of 'Boy Entrants'. These were young boys who for various reasons had been put into the RAF at the age of 15 years and three months and had continued their schooling and trade training for about two and a half years. They were classified as ground wireless mechanics and I had about six of them. They weren't a bad lot really but the worst of them were bloody horrors. Some of them had been orphans in Dr. Barnardos Homes and the like, and seemed to think that the world owed them a living. Of course, being me, I expected the same from everybody regardless of what they had been before they joined the air force.

A couple of domestic incidents come to mind. The first was when a Detective knocked on the door. Pat's father had taken out an allegation against me that I had stolen a Windcheater Jacket from him. The facts were that I had bought the jacket in Holland and loaned it to him. When we left we took it back. The D accepted my explanation and we heard no more of the matter.

I used to go home for lunch, and one day, just before I left to go back to work, Sue, now 9 years old, who had been reading Black Beauty or some such book asked what a gelding was. We told her to look it up in her dictionary. She looked it up and then asked what castrated meant. Again we told he to use her dictionary. Her next question was what are testicles. I said that it was time I went back to work and left Pat to tell her the facts of life. I understand that as a result of these Q and A's when Pat asked her if she now knew what a gelding was she answered "No. But I've learned three new words." Sue kept on learning new words because she is now has a Ph.D. in Plasma Physics.

While we were living at Cowlinge I bought a Honda 50cc motor cycle. It was only a toy really but was very useful and extremely economical. It did 180 miles to a gallon of petrol. I could fill the tank for half a crown. I don't recall too much else about what happened at Stradishall because after a few months my promotion to Chief Technician, following the exam I took at Gan a year earlier, came through. Not backdated I should add! I had hoped that at last I would get to wear a crown but they changed the insignia for Chief Technician to sergeant's stripes with a felt propeller. I'd been robbed yet again!

I do recall however that, on my next to last day there, I was going around doing my clearance documentation. When you arrive and leave an RAF Station due to postings, it is required that you visit various sections, mainly administrative and medical, firstly to let them know that you are there and eventually to ensure that you aren't pinching anything when you leave. I went home after work only to be called by the RAF police to say that the Section Keys had not been handed in to the guardroom. One of the ex-boy entrants, who had been a particularly obnoxious creature, was the key orderly for that week and he 'lived out' with his wife, way out in the country. I had to find his home, in my own time, to get the keys and sign them in. I found his home and I was in a very annoyed state. I said to him "Maloney (not his true name), I'm going to go home after I've done your job, and I'm going to think about you all night. If I can think of just one thing that you have done that has benefited anybody other than yourself, I won't charge you." Next day I told him he was on a charge for failing to carry out his assigned duties. I finished my clearance, wrote out the details of the charge and a written statement from myself and left. I've no idea what happened to him. As a Chief Technician I had now moved from 55th to over 500th on the promotion roster to Flt. Sergeant!

And so I moved on to Abingdon, now as a Chief/Tech. Again I was to be in charge of airfield radio and navigational aids. Abingdon was a Transport Command station home to No 47 Squadron Beverley transport aircraft.

The town of Abingdon lies on the River Thames in Berkshire and is just over the county border from Oxfordshire. Oxford was easily accessible from the camp, it was just a steep hill (Boars Hill) away. From the top of Boars Hill you overlooked the beautiful City of Oxford with all its College spires.

As I now had a lot of years and some rank it didn't take too long for us to get into married quarters. A brand new house just off the end of the runway!

A thing about moving into married quarters which must have helped us to settle down fairly smoothly was that RAF Married Quarters furniture, crockery, cutlery, bed-linen etc was all of just one or two patterns so the bed-covers were the same pattern as those at Coltishall back in 1961. It was just as if you'd moved back into your old home.

Again I reported to an old Warrant Officer so there was no problem there. His office was in Station Headquarters whilst the Ground Radio Section was over the other side of the airfield near Air Traffic Control. The section was mine to do as I wished with. One of my civilian Radio Technicians was an ex Squadron Leader who had been there for some time and he provided the anchor. We got on well from the start. A few things happened during my stay there. I had the usual set of rag tailed staff with which to keep the station operational. Some very serious and others always on the look-out for mischief. Most however were pretty loyal and a pleasure to work with. Having put it that way I suppose that I should mention that throughout my working life, especially after I started to hold positions of responsibility, I always regarded the people who I was to supervise as working with me, not for me. We were working together for, in this case, the British Public. I never owned the Air Force nor any of the companies that employed me in later years.

I recall that one day I was giving the boys a bit of a pep talk about behaviour. I pointed my finger at one of them and said "And that goes especially for you Price." Upon which he leaned forward and took my finger into his mouth and gave a little bite! The Form 252 (Charge sheet) flashed through my mind " ... whereon Price leaned forward and bit my finger" I decided that laughter was the best medicine.

I used to ride my Honda to work around the perimeter track. The lads, some of whom owned big motor bikes, called it my 'motorised sewing machine'. On a freezing cold morning in February '65 I was going to work on it, the peri track was like glass, it slowly slid sideways from under me and I finished up gently sliding on my backside following the bike. No damage either to the bike or me, thank goodness.

A couple of flying incidents come to mind. At one time the World Gliding Championships were taking place somewhere over in the west of England. The course followed by these craft is, to a large extent, determined by the prevailing winds. On this occasion the winds made the track to be followed straight through the Abingdon approach path. Dozens of tiny gliders were being just missed by some very big Beverley aircraft. On another occasion a Beverley was on the approach working with the Abingdon Control Tower. At some point he told the tower that he had the runway in sight. The Controller then waited to see him land. Nothing happened. A short while later the Local

Controller at RAF Benson, a few miles down the road told the Abingdon controller that they had one of his Beverleys on their airfield.

The lads loved to be able to cause consternation on camp, legally. So therefore it came as no surprise to me when I got a furious phone call from the Guardroom one day asking me to get my ----ing Signals truck out of the way, it was blocking all entry and exit from the camp. I went out to see what had happened. There was going to be a very big 'do' at the Officers Mess that night. Lots of top brass would be attending. Whilst they were at the Mess their drivers would be accommodated in the Guardroom cells until called for. This was before the days of hand-held mobiles. We were installing a field telephone from the Guardroom to the Officers Mess. As an officer was about to leave, someone at the Mess would merely ask for Air Marshall X's driver over the dedicated line. No delays. The Guardroom was one side of the Main Entrance to the Camp and the Officer's Mess on the other. There was a wrought iron archway over the entrance. My boys had decided that the cable must go over the archway and used the truck in lieu of a ladder, naturally! I took their side of course and pointed out to the complainant how dangerous a loose wire over the road would be and then quietly told them to get a move on or I'd kick their butts from a ... hole to breakfast time.

On another big occasion, a Battle of Britain Open Day, we were asked to set up a Public Address system inside the biggest of the hangars. I knew very little about the hangar and sent the lads to do the job. It wasn't long before the phone ran hot. This hangar had what was called a 'stressed skin' roof. It wasn't meant to take any weight. My boys were strolling around on the top of the thing risking life and limb and even more serious, expensive damage to the fine new hangar. They knew what they were doing, but it had been too good a chance to miss.

I don't remember the date now but suddenly a group of soldiers and airmen started a special form of drill. They weren't Abingdon people. After about three weeks of this it was announced that Winston Churchill had died. These troops had been rehearsing for his funeral from the moment it was known that he was seriously ill and unlikely to recover. The funeral went off without a hitch and the general public must have wondered how the troops could have learned the drills so fast.

One day I was up in the Air Traffic Control Tower when the Fire Section called to say that there was a fire in a married quarter and asked if they could go and help. The Controller said OK. Then asked which married quarter. The fireman said "26 Cholswell", The Controller said "OK" and I yelled "Hang on, that's my place!" I raced down and hitched a lift on the fire engine. As it happened it was only a chimney fire. There was a blockage at the bend in the chimney. It was said that there had been a labour dispute whilst the houses were being built, and some Irish labourers had deliberately dumped some cement down the chimney! Thus the smoke poured back into the room.

In October '64 I was sent on a Cathode Ray Direction Finding (CRD/F) maintenance course at No. 2 Radio School, RAF Locking which is near Weston Super Mare, about twenty miles past Bristol. I managed a very creditable 78% on that course. CRD/F was one of the many navigational aids (along with ILS) for which I had been responsible over the years without ever having been trained on. It was a V.H.F system so really was nearing the end of its operational usefulness. Else why bother to train me?

I drove home one week-end in November in freezing weather. My Honda had been blown over the night before in a gale and the windscreen had been smashed. I got to the agents in Bristol just as they were closing. The fellow said he could sell me a new screen but it was too late to have it fitted so I sat beside the road, freezing cold and fitted it myself. Eventually after sliding and skidding over a hundred odd miles of icy and snowy roads I arrived home and rang the bell. I stood outside the door fixed in the motor bike riding position. Hoar frost was hanging from my nose, my eyebrows, my ears, arms, gloves, I was frozen stiff. Pat came to the door with the two kids. She stood there rolling up with laughter at the sight I presented. In the meantime Andrew and Susan rushed to run a bath and put on a kettle. Thank God for intelligent kids.

Not a long way from Abingdon town there is an Atomic Energy Research Establishment, Culham Laboratory. They were working on something that required millions of volts being built up and discharged. So what! We had, in common with most big RAF airfields, an Instrument Landing System (ILS). This provided a Glide Path and a Localiser (runway lining up guide) to aircraft using the system. The ILS can only be set up from the ground, it cannot be fully tested without an aircraft. A special flight existed in the RAF for testing and calibrating ILS. Our ILS was ground checked every day and as far as we could ascertain, was perfectly operational. Every so often an aircraft would report that our beam had a bend in it. We said that it was a load of bullshit, we couldn't possibly set it up with a bend. We would do a recheck, request a calibration, the calibration aircraft would do its bit and report nothing wrong. This went on and in fact never ceased up to the time I was posted to my next position. Years later it occurred to me that the offending beam was the one that ran down parallel to the road on which Culham Laboratory was sited. At the risk of showing my absolute ignorance of real life, I now believe that those 'bends' in the beam possibly coincided with Culham doing one of their big bangs.

Whilst at Abingdon we were able to visit quite a few well known places including Banbury (Cross), Malmesbury, Tintern Abbey and Stonehenge. Most Beautiful Village winner Boughton on the Water and many others were within easy touring distance. We took advantage of this. Unfortunately we didn't realise that as we got older our memories would deteriorate slightly. We didn't mark every photo and I now have great difficulty pin pointing some of them. Abingdon itself was on the Thames and had some very pretty scenery close to town

By now we were regretting that we had put Andrew into Boarding School. He was clearly very unhappy there and the Report from the Headmaster's wife changed completely from one term to the next. Her report was pretty scathing almost suggesting that any change was our fault. I wrote a letter telling her that as his place of residence over the past year had been mainly under her supervision, she must share a major responsibility for any change. We decided to pull him out and he then attended the John Mason High School in Abingdon as a day boy. One Saturday we were driving through the town of Witney (famous for its blankets) when we found an old second hand TV shop. I'd heard that you could pick up cheap TVs there so we stopped. Selected one from the bottom of the pile, gave the man ten shillings and kept Andrew quiet for hours with a soldering iron pulling it to pieces. I can't remember that we ever used the pieces for anything but it was as cheap as any toy.

He and Susan got on well with the kids next door and we also got on well with their parents. The father, who was a sheet metal worker, was amazed when I told him that the gardening I was doing was for somebody else; that I would not see the results. I would be away before a year was up. Some trades stayed put for years whilst others, such as Wireless Fitters, were continually on the move. And so, in May 1965 I was on the move again, back to Germany. However, just before I left, Susan was being checked out by the Radcliffe Infirmary at Oxford for her Asthma. Pat was driving her to an appointment one morning when, at an uncontrolled cross-road in Oxford a car smashed into the drivers side writing off the Husky. Luckily Pat and Sue came out of it OK but the other driver, who said that he was rushing to catch a train, was not charged so, as usual, the innocent party lost out. I received a call from Pat and rushed to Oxford but there was little that I could do. Sue had to follow the crash with a whole series of blood-tests. I had to leave Pat to handle all the problems of the smash whilst I once again went away for my fifth overseas tour.

13. Germany 1965-68

Back to Germany and back again to Butzweilerhof. I was with a group of about ten Senior N.C.O.s posted in the same draft. Amongst them was a Flt.Sgt Medic Kipp Cooper who, with his wife Margaret (now sadly deceased), was to become one of our long lasting friends and they have twice visited Australia and we have been able to show them around. But that of course is much, much later and not a matter for this biography.

This time I was posted into No. 5 Signals Wing. A 'hush, hush' unit. Everybody was cleared to at least 'SECRET' level and even the cleaning materials files were classified. The Cold War was still in full swing and everything the other side of the Iron Curtain was of immense interest to us (the Western Powers). As we are talking about 40 years ago I guess it is OK to say what it was all about. I suspect the Russians always knew anyway. We were a radio monitoring unit. At the main base (Butzweilerhof) we had about 50 radio receivers tuned into all the known Eastern Bloc frequencies. All transmissions were recorded whether they were Morse, radio telephony, radio teleprinter or funnies. We had RAF Officers who could talk any language who would translate and if of interest the information was sent on to the Government Communications Headquarters (GCHQ) at Cheltenham in England. At least that is what I believe we did. I never asked questions. I learned, without asking, that the secret was not what we were doing so much as how successful we were at doing it. I tried to make it my rule that I didn't want to be told anything that I didn't need to know to do my job. Pat never knew what I did. She knew that it was secret and never expected me to tell her. She often tells people now that I was a spy.

I put in my application for her and the kids to join me and had to fill in a form to be used for their Identity Cards. I was in the Families Office answering the Clerk's questions. Height? 5' 4 ½", Colour of Hair? Brown, Colour of Eyes? What? Colour of Eyes? "What? I don't know." "We've only been married nineteen years, I've never looked at her eyes ... yet". I had to delay the answering until I got a letter to her asking what colour her eyes were! We soon got a flat at the Volkspark in Cologne, a complex of about four or five blocks of units. The first had 5 floors with about 50 flats, it was known as the Queen Mary, and the others had three floors. They were known as the Barges. We were in a Q.M. ground floor flat.

We had the insurance money for the Husky so before Pat had joined me I ordered a Hillman Minx. It was Tartan Red with Black upholstery. Pat was horrified when I told her what I had ordered. A common colour in England at that time was a rusty sort of red and she thought that was what I was getting. A few weeks after they arrived we were told that the car was being delivered to Ostend in Belgium. Pat, Sue and I took a train to Ostend to pick it up. There was a long freeway between Ostend and Brussels and at the end of it there were dozens of trucks parked. We wondered why, then Pat noticed that all the drivers were having a pee! The trip through Brussels is mainly by-passed by a tunnel. As we pulled out of the tunnel we had to bear left toward Aachen. About five lanes emerged from the tunnel and these merged into two as we turned toward Aachen. I'd never driven in Belgium before! It was dodgy for a bit there. The clutch or gear-box of our brand new car was giving me a bit of trouble so I had to drive with great care all the way to Cologne. Of course, it was a right hand drive on the right side of the road again. We made it OK and we were all delighted with the new car.

Education in Germany for the over 11's was at the British Forces Education Service Boarding Schools at Hamm. The Windsor Boys and Windsor Girls Schools. Andrew was enrolled immediately and seemed to fit in straight away. We used to go up and visit him at half terms and he had really settled in and had good friends. Of course he was now going on for 15 and no longer one of the littlies. I recall that on one visit he and his friend had deliberately placed a textbook carelessly, but impossible to miss, on his bed. Its title was "Groups, Sets and Matrixes"(or something like that). Real higher Maths stuff. He admitted much later that they didn't really know much about the subject at that time, it was only put there to impress. It certainly did that. He eventually graduated (from Sydney University) as a B.Sc. Mathematician. On our visits we would either go into Hamm and have a good feed or we would visit the Mohne Dam, the Dambusters target, and have a picnic. There was, at that time, no speed limits on the Autobahn and we would get the speedo on 160K (100mph) and do the trip up there in just over the hour.

Buses were put on for transporting us to and from work. Needless to say the bus rides were usually fun but I was now a Boss man so had to behave myself.

Now that we were again blessed with a good car we started doing a bit of the old tourist stuff. Unfortunately, due to my job we couldn't visit any of the Iron Curtain countries. This cut out trips to Yugoslavia, Hungary etc. I can't spell Czechoslovakia. Yes I can!!

Of course work didn't stop just because I had a nice new car. I had an 'Aerial Farm' with about fifty 'long wire aerials', feeding into a room full of aerial amplifiers each of which could feed 10 receivers. Halls full of receivers and teleprinters and a workshop with about ten wireless staff. I had my work cut out. I set about organising a controlled servicing schedule ensuring that every piece of equipment was checked out on a regular basis. We were running months behind to start with but the organisation started to bite into the backlog. Imagine my annoyance when one day I came into the workshop to see a civilian wireless receiver on the bench. I asked who it belonged to and was told that one of the corporals was fixing it for a Squadron Leader. I immediately said "He is not!" and put it to one side. Later that day the Squadron Leader turned up for his wireless. I told him that we were months behind with our service work and that no outside work would be allowed until we were up to date. He had a go at me and reckoned that in the old days no Chief Tech would talk to an officer like that. I told him that it probably depended on the officer. He took his radio and went off in high dudgeon. He knew that I was right and he hadn't a leg to stand on.

In addition to our HQ set-up, we also had Direction Finding stations, scattered down the East-West border, monitoring and locating transmissions. The one in Berlin decided to go on the blink. This was a really old piece of equipment that I had studied as a wireless operator under training in 1947. Actually I had studied the later version. The Warrant Officer in Berlin was the same person as the one with whom I had seen the Vulcan loop the loop years before. He specifically asked if I could come up and fix it. RAF Gatow, the British airfield in Berlin, bordered the Russian Sector. It was mid-winter. I travelled up to Berlin on the British Army train. This train ran up to Berlin, through the Russian Zone of Germany every day of the year except Christmas Day. This was the policy to enforce the British 'right of access' following the Berlin Blockade in 1948-50. It was a marvellous piece of propaganda. The train was up to Pullman (Indian Pacific) standard, absolute luxury and filled with British soldiery. Privates and corporals enjoying service they'd never dreamed of. It was timed so that lunch was served in the dining car as the train waited at the checkpoint at Helmstadt. Our Identity Documents had to be handed over to the Russians for checking and undoubtedly for copying. This meant a stop for about half an hour and the Russian soldiers and the East German VoPo's (Volks Polizei) looked on whilst the British soldiers made the most of it. Gorging themselves on restaurant standard food.

Snow lay all around on the airfield at Gatow and I spent the whole night fruitlessly trying to breathe life into an equipment that had died of old age; apart from the fact that I hadn't the faintest idea what I was doing. At about 5 am. I decided to walk back to the Sergeants Mess. The snow was so thick that I was tempted to crawl through the boundary wire near the D/F hut and walk round the road but I didn't want to tear my uniform so I hoofed it through the snow. As it turned out I was lucky. I was later told that outside the boundary wire was the Russian Zone. I'd have stood a chance of being arrested by the Rooskies. In daylight I was able to see that I had been working within about a hundred metres of a Russian border guard tower.

I went up to Berlin twice more over the three years 65-68. Once by air into Tempelhof which was easy and once by road which was again an interesting experience. I drove up in an RAF vehicle. At the Autobahn checkpoint there was first a British Army post which recorded all our details and timed us through, then on to a very long queue of civilian cars and trucks being checked by the Russians and the VoPo's. I'd been told to ignore the queue, drive straight up to the front. This I did. VoPo's approached me and again I'd been told to ignore the VoPo's, the British Authorities did not recognise them as having any authority over entry into the Russian Zone. I awaited a Russian soldier and showed him our passes. I had another airman with me. Again they were taken into a hut and recorded. We then went on into East Germany.

East Germany somehow always felt colder and more dull than in the West. As we passed under bridges civilians would surreptitiously wave their hands to us ensuring first that they weren't being watched. We pulled off into a layby for some sandwiches and coffee which we had with us. Other cars pulled in as well but would not park anywhere near us. We then had to move it for the rest of the trip because, if we were longer than about two and a half hours before emerging at the Berlin end, the Military Police would put out a search vehicle for us.

I realised some years later that, though I'd paid three visits to Berlin, I hadn't had a chance to look at 'The Wall'. I had gone up there to do jobs and that is what I did.

At this time copper was at a premium. The war in the Congo was either in full swing or its results were hurting still and as a major copper producer the metal became scarce and expensive. As I said earlier, one of my responsibilities was an aerial farm. They were mainly Medium and High Frequency aerials which meant long lengths of heavy gauge copper wire. One particular aerial had two 'arms' each about 120 feet long stretching from the top of a mast down to a couple of 6 foot high poles. An inverted V. They then went into the ground and were joined underground by copper braid. This aerial caused me lots of trouble. Because it came down to ground level (almost), the wire could be snipped at the top of the poles, then, at the mast end, could be snipped again giving the snipper two hefty lengths of heavy gauge copper. We would get a complaint from the operators that the aerial was unserviceable, go out to the farm and find it cut. This happened a few times so I decided to do something about it.

I took the aerial off line and told the operators that they'd have to manage without it for a while. I then designed a simple alarm circuit that rang a bell in the 5 Wing Service Police (SP) post if the circuit was broken, and connected it to the aerial feeder with a teleprinter voltage of 80v applied to it. We advised the German Police and they agreed to come on site if our alarm went off. I set it up during the daytime and went home. A couple of mornings later I was told by our Service Police that the alarm had gone off but when they and the Germans had gone out to check the aerial it was OK. I rechecked the circuit, all seemed OK. A couple of nights later same again. After a while the German Police said that they wouldn't come out again. I was beginning to look a bit silly.

I decided to look at the problem more closely. One of the wires in the circuit was the underground copper braid. I got the aerial erectors to dig it up to look at it. It had been there for a number of years and was very corroded. I suspect that at the time that I was checking there was sufficient moisture in the ground to complete the circuit but that at various times it dried sufficiently to effectively break the circuit or it may have been a case of expansion and contraction due to daytime and night time temperature changes. We replaced the braid and a few days later, in broad daylight the alarm went off. I shot off with two bloody big aerial erectors (Rugby players both!) and caught a little man on a bike, on the job. I told the two airmen to bring him in with his bike whilst I went ahead in the truck to arrange for an interpreter. Half an hour later they turned up with the man's coat and said he'd got away from them! I think they must have taken pity on him because there was no way that he could have overpowered these two.

We reported the matter to the German Police and I spent an interesting day at the Police Praesidium in Cologne going through books of mug shots with the detectives. I got to respect their attitude towards their job but they suffered from the same problem as police in most democratic countries. They caught the bandits and the judiciary gave them negligible sentences. That day was also my first experience of continuous motion lifts. No doors. As the floor of the lift draws level you step in and the same to step out.

An example of how careless some people were regarding the security aspect of the job came to light when my Flight Sergeant was on leave. A special top secret piece of equipment that he had responsibility for went unserviceable. The Sergeant Wireless Operator asked me if I would have a look at it. I said OK but as I didn't know anything about the equipment he would have to answer a few questions. I asked him to operate the equipment and then to tell me what he expected to see (on a Cathode Ray tube) and what he was or was not seeing. He then went on to tell me everything that this equipment did. I stopped him and again said that all I wanted to know was what should be there and what was not there. I still remember what that thing did which I didn't need to know. I don't remember whether I fixed it or not. Thinking about it now. We can all do what that machine did on our home computers and the Internet today. It was just 40 years ahead of us.

Another funny security incident concerned the Warrant Officer in charge of the Butzweilerhof RAF Police. They ran the usual Guardroom at the entrance to the RAF Station and various other Police duties. As well there was a special security entrance to 5 Wing at which you had to show your pass before entering. Nobody could enter without a 5 Wing Pass or unless escorted by an authorised 5 Wing person. The W.O. Policeman was generally known as 'The Sheriff' around camp. I had been out of the Wing on some errand and returned to find the Sheriff on the inside of the security gate. "Hello Mr. Xxxxxx" I said, "What are you doing in there?" "Seeing how far I can get" he said. "Right" I said, "You've got as far as you're going to get, please come with me." I then took him into our adjutant's office and told the adj. the story. Of course it soon got round the camp that Chiefy Commons had arrested the Sheriff.

A more serious incident occurred late one night when an operator received a severe electric shock. His mates pulled him off the equipment with a broom and started work on him and others rang for the Medical Officer. The M.O. arrived at the security gate and the copper on duty wouldn't let him in! That incident was one of two serious electric shock incidents that I had to investigate on this tour. It highlighted the fact that a piece of electrical equipment that is supposedly earthed is not necessarily safe. On this occasion the earth lead in the plug (equipment side) had become disconnected and curled round to touch the mains input terminal making the whole equipment casing 'live' and unearthed. The operator had grabbed a handle on the faulty equipment and the casing of another that was earthed, simultaneously. Later the RAF was to introduce 'Earth Free' environments. If nothing was earthed, and there was no earthed object anywhere in the vicinity, it was difficult to accidentally touch mains and earth together.

My Mum and Dad came out for a visit and we showed them around the place a bit. In the middle of Cologne I asked Mum if she liked the place. She replied "It's alright, but aren't there a lot of foreigners." I tactfully told her that she was the foreigner, to which she stated, quite categorically, "I'm not a foreigner, I'm English!" On another day we took them on a ride to the Hague to see the Commonwealth War Graves Commission Cemetery at which Dad's brother Lesley was buried. We found the grave and though the weather was not good, we got a photograph. On our way there we stopped at a cafe for lunch. Dad was a typical English roast beef and Yorkshire pudding man. The menu was, of course, all written in Dutch. Dad saw something that was obviously Beef and chose that. His face when it was served up as slices of beef on bread and some bits and pieces was a joy to behold.

Towards the end of 1966 I applied for membership of the Society of Electronic and Radio Technicians and in March of '67 received notification of my award of membership. This entitled me to put the letters MSERT after my name and to receive a very complicated technical Journal on a regular basis. I don't know why I bothered really. I suppose it may have helped me when I left the RAF and I probably did mention it in job applications but I can't ever remember signing my name and using it. Some years later I decided to not bother about renewing membership. I did make use of it once in the late 70s when I used an article on a technical matter for one of my storemen to use in a fun talk to the Computer Engineers of the computer company that we were employed by. They were at a Seminar in a mountains resort and he was invited to spend a couple of days with them in recognition of his excellent work for them. I recall changing words like 'conductor' to 'conductress' and 'induction' to 'seduction'. When they returned to the main plant one of the bosses came straight to me and asked if I'd written Frank's speech. No use denying it.

In 1967 Chancellor Konrad Adenaur died. He lay 'In State' in Bonn for a few days. On the Sunday night we were returning home from visiting Andrew at Hamm. We came to the junction of the main Autobahn with the Bonn Autobahn. The blackness of the night was illuminated by dozens of red flares burning at ground level and we were stopped by the Polizei. We asked what was wrong and he answered "Adenaur Kommt!" His lying in state had finished and he was being taken to Koln Cathedral for the final ceremonies. It was a very eerie scene but, as first in the queue, we had a grandstand view of an important occasion. It has occurred to me that I witnessed his first visit to Koln as Chancellor (1953) and his last. I wonder if anybody else can claim to have been at both occasions.

Two or three things occurred around this time. The first was probably the announcement that 5 Wing would be moving up to Berlin. I had to set up a 'half' Unit in Berlin whilst keeping the other half going at Butz. I mentioned earlier that we had about sixty aerial amplifiers each capable of producing ten outputs. All of these inputs and outputs were carried in black coaxial cable. I'd never looked into the floor cable ducts before. Now I had to. Confronting me were some 600 black coaxial cables made even more black by the years of soot that had settled on them. I had to carefully identify every cable and either leave it there or pull it out according to whether it would stay or go to Berlin with its associated amplifier. I think I took two weeks to do the job, insisting that I did it alone to avoid any confusion. Not one operator complained about losing his signal so I must have done it right. I was covered in soot every day. Probably the dirtiest job I've ever done and not the sort of job people would think a Radio Technician would be doing.

I was asked if I wanted to stay at Butz or move up to Berlin with the Wing. Me! Being asked! I chose to stay at Butz rather than move the family yet again. Little did I know! I was posted across to my old unit 2nd TAF Forward Repair Unit. At the same time I received my Long Service and Good Conduct Medal. Eighteen Years Undetected Crime! The Acting Station Commander who made the presentation was the C.O. of FRU so he commented that he was looking forward to me joining his Unit. The official photograph of the event looks as if he is giving me a tip. He didn't pin it on my chest and kiss both cheeks, but gave it to me in my hand. At least a hundred or so others had to endure a parade for my benefit.

In FRU I was made NCO i/c Radio Installations. This covered all installations in the British Zone of Germany. They were mainly fairly simple stuff that I had done many times before whilst at REU Henlow, but now I was planning, designing and sending out groups to do the jobs. I did a number of surveys and got a big surprise on the way out, and a very nice compliment from my Squadron Leader on our way back from one. We had a program of installations to be carried out and I was working out the schedule. RAF Wildenrath was a big front line unit and naturally expected a lot of priority. The S/Ldr. said he'd come with me to Wildenrath. As I drove him out he said "I understand that your daughter and my son are engaged." His son had given our Sue a ring at school! They were about twelve years old! At Wildenrath we were confronted by a very high powered crowd of Officers including people like the Command Navigation Officer, Senior Air Traffic Control Officer, the Wing Commander Flying and the Wing Commander this and that. I was the lowest rank, indeed the only non-commissioned rank at the meeting. They all put up their arguments and when they finished my boss said "O.K. Chief, what can we do?" I got out my prepared plan and went through it item by item explaining every part as being the logical point for that particular item. They accepted it like lambs. On the way home the S/Ldr said "Well done Chief, you'd certainly done your homework there." I was quite chuffed.

As a Tactical Air Force, the RAF in Germany had to be prepared to move at any time. As a consequence a great deal of use was made of mobile installations. Until then there had not been a Radio Vehicle Type (RVT) designed for the American UHF equipment that I'd trained on in 1953. I was asked to design two RVTs. A Receiving and a Transmitting Vehicle. I was given a Ford Taunus van to work on. This would be about a three ton van. I started work on them. Of course I still had to run the normal installation programs.

One day I had to send two corporals out to Bruggen about 50 or 60 miles away to do a job that would take about two weeks. They obviously talked it over and came to me asking if they could drive each way every day so that their wives would not be left alone. Pat had been left alone for months at a time over a lot of years and these two were worried about two weeks! I told them that they could not commute and that if their wives wanted to know how to cope just send them along to see my wife. It might sound harsh and even a bit bitchy, but the fact is that they could not be allowed to think that being home every night was a right. They were regular airmen. There would possibly be times in the future when they and their wives would have to experience the type of life that Pat and I had lived and a two week separation was a mild sort of training. Their wives must learn to be able to cope. It was really for their own good ... and it was a chance to be a bit bitchy.

I also got to 'sing' on the British Forces Broadcasting Service program. They used to run a competition about such things as mystery sounds, missing lines, famous radio personalities etc. The prizes were EP records, usually pre-release versions that the stations received free from the record companies. I and another Ch/Tech often sent entries and had an unofficial competition as to who could get the most mentions in the results. One day I decided to record my answer to the music of Anthony Newley's "Mumbo Jumbo, Rhubarb, Rhubarb" from the Musical "Stop the world I want to get off". I had to cut the Anthony Newley parts off where my parts took over. I sent the tape in and got a phone call from the BFBS Studio in Cologne saying that they loved it, but the recording quality was not up to their professional standards. They asked me to come in and re-record in their studios with their Technicians doing the recording. They also mentioned something about making it worth my while. Pat and I duly turned up at the studio and I was taken through to the soundproof room and left there with a pair of phones on my head. Outside through the thick glass windows I could see Pat and the producer and Techo. They laughed half way through the first attempt, so I joined in. Start again. I wasn't allowed to laugh. Anyway the recording was made and played. I didn't get anything other than the winners EP records. I even failed to get a copy of the recording, which I now regret.

One of the funniest vehicle accidents I have ever seen took place in the FRU hangar. One of my Corporals drove a Volkswagen Beetle into the hangar and parked it behind a big Magirus Truck. He went into the workshop and a little while later came out, jumped into the Magirus and backed it straight into the V.W. My funniest incident took place on a very wet day. The hangar doors were slid open just wide enough to allow a vehicle to enter. I was driving a Landrover out of the hangar and eying the width of the door carefully. Another fellow came through the doors in another Landrover so that satisfied me. If he could, so could I. I drove carefully through, keeping my wing mirror as close to the door on my side as I could. I heard a sudden Bang! When I got out to check I found that my Landrover had longer wing mirror stalks than the other one.

Again I can't remember the timing but I returned to camp late one evening from a survey, looked at Station Routine Orders (you never knew when you'd be detailed for Orderly Sergeant) and discovered to my amazement that I had been awarded a C.in.C's Commendation for Meritorious Service in one of the New Years or Queens Birthday Honours List. I have never found out who recommended me or what the citation was. The certificate is stashed away somewhere amongst our important papers. Unfortunately they don't date them. I have since learned that it was for the Queens Birthday Honours List in June 1966, but the Data Protection Act, 1998 prevents me from receiving a copy of the citation. How ridiculous!

By now I was fast approaching 38 years of age, I was going nowhere, backwards, fast. Andrew was now 17 and would almost certainly be a candidate for University. Not as common in 1967 as now. Pat had been talking to a lady from the Australian Embassy in Bonn who had told her what a great country it was. We had considered emigration for a while and my brother Peter was now in Australia. Whether we emigrated or not, retirement would provide a more stable environment for Andrew's later years of education. Of course, it was also pretty certain that Susan would follow him into Uni. Her results were always top level. Either retirement or me moving around on my own, leaving Pat settled somewhere. We decided to take the option of retirement with a pension at the age of 40. I put in the application Form.

I'll never forget receiving a call from the Station Commander's P.A. He was a friend of mine and told me that the C.O wanted to see me next day. I'd forgotten all about the retirement application and couldn't think of what the C.O. would want to see me about. I went into his office and he told me to take a seat. I knew then that I wasn't in any sort of trouble. There are two ways of 'taking a seat'. One, if you want the other person to know that you are worried, is to sit on the front edge of the chair. The other, which I always tried to adopt was to sit well back in the chair and look attentive but relaxed. He told me that it was about my decision to retire. I immediately started to think of all the arguments we'd stacked up to justify retiring when he threw in the bombshell by saying that the Air Ministry were worried about the number of men of my age and rank who were suddenly deciding to retire. They'd asked the men why and had been unable to draw any conclusions. They had then decided to ask instead "Why did you join?" Oh!

I was completely thrown. I was only 17 ½ years old when I joined. I'd seen a movie about the Air Sea Rescue Service, I'd missed out on the chance of a big job promotion. I'm buggered if I know why I joined. It seemed a good idea at the time. And anyway it was fairly safe because the war had finished. Couldn't mention that bit though. I doubt that I helped Air Ministry much in their research on that particular topic.

Shortly after this it was decided to move the FRU to Bruggen on the Dutch border. I might just have well have moved up to Berlin with 5 Wing. I had an office in a big hangar and a very big workshop. I was in charge of all the wireless servicing now and we had about a hundred mechanics and fitters on strength. The jobs that we'd been doing at Butz came with us including the construction of the RVTs, each now with its own official RVT designation. I had a bit of a contretemps with a Flight Sergeant who was responsible for the mechanical engineering aspects of the job. He worked in another hangar and complained that there was not sufficient cooperation from me. I didn't go across to his hangar to see him about things. I merely told the C.O. that the distance from his hangar to mine was precisely the same as that from mine to his, so why didn't he come over to consult with me. That ended that problem.

By now Susan was also at Windsor School. She had a go at running away but got caught before she got out of the gate, thank goodness. We were rather farther away than when Andrew did it. Andrew later boasted that at least he'd made it home.

We did a bit of camping including a trip down to Italy via Vienna. In Vienna we were amazed when a tram conductor stood Sue against a measuring stick to decide whether she was a child's fare or an adult. I stood there muttering about "come the revolution". Andrew showed that there was nothing camp with him by following a nice bit of stuff in tight mauve slacks around the gardens of Schonbrun Palace and later fancying a bird whom we nicknamed Roses, because her swimming costume looked like a box of Roses chocolates, on the beach near Ravenna.

We also got a taste for Indonesian food at Vroom and Driesmann in Holland. We would have a great plate of Nasi Goreng in the middle of the table and not a grain of rice would be left. On the way home at nights there would be a Wurst and Pomme Frittes wagon on the road near the camp and we acquired a taste for chips with mayonnaise. They also sold 'CurrieWurst' which was delicious.

For a while we travelled from Cologne to Bruggen on RAF buses. These would pick us up at the Queen Mary waiting there for about 15 minutes. During this time Kipp Cooper would beat me about 5 times at chess. I wasn't very good at it! Again Kipp and I had to try to keep order in a bus full of wild airmen. It wasn't easy. Regular incidents included the wolf whistles out of the windows each morning as we passed an obviously 'Gay' man walking along the road. Of course they weren't known as Gays then. He was a Poofter to the boys.

At another corner there was a big filling station and we would frequently see a lady with her dog on a lead there. The boys would all make barking noises and the dog would go mad racing round and round her till both legs were literally tied up. On another occasion we caught up with a sports convertible in which there was a beautiful bit of stuff showing all her legs and then some. Her 'boyfriend' was driving. The lads all rushed to the front of the bus and the comments were certainly not repeatable in family oriented literature such as this.

There were two or three buses doing the run each day and once on the Autobahn the drivers would put their feet down and have a race. The lads on our bus discovered that if everybody leaned back in their seats and then forward simultaneously the bus jerked forward. This would give it the edge over the other bus. Thus in our bus you would see forty or more airmen throwing themselves backwards and forwards whilst yelling "In…Out, One…Out, Two…Out, Three…Out" and so on. It was just a little bit scary actually.

One winters day I had driven the car to work for some reason and that evening I had a premonition whilst driving home. It was very dark, very cold and it was raining. I didn't like the look of the rain, or the sound of it as cars and eventually the buses went by me. I drove very carefully and parked the car on a sloping part of our road set aside as a nose to kerb parking lot. As we got out and stood on the ground our feet just slid from under us. It was so cold that the rain was freezing as it touched the ground. I had been right to feel that something was wrong.

Eventually we moved into a house in Volkspark in a street which Pat assures me was known by most of us as Dustbin Alley. Then later we got a quarter on the camp at Bruggen. Bruggen also housed a USAF unit and consequently had a Post Exchange (PX) which was their equivalent of the NAAFI Shop but, strangely different to my experience in the US Zone in 1953, much cheaper. We were allowed to shop there. I remember buying some excellent quality bed linen and the like ready for the day when we would have to supply our own.

I usually managed to get on fairly well with my Officers. They knew that I was a hard worker and, if not brilliant, at least had a grasp of what was going on. I also had a very good working relationship with my section lads. Of course I now had ranks up to Sergeant working under my supervision. My boss at Bruggen was an Irish Flt/Lt. named Houston. We had a very good working relationship and could swap a few personal comments as well. I was in his office one day telling him that Andrew was studying for his 'A' Levels. He asked me how many and I told him three. He reckoned that studying for eight was harder. I asked him who he knew that had eight 'A' levels and he said that he did. I immediately dropped on to my knees in a Moslem prayer attitude and backed out of his office. Afterwards I wondered just what any senior officer who may have come in at that moment might have thought. He gave me an excellent personal reference to bring out to civvy street, even though that sort of thing was not really approved.

By now we had definitely decided to emigrate and I put in an application for my last year, on completion of this overseas tour, to be at Edinburgh Field in South Australia. The RAF had a detachment there and it would have given me a chance to settle into Australia during my last year. The CO was quite happy to pass it on and dictated a letter to his Dutch secretary supporting my application. The letter should have included the phrase " ... a Southern

Hemispherical posting ... ". The Secretary misheard this and typed it as " ... a sudden hemispherical posting ... ".! Of course I didn't get it.

Pat and I did some more trips into Holland and went to visit the tulip fields. They were fantastic. We went to Keukenhof which is the showpiece of the Dutch Tulip Industry. Everything is decorated with tulips. I shot off picture after picture and thought that we had a superb record of our trip until my film counter reached about 45 on a 36 exposure film! I opened the back and, of course, I hadn't ensured the film was properly engaged in the take-up spool. We finished up with about three pictures. Very disappointing but we still have the memories of the trip. One of these memories is the Delft china tea service which we bought in the village of Delft on our way back to Bruggen. Not a completely wasted journey.

On another trip we went into the reclaimed land of the former Zuider Zee. The Dutch had built a massive dike across the entrance to the Zee, determined that never again would the North Sea inundate their country. It was a very interesting journey and included the Maritime Museum at Lelystadt. In the museum they had all the wrecks and pieces of naval equipment which had come to light as they drained the former Zee. The Dutch were experimenting with an interesting Social set-up in the Ost-Flevoland as the area was known. They were bringing in residents who showed indications of being capable tradespeople with proven social skills as well. If you didn't have these capabilities then you didn't get land. I wonder how it has worked out. The roads through the area were long and dead straight and that day I discovered the danger of driving on such a road. A car was coming the other way. It had probably been in my view for miles but I didn't see it until it was about a hundred yards away. I'd been mesmorised. I learned a very lucky driving lesson. I remember this drive whenever we get onto the miles of endless straight roads of the Australian outback.

My three years were coming to an end and we had a few family matters to sort out. Andrew was half way through his 'A' levels, the English equivalent of the Australian HSC. There were a number of 'A' level syllabi in England administered by the various major Universities, London, Oxford and Cambridge. If Andrew came home with us he would change his course at the half way mark. Educational suicide according to his Headmaster. I applied for permission for him to stay on at Hamm. Hamm, to non-service people, was a very expensive Boarding School with fees equal to some top English Public Schools. Children of servicemen were educated at greatly reduced fees whilst their parents were serving in Germany. No one could tell me what it might cost if he stayed without some special permission. Nor indeed if he could stay. We waited and waited and I received no word. Eventually I told the Headmaster that he would be leaving at the end of the term. The Head pleaded with me to let him stay but could not give me any assurances. I told him that someone had to make a decision and if nobody else was prepared to then I would have to.

I was given my new and what was to be my last RAF posting. I was going back to RAF Coltishall in Norfolk. My third time there and the family's second. I drove the car home whilst Pat and Sue went by air. Pat reckons that she was at last getting some service as a Ch/Tech's wife. She had her luggage carried into the aircraft for her. Andrew was to follow at the end of term.

14. Coltishall 1968-69

Coltishall again! Well at least I knew where I was going. As well I knew that it would be my last year in the RAF. It would be nice to say that I also knew that it would be my last posting but with my record that was never on the cards.

Pat and Sue went to live in family temporary accommodation at RAF Warton near Lytham St. Annes in Lancashire whilst I went to my new position. Again I was in charge of airfield wireless and non-radar navigational aids. Ground radio servicing flight (GRSF). I shared an office with the F/Sgt. in charge of Ground Radar Servicing and it was all in a wooden hut with the workshop taking up about three quarters of the hut. Our Flight Commander a Flt./Lt had the office next to ours, just inside the door to the hut. This doorway had a porch built over the outside, probably to protect the doorway from driving rain. I had a Sergeant, some Corporals and a load of airmen and of course my old friends Nick and Horrie the civvy radio mechanics from way back. Old Mr. Fisher was also still there running the transmitting station. It was just like coming home again. Because my position was considered essential I had an ex-officio Married Quarter and got into a small one fairly early in the piece.

Andrew came home from Germany and was enrolled with Sue into Thorpe Grammar School, Norwich, where he resumed his studies for the GCE "A" Levels.

I suppose the most memorable thing about our last year in England was that the ground never ever dried out. It was a very wet year. We were later allocated a brand new home in Sprowston just outside of Norwich. The RAF were beginning to take up homes in outside housing estates. It was very nice and very convenient for shopping.

We now started the process for emigration in earnest. We went down to Australia House in The Strand in London and spoke to the people there and started the application process. We were not used to the idea of every household getting a phone book every year and to see the people at Aussie House go through the Yellow Pages and rip out a whole section (Radio and Wireless manufacturing for instance) and push it across the desk to us came as a bit of a surprise. It was the easiest way for them to give us a whole list of relevant companies for prospective employment without having to write it all out.

We had a bit of money in the bank so we went to The National Bank next door to Aussie House and opened an account in Perth. This was later to prove a worthwhile exercise. Later we were called for an interview with some immigration officials. All the family had to attend. We've always been convinced that the purpose of this interview was to look us over and ensure that we weren't a crowd of down and out black, brown or yellow imbeciles. As it happened the officials, after listening to our history, told us that we were the perfect material for emigration. As we've settled down pretty well I suppose that they did know what they were talking about.

Back at Sprowston buildings were going up all around the estate. In England they didn't do the Kerb and Guttering first as in Oz. The homes are built and are then followed by the roads. We moved in at the early stages and the roadway was full of bumps and holes, all filled with rainwater. Andrew and Susan were horrified (or proud) to hear me swear for the first time (within their hearing), when my front wheel went into a hole and the bottom of the car grounded. A poor labourer got the lot from me. It included the word "BLOODY". So Dad was the same as others. He did know swear words. Good job they didn't have to work with me.

In the meantime there was a job to be attended to. My boss was shocked when I told him that I didn't know anything about ILS. How could I be a Chief Technician and not know? I told him that my job was to keep the airfield radio serviceable. On my staff there were people trained on everything we had. My job was to get the right person to the right place at the right time. He had to accept that. Couldn't do much else when you think about it. If we had a really difficult problem on a piece of equipment that I wasn't familiar with and the appropriate technician was beaten by it I would go out to the site with him, open up the circuit diagrams and get him to talk me through it. At various vital points I would say "Have you checked for that?" If he had we would continue if not he'd do that check. We always sorted it out.

Coltishall was a very important fighter station and 74 (Tiger) Squadron was still there with its Lightnings. These were fantastic aircraft which were capable of reaching the Dutch Coast at 40,000 feet within four minutes of a 'Scramble'. Of course the scrambled aircraft were on what was known as QRA (Quick Readiness, or Reaction, Alert) status and the pilots were strapped into their cockpits at the end of the runway, plugged into power and to the Controllers at the Sector Operations room as well as to our own Air Traffic Control. The Lightning's landing speed was so high that it deployed a tail parachute on touch down. There was also a Javelin night fighter squadron, possibly 23 Sqdn. stationed at Coltishall.

A few incidents are worth recalling. In their way serious and potentially fatal but, as things panned out, all have their humorous side. The first concerned a Lightning that was taxiing around the peri track and came to a right hand bend. The pilot tried to throttle back to approach the bend but his throttles stuck. He couldn't turn and instead ran straight onto the grass and into the offices which are built into the side of most hangars. It happened to be his C.O.'s office. The top of the nose of the Lightning came just above the roof of the office. The Lightning was stuck firmly into the side of the hangar, engines roaring away, sucking brick dust through its engines, out through the tail pipe, onto the airfield. The pilot, who was uninjured, immediately scrambled out of his cockpit, walked along the top of the engine onto the office roof and was last seen backing away at a rapid pace. In the meantime the engine roared away. Eventually a plucky Fire Fighter Sergeant went to the side of the aircraft, removed a plate and turned a fuel switch. Fun over.

The second event was when we had an air display on camp and the Chief of Air Staff (the RAF's top man) was on the roof of Air Traffic Control, with lots of reporters, watching the Lightnings do their bit. A Lightning was due to do a low level run up the airfield. We could see him approaching at about 650 miles per hour just behind the ILS hut on the airfield. He swept past, and just in front of, the hut then screamed up the peri track between the Tower and the hangars. He was still below the level of the Tower roof as he went past it. The C.A.S was not amused. He immediately left the Station stating that he didn't want to see his pilots spreading themselves over the peri track. The funny parts were that we radio people were on the ground immediately below the tower and, as we looked up, we could see the reporters all picking themselves up from the roof. What the CAS didn't know was that, as the Lightning swept past the ILS hut, he had passed between the aerials (about ten feet above ground level) and the monitor aerial (about twenty odd feet high), causing the system to fail and bring on the secondary system.

A third incident concerned the Lightnings doing a squadron reheat take-off. The cloud base was at about 500 feet. The reheat take-off was the one used when they scrambled. It is fast, steep and spectacular with a long trail of flame issuing from the tail-pipe. When there's no cloud the planes can be seen literally clawing their way almost vertically into the sky. On this occasion they vanished into the cloud almost immediately. I was in the Tower watching them and hearing the radio. The Flight Commander was asking each of the other pilots where they were and eventually asked if any of them had seen George. Nope! George was nowhere to be seen. Then we saw George literally falling out of the sky backwards as he descended from the clouds. He pulled out of his fall just above ground level and roared away. I heard later that he had suffered from a 'power stall'. I was scared. George must have been terrified.

I knew I mentioned that porch over the front door of the hut for some reason. One of the wireless mechs used to drive the rest of the lads to and from lunch in the sections gharry. I had told him previously that he approached the side of our hut too fast but I was only a Chiefy. One day he was driving the others back from lunch when his brakes failed, or he left them too late, and he slammed the Signals Gharry straight into the porch. Damage to a RAF vehicle and a building. Of course we went out of our way to keep him out of trouble. He gave me a good reference later.

Winter 1968 arrived and convinced us that Oz was the place for us. Driving up to work every day on icy roads was not my idea of fun. What was my idea of fun was sending Andrew out of the car one evening as we drove back from shopping in Norwich. It was uphill, all the traffic ahead had stopped, the road was like glass, and cars the other side of the road were sliding towards us. There was very little hope of starting on the hill so I told Andrew to get behind and push as I tried to go forward. It worked, but when Pat then said that I should now stop to let him get back in the car I just laughed. He had to jump in whilst I stayed moving, or walk home. He made it OK.

One day I got a telegram saying that Dad was seriously ill in hospital. I took some leave and went to see him. We had never been close so it was fairly easy for me to sit with him in hospital. He was obviously never going to come out. The others boys in the family who had always smoked and drank with him couldn't do this. He had been so much closer to them. I had always been a near teetotaller and had only smoked for about six months before Andrew arrived. Dad was still alive when I returned to camp. A few weeks later, as I was addressing the assembled crew, the boss touched my elbow and handed me a piece of paper telling me that Dad had passed away. I merely nodded my head and carried on with what I was saying. He must have wondered what sort of a son I was. We went to the cremation and I still felt nothing until the coffin went into the furnace. I did feel something then. I also felt sorry for Jacky Almy, Rita's ex husband who had possibly saved Dad's life in the accident during the war. Jacky was standing apart from the rest, alone. I left the others and went over to thank him for coming. I think it may have helped him just a little.

Back at camp my time was drawing to a close. One of the wireless mechanics, an ex Boy Entrant who was not the brightest lad but a genuine person for all that, asked me about the exchange rate for the Pound. I'd recently done some transfers of cash so I was able to tell him to the Cent just how much I would get for £1,000. He looked at me in admiration and said "Gee, Chief, you know everything don't you." I assured him that I didn't and wished that I did.

When an airman of long service is about to leave the service he is entitled to one months resettlement training leave. The normal process is to write to a company that would be interested in employing you on your discharge and work for one month with them, familiarising yourself with their procedures so that you are ready to fall straight into a useful position with the company. Using the Yellow Pages of the Sydney Telephone Directory as my guide I had been trying to get some resettlement training with Radio Companies that had

Australian subsidiaries but they weren't interested. I decided that I wasn't going to lose the training opportunity so I took on the Painting and Decorating Course run by the Army at Catterick in Yorkshire. As its title suggests it trains you for a career as a Painter and Decorator. It included other items such as glass cutting. It has proved very useful over the years both domestically and professionally (for a few months). On the last day of the course, as I returned to Norwich, I saw that I was going to arrive before Pat finished work so I parked the car in the middle of Norwich and walked across to her office. When we got back to the car a Traffic Warden was writing out a ticket for it. I asked him what I had done wrong and he pointed out that the spot where I had parked was, in fact, a gap between parking spaces. I said that I was sorry about that. I'd seen someone pull out and had parked in his place. I then asked him how I could pay the fine as I'd never had one of these before. He said that we didn't have to hurry as we'd have a few weeks to pay in. I then told him that we were leaving for Australia before that. He apologised for giving me the ticket, and of course I said that he was only doing his job. By now he was almost in tears. Nobody had ever been nice to him when he'd given them a ticket before. There was no way that he could change it once it was started. I said not to worry just as long as I could clear it before leaving for Oz. I didn't want the police chasing me out there. Be nice to Traffic Wardens. The bastards are only doing their job.

We now had to make arrangements for Andrew. If we waited until he finished his 'A' Levels we would have to set up home in Britain somewhere and then start all over again in Oz. We couldn't afford to do that. His Headmaster suggested that we leave him with a Canon in the Church of England in Norwich, who had sons of his own around Andrew's age. This we agreed to do. Andrew's stories of the antics he and the Canon's sons got up to are hilarious.

On my last day I was amazed when the Flight Commander, against all military regulations, got the whole section together and presented me with a clock with the signatures of most of the section on the back. That clock is still with me. It has had a new movement fitted but the signatures are still clearly there. At that same presentation one of the lads, he who'd crashed the Signal Gharry earlier, came up to me and said "Chief, when we heard you were coming back here I asked Nick and Horrie what you were like. They said you were a bastard. And they were right." he said, "But you are the fairest bastard I have ever come across." I'm rather proud of that reference.

Pat, Sue and I went down to Brighton to say goodbye to the families and then on to Southampton to join the TV Fairstar which was at that time a migrant ship. We'd joined the £10 tourists. Andrew followed in August.

A change of medium

Well that's it! My typing fingers have run out of puff. As it happens though, we've bought a good Mac computer which has applications for making movies and DVD's. There are lots of slides and photos which adequately show our life since 1969, and since 1969 it has been much more 'our' life than 'my' life. We've also bought a MiniDV movie camera which can feed straight into the Mac and the whole lot can then be downloaded on to a VHS tape or burned onto a DVD. What I'm saying is that, if you want to know the rest of our story, you'll have to buy the movie.

Cheers!

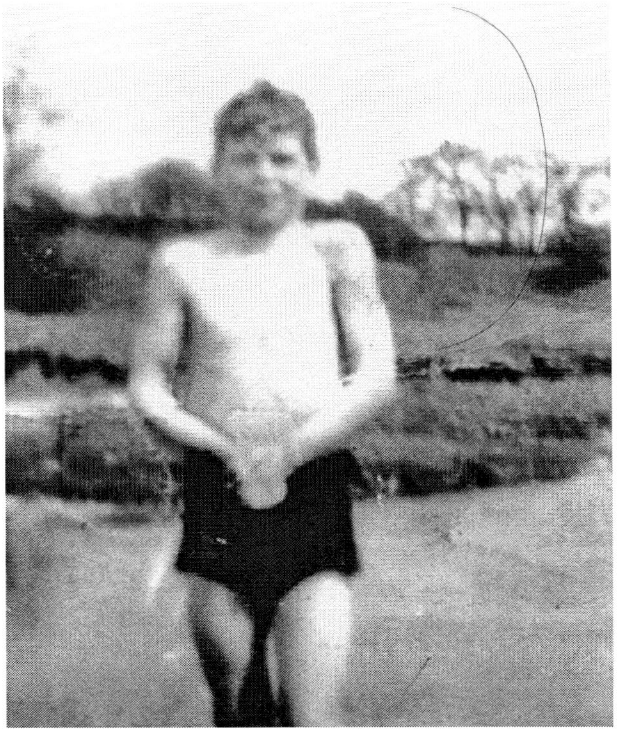

'41 Breaking the ice.

'42 Varndean boy.

Carlyle St. Mum, Dad & 7 kids. 2003

Moulsecoomb Way. Luxury. 2003

'42 Morrison Shelter.

'41 Heinkel HE 111

Hitting back – Lancaster

Hitting back – Mosquito

Varndean Trenches. 2003

Varndean Quad, Hall & Physics labs. 2003

Malham. 2006

Church at Gargrave. 2006

'46 Pat (Just 1 of 5 birds)

'46 RAF Recruit.

'47 Those slacks.

'48 Bedspace C.B. (Oiled floor)

'48 HF/DF Castel Benito

'48 B29 landed safely

'48 Chunky

'48 SHQ Signals W/op

'48 Jimmy and me at the Lido.

'48 Strolling around Tripoli

'48 Mickey, Strictly platonic.

'48 Piazza Italia. Tripoli

'48 Gharry on Tunis Rd. Tripoli

'48 Signals and Briefing crew off watch

'49 Snow in Tripoli

'49 My -GOD, it's crashed!

'49 Four days later!

'49 1st Class (C in C's Dakota) to Malta

'49 Sick Class (Lancastrian) to U.K.

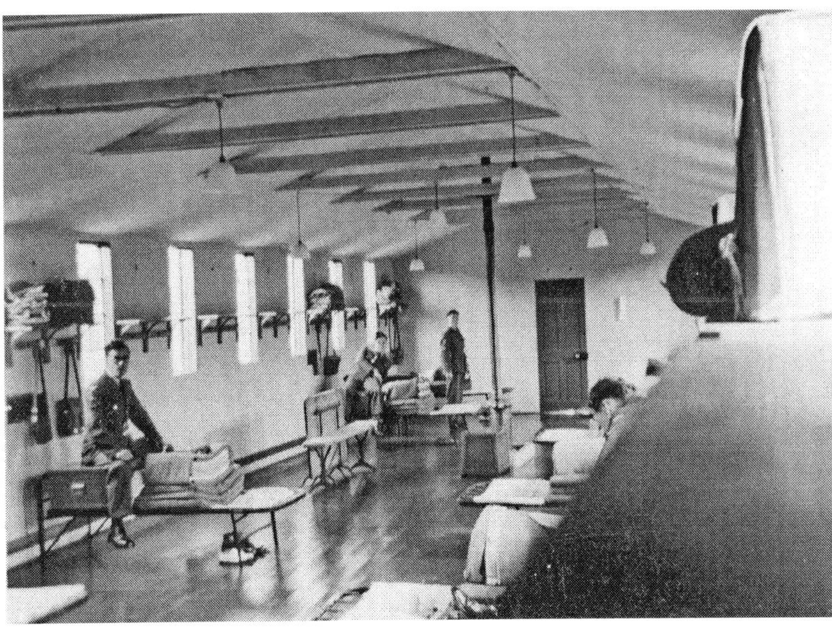

'49 Bull.... in the billet

'49 Concourse 1

'49 Rich football team

'49 Pat affecting my life

'49 Wedding Group (someone blabbed)

'49 Rye honeymoon

'51 Then there were three

'52 3500 F.C.U. Margate

'52 3500 RAF Junior Cup

'52 3500 on parade

'53 Hangar at Schwechat

'53 Moth pilot – I wish!

'53 Konrad Adenaur arriving

'53 Koln Dom from a Meteor NF11

'54 NATO course, with Instructors

'54 UHF Group in class

'54 Greek Air Force Corporal

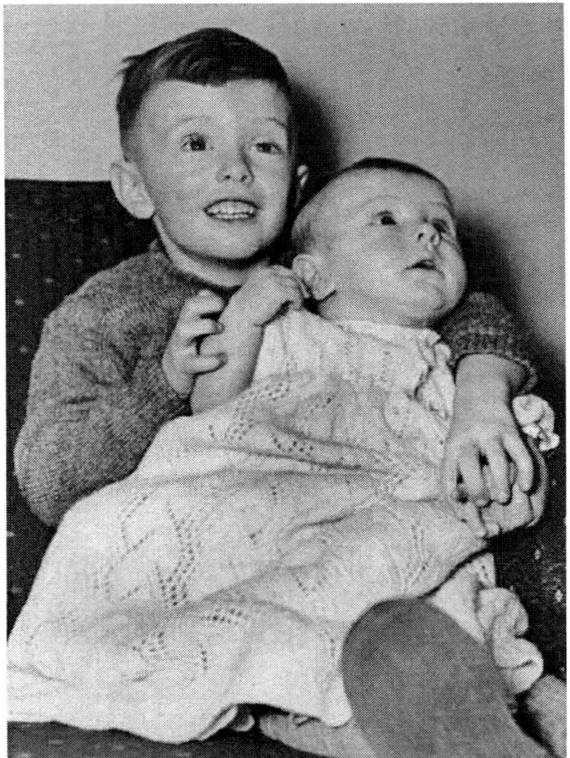

'55 Time to buy a car

'55 Source of petrol coupons

'55 Pat with Eifel

'55 Pat with Merc

'56 Model aircraft

'57 Our last 'banger'

'59 Home in Limassol

'59 Moving our garage

'60 Curium

'60 Kolossi Castle

'60 Temple of Apollo

'60 Cooking at Anoyira

'60 Troodos Mtns picnic

'60 St Hilarian Castle

'60 St. H. Penthouse view.

'61 Fossicking

'60 A good day

'60 Our neighbour's house. Future C.A.S

'61 H.M. The Queen visits

'61 Cheerio Cyprus

'61 Aegean Sunrise

'61 Approach to Corinth Canal. All breathe in!

'61 Dolomites

'61 Husky on Silver Cities freighter

'61 Our Cottage at Happisburg

'61 Slipping a disc in Brighton

'61 Snow in Norfolk – December 1961

'62 Modern History Castel Dorn

'62 Natural History Arnhem

'62 War Memorial Heelsum

'62 War Graves Commission Cemetery Arnhem

'62 RAF V- Bombers

'62 "Tigers. Tigers. Break!"

'62 Red Arrows Bomb Burst

'62 Over the hedge - Hunter

'62 Over the hedge - Hunter

'62 Battle of Britain Display

'63 Bridge HMS Cavendish.

'63 Dunidu ahead.

'63 UK Rep's. residence. Dunidu.

'63 W/T Cabin Dunidu.

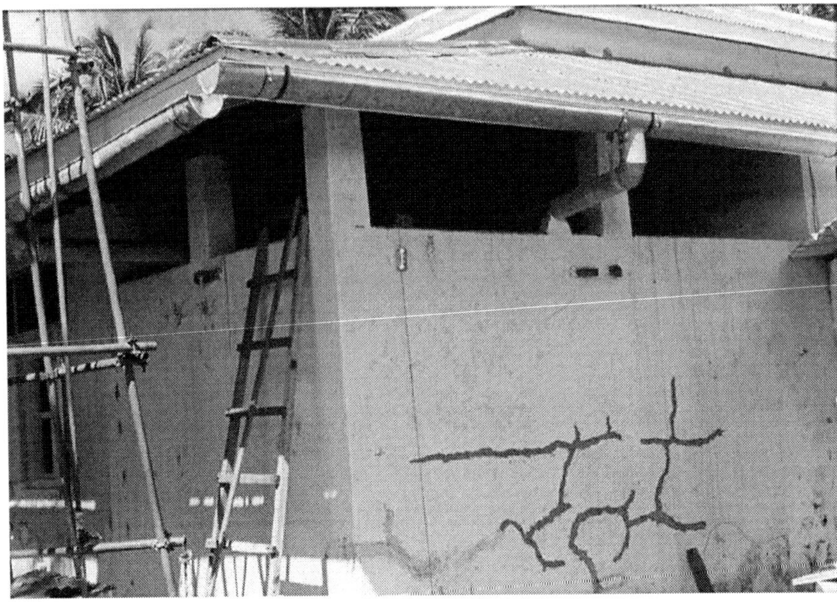

'63 Drinking water supply.

'63 Buggalo.

'63 Male Dwelling.

'63 Victoria.

'63 Shoreline at Hulele.

'63 Varsity arrives.

'63 Boatyard, worker and guard.

'63 Next weeks breakfast.

'63 Invasion fleet?

'63 Hazardous Duties volunteers.

'63 Curried fish for dinner.

'63 I've dug it out, will it fly?

'63 Water below! Yesss!

'63 I took off from that ?

'63 A few of the young ones.

'63 Last laugh.

'63 All men home going.

'63 Packaging for two valves.

'64 Top Cottage, Cowlinge.

'65 Nice new Minx.

'65 Castle on the Rhine.

'65 Mosel town scene.

Royal Air Force, Germany (2TAF)

Commendation by the Commander-in-Chief

This certificate is awarded to

R4014453 Chf Tech M.W. Commons

in recognition of meritorious service rendered to the Royal Air Force whilst serving in Royal Air Force, Germany

Commander-in-Chief

'67 C in C's Commendation.

'68 18 Years undetected crime.

'68 Last visit to Mohne Dam.

My last big job. Battle of Britain Display 1968.